PENGUIN CLAS

STUDIES IN HYSTERIA

SIGMUND FREUD was born in 1856 in Moravia; between the ages of four and eighty-two his home was in Vienna: in 1938 Hitler's invasion of Austria forced him to seek asylum in London, where he died in the following year. His career began with several years of brilliant work on the anatomy and physiology of the nervous system. He was almost thirty when, after a period of study under Charcot in Paris, his interests first turned to psychology; and after ten years of clinical work in Vienna (at first in collaboration with Josef Breuer, an older colleague) he invented what was to become psychoanalysis. This began simply as a method of treating neurotic patients through talking, but it quickly grew into an accumulation of knowledge about the workings of the mind in general. Freud was thus able to demonstrate the development of the sexual instinct in childhood and, largely on the basis of an examination of dreams, arrived at his fundamental discovery of the unconscious forces that influence our everyday thoughts and actions. Freud's life was uneventful, but his ideas shaped not only many specialist disciplines, but also the whole intellectual climate of the twentieth century.

NICOLA LUCKHURST is Lecturer in Literature at Goldsmiths College, University of London, and Distinguished Visiting Fellow at the European Humanities Research Centre, University of Oxford. Her publications include *The Reception of Virginia Woolf in Europe*, *Science and Structure in Proust's "A la recherche du temps perdu"* and *Stéphane Mallarmé Correspondence*.

RACHEL BOWLBY'S books include *Carried Away: The Invention of Modern Shopping* (2000), *Feminist Destinations and Further Essays on Virginia Woolf* (1997), *Shopping with Freud* (1993) and *Still Crazy After All These Years: Women, Writing and Psychoanalysis* (1992). She is professor of English at the University of York.

ADAM PHILLIPS was formerly Principal Child Psychotherapist at Charing Cross Hospital in London. He is the author of Several books on psychoanalysis including *On Kissing, Tickling and Being Bored*, *Darwin's Worms*, *Promises, Promises* and *Houdini's Box*.

SIGMUND FREUD AND JOSEF BREUER

Studies in Hysteria

Translated by
NICOLA LUCKHURST
With an Introduction by
RACHEL BOWLBY

PENGUIN BOOKS

PENGUIN BOOKS

Published by the Penguin Group
Penguin Group (USA) Inc., 375 Hudson Street, New York, New York 10014, U.S.A.
Penguin Books Ltd, 80 Strand, London WC2R 0RL, England
Penguin Books Australia Ltd, 250 Camberwell Road, Camberwell, Victoria 3124, Australia
Penguin Books Canada Ltd, 10 Alcorn Avenue, Toronto, Ontario, Canada M4V 3B2
Penguin Books India (P) Ltd, 11 Community Centre, Panchsheel Park, New Delhi – 110 017, India
Penguin Group (NZ), cnr Airborne and Rosedale Roads, Albany, Auckland 1310, New Zealand
Penguin Books (South Africa) (Pty) Ltd, 24 Sturdee Avenue, Rosebank, Johannesburg 2196, South Africa

Penguin Books Ltd, Registered Offices:
80 Strand, London WC2R 0RL, England

"Über den psychischen Mechanismus hysterischer Phänomene (Vorläufige Mitteilung)"
first published in 1893 in *Neurologisches Zentralblatt* 12 (1) and (2)
Studien über Hysterie first published 1895 (Leipzig and Vienna: Deuticke)
"Hysterische Phantasien und ihre Beziehung zur Bisexualität" first published
1908 in *Zeitschrift für Sexualwissenschaft* (1)
This translation first published in Penguin Books (U.K.) 2004
This translation published in Penguin Books (U.S.A.) 2004

1 3 5 7 9 10 8 6 4 2

Sigmund Freud's German texts collected in *Gesammelte Werke* (1940–52)
copyright © Imago Publishing Co., Ltd., London, 1952
Translation and editorial matter copyright © Nicola Luckhurst, 2004
Introduction copyright © Rachel Bowlby, 2004
All rights reserved

LIBRARY OF CONGRESS CATALOGING IN PUBLICATION DATA
Freud, Sigmund, 1856–1939.
[Studien über Hysteria. English]
Studies in hysteria / Sigmund Freud and Josef Breuer ; translated by
Nicola Luckhurst ; with an introduction by Rachel Bowlby.
p. cm.
Breuer's name appears first on earlier editions.
Includes bibliographical references.
ISBN 0 14 24.3749 2
1. Hysteria. 2. Psychoanalysis. I. Breuer, Josef, 1842–1925.
II. Luckhurst, Nicola III. Title.
RC532.F73813 2004
616.85'24—dc22   2004044287

Printed in the United States of America
Set in Adobe New Caledonia

Contents

Contents

Introduction
Never Done, Never to Return

Near the start of the *Studies in Hysteria*, Breuer and Freud describe what they have newly understood to be the sequence by which hysterical symptoms are cured:

> The psychical process that had originally taken place has to be repeated in as vivid a way as possible, brought to its *status nascendi*, and then 'talked through'. This makes any phenomena involving stimuli – cramps, neuralgias, hallucinations – appear once more at full intensity and then vanish [*schwinden*] forever. (p. 10)

The order outlined here involves a return to a point of origination; a repetition or re-reaction; and a final ending. Past, present and future interfere with one another and reconnect; a painful 'return' of or to a past, resurrected and relived, makes possible a future 'forever' free of the symptom. 'Hysterics suffer for the most part from reminiscences' (p. 11), in Breuer and Freud's resonant phrase; for their suffering to be relieved, the sore past must be allowed to emerge into the present, its pressure relieved.

What happens in this is dramatic. A performer makes a final appearance, a reprise for one last time, charged with the built-up emotion ('at full intensity') of the finale. A rebirth (going back to the *'status nascendi'*) is followed by sudden death. This is a twofold drama, made up of the patient's retrospective telling or reliving, now, during the therapeutic conversation, and the recovered history, now seen by the patient for what it was: for its subsequent significance. This recalls, or anticipates, what was to be the future role in psychoanalysis of an actual play: Sophocles' *Oedipus Rex*. Oedipus' story gives Freud the model of (male) childhood development in the structure of the Oedipus complex, but this is not all that the play suggests. Its action, as Freud points out in *The Interpretation of Dreams* (1900), consists of nothing other than dialogues that ultimately rewrite Oedipus' history by showing it up in a completely different light: the combination of present conversation coupled with a reinterpretation of the past is exactly what happens in psycho-analysis.

The theatrical language of Breuer and Freud's exposition points to both a connection with and a departure from the treatment of hysteria at the time. In the mid-1880s, Freud had spent six months in Paris following the work of Charcot, the renowned psychiatrist who gave public presentations of hysterical patients at the Salpêtrière hospital. The patients were exhibited before an audience; their illness was seen in the form of a repeatable performance, in the four characteristic 'phases' of a hysterical attack. Charcot used hypnosis to induce hysterical acts and attacks as a means of demonstrating their typical features. The effect was also to suggest that the illness, if it could be stimulated artificially in this way, was not primarily organic or hereditary. Breuer and Freud followed him in this theoretical postulate, but their treatment took a different course. The stress fell on the auditory not the visual; not on the patient as a bodily spectacle for assembled observers, but on her words to a single trusted interlocutor. Here the rehearsal of the symptoms is not didactic (for an audience) but therapeutic (for the patient). The theatre, as in the first quotation, is no longer a real one, in which symptoms are made to appear, but an analogical one in which they spontaneously perform for one last time.

The move from the real to the analogical theatre is also a passage from public to private space. In one of her many striking verbal inventions, Breuer's patient 'Anna O.' speaks of her 'private theatre'. She is referring to the sometimes painful daydreaming through which she drifts away from the here and now into what the (German) text calls (in French) her *absences*. In this 'double consciousness' she is carried to another place and time, imagined or past. This other world is set apart from present reality, but not inaccessible to it. It is described as occurring through a form of self-hypnosis, in which Anna O. creates for herself the second consciousness that Breuer's use of hypnosis in treatment was meant to bring about. But the private theatre worked quite differently when it was presented to someone else: instead of being the sign of the illness, the second mental state could be made the means of the cure. Anna O. got into the habit of regularly describing the scenes she saw. The one-woman show with the same person doubling as audience thus changed its register, taking on a restricted public form through the communication of words and feelings to another. Another patient, Frau Emmy von N., instantly produces a whole set of parallel memories 'in such swift succession that it was as if they were a single episode in four acts' (p. 59). Continuing the dramatic analogy, the traumatizing moments in the past that return, eventually, to Miss Lucy R. are described by Freud as 'scenes'. When they have appeared to her in their relatedness, and she has reported on them to Freud, she is freed of their impact. She becomes the spectator and critic of these extracts from her history that, in being represented, can be both recognized and set at a distance; setting them out in words could operate as a form of relief. It was Anna O. herself who, famously, named this the 'talking cure', surely the mother of all soundbites, and as telling a catchphrase for what was not yet psychoanalysis as anyone could have dreamt up.

With its combination of a palindrome and a big circle, the name 'Anna O.' might seem to have been invented expressly to serve as the alpha and omega, the *fons et origo* of the new therapeutic method. Hers is the first of the five case histories presented in the *Studies in Hysteria* as they appeared in 1895; she had been a patient of Breuer's some years before that, at the start of the 1880s. Later on, Breuer had lengthy conversations about the case with his much younger friend and colleague Sigmund Freud, who persuaded him to write it up. In 1893 the two men published an article on hysteria which then became the 'Preliminary Communication' to the book of 1895; and the rest is psychoanalytic history.

Anna O. in one way never did exist in that indeterminate sphere known as real life: she is a character in Breuer's story, later a character in the history of psychoanalysis. Like all the other heroines of the book she was given a pseudonym to protect the identity of the woman now known to have been Bertha Pappenheim, who subsequently became well-known in her own right. After her treatment by Breuer, and some later mental troubles, she went on to live an exceptional and fruitful life as a social worker, feminist and Jewish activist. Meanwhile Anna O.'s story, and her inventions, as told and interpreted by herself and by Breuer and by Freud, went on to have a life of their own independent of Bertha Pappenheim's. It was Anna O., not Bertha Pappenheim, who would figure for psychoanalysis as its ambiguous ghost or largely forgotten mother.

The Anna O. case became a focal point for Freud's later returns, in works like *The History of the Psychoanalytic Movement* (1914) and *An Autobiographical Study* (1925), to the moment of the *Studies*, now retrospectively seen as that of the origin or birth of psychoanalysis. In looking back at Anna O., and at the other case histories of the volume, Freud was also looking back at, and reinterpreting, the partnership with Breuer that was not to last. Initially, psychoanalysis had two fathers. But already by the time of the second edition of the *Studies*, in 1908, Breuer's preface (p. 3) clearly marks his distance from what had by then become firmly established as Freud's psychoanalysis.

Breuer had renamed Anna's innovatory talking cure the 'cathartic method'. The new phrase translates her words into a more technical language and shifts the perspective from the patient, the one who gets talking-cured, or talking-cures herself, to the physician, who applies a method of treatment. Breuer's change is one of many different kinds of translation that are at issue in the *Studies in Hysteria*. What are the implications of moving from one linguistic register to another – from ordinary speech to a clinical vocabulary? What is the right kind of language for talking about psychological matters, when the patients' own words are the medium of the treatment? How do feelings get carried over from mind to body, or in the other direction?

The relationship of actual languages to one another is also at issue.

It happens that the phrase 'talking cure' was first uttered in English, although Anna O.'s first language was German. Breuer's German text quotes the English phrase, and the foreign expression in the middle of the sentence, just like the foreign body to which Breuer likened the hysterical symptom, is noticeably at odds with its environment. In the story of Anna O.'s treatment, the English phrase comes out of a moment when she was compulsively speaking in languages other than German – Italian, French and in particular English. Languages are multiplied, set alongside one another, as if to exhibit their separate meanings for the speaker. In the talking cure, there is no one language, but a constant movement of boundaries between languages themselves and between language and other domains. In one case, that of Freud's patient Fräulein Elisabeth von R., bodily symptoms are said to 'join in the conversation' (p. 152), reacting to the memories that the patient is coming up with. Words are far from being just a neutral tool for stating a fact or communicating a message. Like weapons they may hit and hurt (and it is by the same logic that they can also heal). Here Freud is speaking about Frau Cäcilie M., who was treated by both him and Breuer:

> The patient . . . reported a conversation that she had had with him [her husband] and an observation on his part that she had taken to be deeply offensive, then suddenly she grabbed her cheek, cried aloud in pain, and said, 'That was like a slap in the face.' – At this, both the pain and the attack were over. (p. 181)

Without her being aware of it, the body has translated the patient's identification of verbal and physical injury by 'symbolizing' it, the word that Freud goes on to use. Once Frau Cäcilie has recognized her own unconscious connection – it was *like* a slap in the face – she is free of its effects.

In the dominant account of the *Studies*, an unwelcome thought or memory is split off from consciousness and 'converted' by unknown means into a physical symptom that may be trivial or quite debilitating – a persistent cough, an intermittent stammer, or, more severely, a paralysed limb. This symptom may (but need not) have some discernible relationship to the precipitating event – in Frau Emmy von M.'s case, the clacking sound that came out just when she was trying to stay quiet by her sick daughter's bedside; in Miss Lucy R.'s, the hallucinated smell of burnt pudding associated with the distress of a moment when that smell had been really there. For Freud, the forgetting occurs because the perception is unbearable; it is associated with something the patient cannot *admit* to herself, cannot allow into her conscious mind. The person does not want to know and so the memory subsists in the altered, 'converted' form of the symptom, translated from a mental to a physical status, and kept well away from conscious awareness. It was Miss Lucy who gave Freud what he praises as the perfect formulation of this phenomenon: 'I didn't know, or rather, I didn't want to know' (p. 118).

The Greek word *cathartic*, adopted to describe the new therapeutic treatment, carries the connotation of a (good) riddance of bodily or emotional matter that would otherwise clog or interfere with a person's health. It is also evocative of high drama. In Aristotle's theory of tragedy, the *Poetics*, this word, also associated with bowel movements, is used to describe the freeing effect of watching a tragedy, vicariously letting out emotions that would otherwise accumulate and cause pressure.[1] The notion of catharsis involves an evident tension between tragic grandeur and everyday bathos, between higher and lower species of human event. This tension, as we shall see, is to be found throughout the *Studies*. This can be seen already at the level of vocabulary. As well as speaking in newly forged technical terms of 'cathartic' treatment and 'abreaction', Freud and Breuer also use ordinary words for clearing away or cleaning up, like *Ausräumung* or *Reinigung*; while another word, *entledigen*, 'to rid oneself of', has more of a connotation of distress and invasion.

Aristotle's exemplary play for his theory of the cathartic effect of tragedy is none other than *Oedipus Rex*, which became the paradigm drama of psychoanalysis too. In it, the roles of the investigator and the one interrogated become switched and confused. Oedipus begins as the one in authority, seeking the cause of a 'plague' – a foreign body – infecting the city, but finds he is himself unwittingly the object of his own judicial search. One of the effects of this is to undermine the position of the investigator, who is not situated securely outside the problem. In a related way, the one-to-one dialogue between patient and doctor is based on a premise of equal exchange and potential vulnerability on both sides that is quite different, as we have seen, from the situation in which patients are presented as exhibits before an audience.

Repeatedly, Breuer and Freud stress not only the active collaboration of their patients in the therapeutic process, but also their contributions to the development of the new method of treatment. Proclaiming the intelligence of their patients went against the usual view that hysterics were weak-minded and tended to inherit the 'degenerate' tendencies of other members of their family. This doxa was partly a mistaken inference from social circumstances: the thousands of patients confined in the Salpêtrière hospital where Charcot worked were almost all poor and uneducated. But with the exception of Katharina, the down-to-earth working girl who follows Freud up a mountain to ask his advice and take her lofty place in psychoanalytic history, Breuer and Freud's experience, as they point out themselves at the outset, is with 'private practice among an educated and literate social class' (p. 1). And they insist, against the prevailing view, that hysterics may be exceptionally gifted. Fräulein Anna O.'s 'powerful mind' is praised at length on the opening page of her chapter; it is also suggested that, as a woman, her sufferings are partly due to her not having received an education commensurate with her intellectual capacities. In relation to their joint patient, Frau Cäcilie M., mentioned intermittently throughout the book, Freud in particular expresses fulsome admiration for her exceptional talents, from chess to poetry.

Freud never rejected heredity as irrelevant, but he consistently spoke against the prevailing idea that it was the sole or even the dominant factor in the development of mental illness. Nor did he reject the significance of major traumatic events, including early sexual abuse. (In the *Studies*, the 'reminiscences' from which hysterics suffer range from unacknowledged romantic love of a sister's husband to the sexual advances of an uncle/father in adolescence.) The practical difference between heredity and events is that events, in their contingency, leave open a possibility of cure: just as they might not have happened, so their effects are not fixed once and for all. It is possible, through the process of conscious remembering discovered in the talking cure, to relive a disturbing past event in such a way as to rid it of its pain. In this volume, we see Freud and Breuer postulating more modest kinds of 'precipitating event' (p. 11.) in the common experiences of grief and longing, love lost or unrequited, that filled the lives of middle-class women at the time. Breuer identifies 'being in love and nursing' as 'the two great pathogenic factors' in hysteria (p. 220). The two are linked by the concentration on a loved one: the lover's 'state of "rapture"' causing 'external reality to fade'; 'the twilight states' (p. 219) of the bedside vigil.

Together with its dramatic overtones, the opening quotation (p. viii) also carries the suggestion of magic, as mysterious symptoms emerge one last time before disappearing forever. Freud often returns to this semi-supernatural phenomenon: 'Nor will a reminiscence return for a second time if it has been dealt with and an image that was talked away will never be seen again' (p. 297). Elsewhere, the last moment is described as the end of a haunting: 'the image vanishes, like a rescued spirit being laid to rest' (p. 282). We shall come back to the question of the final ending of the analysis. But for the moment, I would like to consider the hypothetical 'end' of hysteria as a disease, and the hypothetical replacement of the *Studies in Hysteria* by later psychoanalytic theory. In both cases, it would seem – the illness and the theory – hysteria seems to disappear, but disappears only to reappear. It vanishes, and it returns.

From later perspectives, hysteria has frequently come to acquire a second, and secondary, significance. Whether considered primarily as a diagnostic category, or historically, in relation to its own time, it figures as the backcloth and the warm-up act for the full production of psychoanalysis. It appears as the dress rehearsal, in colourful late Victorian costume, of a settled performance that was to run and run through the twentieth century. Yet there have been constant changes of cast and direction, some more fundamental than others, and there have been comebacks and revivals and reinventions of concepts and

practices that had been discarded long before, some more apparent
than others. Far from having definitely gone away, hysteria keeps
on coming back. Over the past decade, in particular, it has been
the subject of a strong reprise, a century after Breuer and Freud's
book and its previous *fin-de-siècle* flourishing and decline. The focus
is sometimes more clinical, sometimes cultural, with each involving a notion of *return* – going back to hysteria, or hysteria itself
coming back.

At the start of the twenty-first century, hysteria is still, or once
again, out and about, both as a questionable and potent name for
forms of contemporary malaise, and as a topic for historical research
that may also have a bearing on issues of today. Some contemporary
writers about hysteria adopt the ambiguous label 'new hysteria
studies', indicating the double return both to, and of, hysteria.
Reinterpretation of the initial nineteenth-century moment of the
phenomenon is combined with questions about its persistence or
resurgence in the present. Elaine Showalter's book *Hystories*, for
instance, explores contemporary parallels to, or manifestations of,
hysterical imitation, in the recent large-scale outbreaks of illnesses
like Gulf War syndrome, multiple-personality syndrome, or ME. It
is as though hysteria is always surrounded by the question of its
putative disappearance and possible return or remaining, perhaps
in unrecognized forms. Psychoanalysts such as Christopher Bollas
and Juliet Mitchell question the putative fading away of this most
protean, amorphous of illnesses as a diagnostic category, and so help
to bring it back by giving it a place in present discussions. In *Why
Psychoanalysis?*, Élisabeth Roudinesco argues that the widespread
existence of depression is the late twentieth-century cultural equivalent of hysteria. But its habitual treatment only by drugs indicates a
denial of Breuer and Freud's initial insight that hysterical symptoms
represent not a chemical imbalance but a mental conflict that can
be freed up through an active process of thinking and talking.

This centennial phenomenon appears itself to be re-enacting
the ritual anniversary commemorations and revivals of past events
described in the *Studies* a hundred years ago. Anna O. relives the
period of her father's final illness, exactly a year later, as though to

complete an event from which, through her own illness, she had been both physically and psychologically absent at the time. At another point, Freud draws a connection between the striking anniversary restagings of hysterics and other ways of suffering from reminiscences, by knowingly living simultaneously in the past and the present. In one of the vignette accounts of other cases that are interspersed with discussions of the principal patients, he gives a detailed description of how a woman he knows has been able to deal with the many deaths in her family in part by reviving and reliving the days of their dying as anniversaries and memorials (pp. 166–7). The difference from Anna O., what makes this patient other than hysterical, as Freud is careful to underline, is that the remembering is conducted quite consciously, as a deliberate ritual of bringing back and laying to rest.

Anniversaries both mark and make meanings. This return to and return of hysteria, the sleeping beauty awakened again after a hundred years, seems uncannily to be occurring like an enlarged version of the conscious and unconscious anniversary rites of Breuer and Freud's women of the last century. Related to this return, however, is another sense of hysteria, and by extension the study of hysteria, as second: not as repetition or return, but as occupying a secondary, subordinate place. In this context, hysteria and the cathartic method are seen as decidedly pre-psychoanalytic, the before of an achieved after.

Hysteria preceded analysis; it was something else and it also opened the way towards psychoanalysis. But in the light of a more fully developed analytic doctrine, hysteria – the illness itself and the experiments in its treatment – was overlaid and relegated to a preliminary status. Where Breuer and Freud, to return once again to the first quotation, speak of going back to the *status nascendi* of a symptom, so hysteria itself becomes, subsequently, the embryonic moment of psychoanalysis. Without hysteria, without Anna O., without the collaboration of Breuer and Freud and the publication of the *Studies*, there would have been no psychoanalysis. But all that was superseded when Freudian psychoanalysis became a settled institution, practice and theory. A century on, it is hard not to read the *Studies in Hysteria* as an in-between, a twilight or dawning state between a pre-psychoanalytic darkness and the new ways of thinking that psychoanalysis opened up for those treating and those undergoing mental suffering. When we look back with psychoanalytically anchored attention, we seem to encounter the hazy dream or daydream of the theory that was yet to develop the firm lines it had established by the first years of the twentieth century.

We also see as out of place many elements that the new science – as it wished to see itself – came to reject as superfluous or superstitious or worse. Freud himself cannot resist, when he rereads the text for a later edition, adding the occasional embarrassed footnote, here in relation to the first of his cases in the volume, that of Frau Emmy von N.:

> I am aware that no analyst can read this case history today without a smile of pity. But it should be borne in mind that this was the first case in which I made extensive use of the cathartic procedure. For this same reason, I want to leave the report in its original form, advancing none of the criticisms which can so easily be made today, and making no attempt to fill in the numerous gaps retrospectively. (p. 108)

'No analyst': Freud coyly pretends to forget that without himself or the now pitiable *Studies in Hysteria*, the profession would not exist. It is the subsequent development of psychoanalytic theory that has produced the 'numerous gaps' that can now be closed: literally, the passage speaks of their 'later filling', *nachträglichen Ausfullung*. This model of a delayed fulfilment and a changing relation to past events evokes a temporal and interpretative structure which, by the time of the belated footnote itself, applied both to the psychoanalytic theory of a life-story and, as here, to the history of psychoanalysis as a practice. In psychoanalysis as a whole (as with other disciplines), advances in knowledge retrospectively reveal gaps in the notions of an earlier moment. But later developments can also bring out anticipations as well as absences in the earlier theory. According to Freud's 'afterwards' logic of *Nachträglichkeit*, old events are newly translated, take on a different significance, at a later point. In the same way, it is as though we have never quite done with hysteria; it is always, repeatedly, necessary to return to it, to see what it lacked or promised, to try to understand what is going on in its own apparently unprompted return in the present time.

Rereading the *Studies* in this way, we find that the two-time structure is already identified in the case of Fräulein Elisabeth von R., for whom an earlier, forgotten scene turns out to have laid the foundations for her distress at a second event which is unconsciously recognized as comparable. The first moment now appears as a forerunner and first instance of the second, in relation to which its meaning is established. In such contexts Freud often uses the archaeological analogy that he would continue to deploy for the process of analysis: 'This procedure involved a level-by-level clearing out [*Ausräumung*] of the pathogenic psychical material, and we liked to compare it to the technique of excavating a buried city (p. 143). It is as if the *Studies* themselves become the buried beginnings and foundations of the fully elaborated theories and therapy of psychoanalysis. Re-reading the book, we cannot but spot many 'seeds', as Freud calls them in the Preface to the Second Edition, of the later plague or plant that would come to establish itself in so many parts of the world in the course of the twentieth century.

In some instances, what had first been seen as neurotic features of hysterical behaviour made their way into psychoanalytic accounts of subjectivity in general. After Anna O.'s 'private theatre' and double consciousness, the strange 'second' states of hypnosis and reverie, Freud proceeded, over the following years, to develop the theory of the unconscious as a universal feature of human minds. The division of conscious and unconscious, with the obscure pressures and deflections of inadmissible thoughts, became for Freud the pattern for human psychology in general, not just for the hysterical patients who had first pointed it out to him: 'I didn't know – or rather I didn't want to know.' A related move from (neurotic) exception to (normal) generality, or ordinary neurosis, takes place with the notion of psychical conflict. In the *Studies*, this conception is more Freud's than Breuer's, and its deployment by the end of the book anticipates the parting of their ways. Where Breuer keeps to the idea of a missing reaction, an experience that has not been properly dealt with, Freud increasingly adopts the idea of a dynamic rejection from consciousness of what is incompatible with it. The symptom that results retains but distorts the memory of its cause; it allows a provisional resolution of the conflict. Over the next few years, this notion of compromise – a stabilization that is always at risk of breaking down – would come to be central to Freud's view of psychical mechanisms. Conflict and compromise would come to seem the norm rather than the (neurotic) exception of mental life, now thought of as an inevitable and perpetual struggle between what instincts may seek, and what consciousness or circumstances may refuse.

The question of women is another area in which the *Studies* appear retrospectively as buried anticipations of later theories. Although all the case histories, including the minor ones, are about women, the *Studies in Hysteria* are not presented as studies in femininity. After the 1890s, not only did hysteria fade from psycho-analytic focus, but the default psychoanalytic subject underwent a change of sex from (aberrant, hysterical) female to (ordinary, Oedipal) male. And then much later, when the question of women's difference was raised as a separate issue in the 1920s, the old theory of hysteria was itself like an unexcavated 'buried city', underlying the emergent theory of women's early development, now in contrast to men's.

In these later writings, on femininity, Freud considers the centrality of the early relationship of mother and daughter, again using an archaeological metaphor. The newly discovered significance of the first importance of the mother–daughter relationship is compared to the recent retrieval of the remains of the Minoan-Mycenaean civilization beneath and before that of the golden age of Athenian culture. In thus rectifying what is now exposed as an omission, Freud makes visible the sparse attention to mothers and to relationships between women more generally in the *Studies in Hysteria* (and the 'Dora' case of 1905). Anna O.'s mother, for instance, has only a fleeting role in the case history, as the author of the diary that testifies to the accuracy of Anna's relivings of the same days of a year before when her husband, Anna's father, was dying. Because he is interested in the mother's words only as evidence for what actually happened, Freud does not look at how mother and daughter have each in one sense been engaged in the same process, with their own times and ways of marking and remembering those days. There is no discussion of the mother–daughter relationship itself. Similarly, Frau Emmy von N.'s relationships with her two daughters, her only immediate family at the time of her analysis, are explored much less than the connection of her present illness to her husband's untimely death, and the possibility of a practical cure if she were to remarry.

But from the point of view of the larger issues surrounding women's development in Freudian theory, the discovery of mothers is not necessarily a happy addition to the family. Mothers are identified with a moment of prehistoric exoticism, with a little-known and less sophisticated culture that came before the democracy and the intellectual achievements of fifth-century Greece, regarded in Freud's time not just as the beginning of European culture but as a high point of civilization that would never be equalled. This pattern fits perfectly the Freudian theory of femininity as it came to be settled in the 1920s and 1930s: women never have the chance to move out of the restrictive world of the family into the wider republic of equal citizens who have gone beyond the princely period of their infancy at home. Hysteria here makes a kind of return, incognito, in the interwar decades, when some of its features reappear in the form of a protesting, inherently unsatisfied and misfit femininity. This femininity is like a mythicized version of the situations of most of Breuer and Freud's nineteenth-century women patients. It puts women into a necessarily subordinate, secondary role: not men, not full subjects and never quite reconciled to their situation. At the same time, unlike the *Studies*, it sees women's troubles not just individually but in structural terms. Women suffer not only from reminiscences, but from the difficulties of being women.

In the femininity papers, the significance and complexity of sexuality in male and female development is axiomatic. By contrast, we might imagine from much of the literature that relates to the *Studies in Hysteria*, and in particular to the Anna O. case, that sexuality was yet to emerge as an explicit issue in Freud's, and especially in Breuer's account. It seems to be there and not there, appearing for a moment only to be quickly tidied away again. Speaking of Anna O., Breuer famously declared that 'the element of sexuality was astonishingly undeveloped' (p. 25). Starting with Ernest Jones in his biography of Freud, generations of subsequent commentators have gone back to this fateful remark. It would be interesting for Breuer to have said that Anna O. happened to lack one admittedly major feature of normal human character, when that very 'element' later came to be seen as so central to the psychoanalytic conception of human development. But it was another thing entirely that he subsequently seemed to have made his claim defensively. Breuer's account does not report the alleged final episode of Anna's consultations with him, when she announced the arrival of 'Dr Breuer's baby'. Breuer's failure to acknowledge this putative event in his write-up then stands in sharp contrast to Freud's remarks at the end of the book, where he begins to explore the curious way in which patients 'transfer' to the doctor feelings they have experienced in relation to someone else. In his own *dénouement*, we can see Freud on the way to what would become the fully fledged theory of transference as a vital component in analytic work. Rather than the new symptom adding to analytic work, as a further 'obstacle', it could instead provide an alternative means of understanding what was essentially the same problem:

> The patients, too, gradually learnt to see that these kinds of transference to the person of the doctor were a matter of a compulsion and an illusion that would melt away when the analysis was brought to a close. (p. 305)

Again, there is a magical element, with an involuntary 'compulsion' and 'illusion' apparently dissolving into thin air. But from this perspective, the difference between Breuer and Freud would be that Breuer himself repudiated, chose to ignore, what he regarded as the embarrassment of Anna O.'s feelings for him: Bertha Pappenheim falling for Josef Breuer, not a patient naturally making a transference onto her doctor. So the narrative sequence of the *Studies* themselves seems to foreshadow the breaks that were about to occur. Breuer, it appears, withdraws from the awkwardness of a personal involvement, whereas Freud comes to see that 'the whole process followed a law' (p. 305): what had seemed at first to be another difficulty in the way of the therapeutic process turned out to herald a breakthrough.

The idea that it might make no difference whether what you explore is the present transferential symptom or its real-life original implies a move away from the question of what happened or what the patient thought (in reality) to that of how events and feelings that occur to the patient are experienced. The point of an analysis would then be not so much to get at some ultimate precipitating cause – the 'foreign body' or 'buried city' of Breuer and Freud's metaphors – as to enable the patient to understand, through the 'transferred' relationship to the analyst and the artificial situation of the sessions themselves, that she casts both herself and those around her in characteristic kinds of role. For the patient to see her own active share in affecting the parts and the script is the start of change. Here, for instance, the terms point to much later formulations:

> Even when everything is over, when the patients have been overwhelmed by the force of logic and convinced of the curative effect that accompanied the emergence of precisely these ideas . . . they will often add, 'But *remember* that I thought that? That I can't do.' . . . Should we suppose that we are really dealing with thoughts that did not materialize, whose existence was only ever potential, and that the therapy consisted in accomplishing a psychical act that did not occur at the time? (pp. 301–2)

Conviction takes precedence here over the actual occurrence; the emphasis is on a mental event, 'accomplishing a psychical act', here and now. What matters is the sense of completion, a process allowed to come to an end.

In that notion of a 'psychical' act lies one germ or seed of the end point of Freud's rapidly changing hypotheses at this time about the significance of sexuality. For a while, in the years immediately following the *Studies*, he took seriously the hypothesis that such children's 'seduction', pathological on the part of the perpetrators and harmful to the victims, was in reality extremely widespread. Then, in what came to be quaintly called his 'abandonment' of the seduction theory, he changed his mind. Sexuality was indeed at the centre; but as something imagined, rather than actually undergone, by the child. This move ushered in the concept of psychical reality that we can already see adumbrated in the preliminary idea of transference and the primacy of a 'psychical' act. The argument about the reality or prevalence of child abuse returned with a vengeance in the 1990s as a controversy about the truth or falsehood of patients' claims to have recovered memories of childhood sexual abuse in the course of therapy. But for Freud, by the time of 'Hysterical Phantasies and their Relation to Bisexuality', in 1907, the constitutive role of fantasy, or psychical reality, was largely taken for granted.

Before looking in more detail at that essay, we might consider how sexuality appears in the earlier world of the *Studies in Hysteria*. There is Breuer's revealing remark, raising and dropping the question in a single sentence. Yet elsewhere, and by both authors, the importance of sexuality is affirmed as clearly as it ever would be in subsequent Freudian writings, and almost as a matter of course. In speaking about Frau Emmy von N., Freud sounds like Breuer in relation to Anna O.: 'among all the intimate information which the patient communicated to me, the sexual element, which is after all more liable than any other to give rise to traumas, was completely absent' (p. 94). 'After all' makes it seem uncontroversial and obvious.

Freud goes on to say that rather than take Frau Emmy at her word, or her silence, he assumes that there must have been a process of censorship involved, a gap or erasure of what was undoubtedly there. Censorship was to be a persistent analogy of Freud's for thinking about how one part of the mind bans the thoughts of another. Here it is taken to be motivated by embarrassment; but beneath this, it is assumed that Frau Emmy von N. has 'sexual needs', 'and had sometimes reached a point of severe exhaustion in her attempt to suppress this most powerful of all drives' (p. 95).

As in later Freudian theory, sexuality is acknowledged to be of pre-eminent importance, and in women as much as in men. But unlike the later view, sexual satisfaction is not in itself a complicated matter. 'Abstinence' and 'celibacy' are the terms regularly used in this context: get Frau Emmy a new husband, Freud implies, and her troubles might be over.

This view of the sexual instinct as naturally needing a fulfilment, thwarted only by lack of opportunity, or by forms of shame, is neatly articulated by Breuer:

> Sexuality appears at puberty ... as a vague, indefinite, aimless increase in excitation. In later development (in the normal course of things) this endogenous increase in excitation caused by the functioning of the sex glands becomes firmly connected with the perception or idea of the opposite sex and, of course, with the idea of a particular individual, when the wonderful phenomenon of falling in love occurs. (pp. 202–3)

Breuer describes the gradual direction of a bodily instinct towards an appropriate social and personal end, so that perfect union with someone of the other sex perfectly fits and fulfils the growing urge. By the time of 'Hysterical Phantasies', and especially in the *Three Essays on Sexual Theory* (1905), Freud had elaborated a view of sexuality diametrically opposed to this one, which survives only as the starting point to be debunked and dismantled. Human sexuality does not naturally seek or find the outlet or partner that, from a biological point of view, should secure the reproduction of the species; instead, what needs to be explained is how it comes about that most humans ultimately do behave according to the norm.

'Hysterical Phantasies' begins with a classic daydreaming scene – straight out of *Studies in Hysteria*, it might seem, except that here the dreamy girl is not sitting up at night by a sick-bed, but walking down the street. It is tempting to read this as emblematic of a move from the nineteenth to the twentieth century. The woman has left the house and is now moving in the urban, public spaces that had previously been largely out of bounds for ladies. And yet, for the time being, the tale the woman is telling herself is a classic love story of feminine abandonment by a more powerful man. As though watching a silent movie, the dreamer works herself up to climactic tears as she walks along, sympathizing with herself as pitiful, devoted victim. The driving force of the dream is the fantasy, if not the reality, of a romantic completion like Breuer's version.

In its last section, though, the essay moves beyond the habitual or conscious fantasy. Freud postulates that bisexual fantasies, where the subject alternates between one identity and the other, are 'common enough'; he gives as examples a person who while masturbating 'tries in their conscious phantasies to empathize with both the man and the woman in the imagined situation', and the woman who, during a hysterical attack (and so unconsciously), 'plays both parts in the underlying sexual phantasy at once' (p. 315). Both parts, not all four: implicitly the man and woman with whom both subjects identify themselves are each involved in sexual encounters with the other sex, not with another man or another woman. In other writings, Freud would also explore these further permutations of the normal pairing, which follow from his own undoing of its naturalistic premises. And the breakdown can go further than the three possible couples (man–woman, man–man, woman–woman), beyond the assumption of two participants and beyond the specification of one sex or another. In 'A Child is Being Beaten' (1919), for instance, which analyses a number of conscious and unconscious fantasies, the sex of the participants is often unclear, and so is their number.

In moving from the old-fashioned daydream to the modern performance of sexual roles, 'Hysterical Phantasies' can seem, very neatly, to recapitulate the phases of development in Freud's thinking about sexuality up to that point, just as he tends to claim, in a would-be evolutionary mode, that human maturation, both biologically and socially, 'recapitulates' the development of the species. From the perspective of a century later, it can also appear that Freud's stress on sexual identity as role and performance, rather than as nature or final destiny, is a striking anticipation both of the theories and of the new existential situation of a post-modern world in which it is possible to opt for forms of sexual identity and sexual practice that would scarcely have been thinkable, let alone livable, for Freud's contemporaries. The present language of options and preferences, in every field from sex to computers, naturalizes a world imagined in terms of mobility and multiple choices.

There also seems to have been a change of emphasis, from 'Hysterics suffer mainly from reminiscences' to something like 'Hysterics suffer mainly from fantasies'. The last section of the essay gives a list of some characteristics of hysterical symptoms. It is full of bizarre overlapping categories, as Freud points out himself. Only the first two numbered points bear a trace of the hysteria of the mid-1890s, mentioning mnemic symbols, traumatic experiences and conversion. And of these the first and last are placed in quotation marks – now as if doubtfully, whereas in the *Studies* the same punctuation had been used to highlight a new term in need of explanation ('If, for the sake of brevity, we adopt the term "conversion" . . .' [p. 81]). The following seven points then draw on the general psychoanalytic theory that has been elaborated in the interim period. From the new perspective, hysterical symptoms represent the fulfilment of a wish; they are substitute formations, compromises between a sexual wish and its suppression. Sexuality has become, as it would remain for Freud, both the cornerstone and the stumbling block of mental life.

Another change apparent from the nine points is that hysteria has ceased to be treated distinctly as an illness. In one way this is indicated by the fact that the noun does not appear, only the adjective, 'hysterical', describing 'symptoms' or 'phantasies'. By this point, hysterical phenomena, like other neurotic symptoms, are primarily of interest not in themselves or in their differences from what is normal, but rather for their capacity to show up, as though in an exaggerated form, what is true of all: here, that 'man's postulated bisexual disposition can be observed with particular clarity in the psychoanalysis of psychoneurotics' (p. 314). This changed perspective is occasionally to be glimpsed in the *Studies in Hysteria*, as with Breuer's suggestion that behaviours like blushing or crying are ordinary examples of the bodily manifestation of feelings found in hysterical conversion. But the weight of this argument has shifted. The point now is not primarily to understand an illness whose mechanisms may have small-scale analogues in ordinary oddities, but to see how the sexual peculiarities of neurotic people are only a particularly 'visible' manifestation of a universal potential.

It is as though the revolutionary new theory of hysteria had rapidly run its course, to be left behind as the confused beginnings of what was not yet psychoanalysis. In the years since the *Studies in Hysteria*, Freud had written extensively on such topics as dreams and fantasy, jokes and the madness of everyday life, each the subjects of best-selling books that reached an audience far beyond the medical community. So his own interests, and the broader theory of psycho-analysis, were moving beyond hysteria, beyond mental illness, and beyond particular cases, to the psychology of ordinary life.

In one way, madness was being brought down to earth; in another, real life was being rendered sensational. In the *Studies*, before psychoanalysis had itself become the talk of the town, Freud expresses anxiety about the generic category into which his writing might fall and the kind of reading experience it might attract. He worries about whether what he is writing is more entertaining than scientific: 'I myself still find it strange that the case histories that I write read like novellas and lack, so to speak, the serious stamp of science' (p. 164). But he also likens the course of a psychotherapy to a popular modern form of literary suspense:

> [T]he interruption that is dictated by incidental circumstances of the treatment, such as the hour being late and so on, often occurs at the most awkward points, precisely when we might be able to approach a decision or when a new theme emerges. These are the same difficulties that spoil anyone's reading of a novel serialized in a daily newspaper, when the heroine's decisive speech or, say, the ringing out of a shot is immediately followed by the words: 'To be continued'. (p. 299)

Here, far from appearing apart, the everyday and the dramatic are inseparably joined.

As this passage also suggests, with most of the patients described in the volume there are no formal boundaries to therapeutic sessions. Their hours are not fixed, sometimes seeming infinitely elastic, and meetings with the doctor happen not in a professional consulting room but in the patient's own home, where he is known to the family. Miss Lucy R. is the patient who happens to initiate the beginnings of future therapeutic formalities. As a governess, neither her time nor her home is her own. It is therefore she who visits Freud rather than the other way round, for sessions that are at set times and of more or less fixed duration. The different kind of thinking and experience of the analytic session is thus partitioned off, and ideally the patient acquires the ability to use this differentiation so as not to be 'obsessed . . . in the interval between two sessions of treatment' by something that has come up, and instead to 'learn to wait for the doctor' (p. 299). But theatricalization does not disappear with the development of more formal separations between the time of therapy and the ordinary life that continues to be lived on either side of it. The theory of transference, which Freud is beginning to develop at the end of the *Studies*, consolidates these kinds of change. The real-life doctor exits from the analytic stage, to be replaced by whatever cast of characters, seen as such, the patient may put in his place. The impersonal suspension of normal social exchange then provides the space for the patient to be able to see the roles into which she is casting both herself and the analyst in the conversation. And at the same time, the newspaper serial comparison takes the dramatic focus to a form that is at once modern, quotidian and never-ending.

At the very end of his concluding essay, Freud announces: 'not until the last words of the analysis does the clinical picture disappear in its entirety (p. 300)'. This conjures up exactly the same theatrical and magical scenario as with the hypothetical disappearance of the symptom gone 'forever'. We have seen how the ghost of hysteria, vanished if not banished from the horizons of twentieth-century psychoanalysis, has never stopped coming back, in every kind of guise and disguise. And in one way, perhaps the only element that really did vanish for ever was the belief in the possibility of a total cure, once and for all. More than forty years after the *Studies*, in 'Analysis Terminable and Interminable' (1937), Freud stated clearly the limits of psychoanalytic treatment, which can never produce, nor should it, a patient immune to the unforeseeable experiences that may come her way in life after therapy. The subsequent histories of the patients we know about suggest that the end of the treatment with Breuer or Freud did not render them proof against further mental troubles. And already at the end of this text, Freud delicately shifts the focus away from a putative invasive element to a more or less favourable environment. He deploys a direct analogy with surgery:

> I have frequently compared cathartic psychotherapy with surgical interventions, describing my treatments as *psychotherapeutic operations*, which in turn leads to analogies with opening up a cavity filled with pus, scraping out a carious area and so on. Analogies of this kind are not so much justified in terms of removing what is diseased as they are in terms of establishing conditions that in the course of the process are more favourable to the cure. (p. 306)

Here Freud is overtly moving away from the 'cathartic' model with which he and Breuer had first sought to explain the success of their new mode of treatment. The aim now is not so much to cut out a noxious element that can be isolated and permanently removed, but to alter the environment within which the patient will deal with what she encounters in her present and future life. (It is ironic that here and often elsewhere Freud chooses a strictly medical analogy for talking about the hysteric for whom, in particular, the body is troublingly implicated with the mind.) The job of the surgeon/ therapist sounds much more like a routine operation of clearing out, clearing a passage. It is not very exciting; and it will eventually need doing again.

At another stage in the elaboration of therapeutic practice, Freud speaks of the curative effect, as more symptoms are generated during the course of an illness, of a 'regular removal' [*die jedesmalige Beseitigung*] (p. 265). It is, as he says, 'a Sisyphean task' (p. 265), characteristically turning to Greek mythology for something that Anna O. herself presented in rather more modern and mundane terms when she called it 'chimney-sweeping'.[2] This expression is recorded in the same breath – of Breuer's, if not hers – as the talking cure, and it too is in English in her utterance and in the German text: 'the apt and serious "*talking cure*" and the humorous "*chimney-sweeping*"' (p. 34). Breuer thus brushes off the chimney-sweeping as just Anna's little joke, and pursues it no further. But in fact it is suggestive in a number of ways.

Chimney-sweeping might, at a push, have something in common with the dramatic model. As secret conduits between the interior and the outside world, chimneys do evoke something of the ghostly ambiguity of the hysterical symptom as 'foreign body', a nebulous and unwelcome visitor to the patient no longer master in their own house. But chimney-sweeping is not normally to do with getting rid of intruders. What is removed is only the unmourned ashes and dust of daily life. And the blackness of the chimney is not in itself threatening or ominous; it is the remains of a warm hearth. So chimney-sweeping might point towards the move away from the rigid separation implied by the metaphor of the foreign body. No house (or body, or subject) is at any time complete and whole, without openings through which outsiders, welcome and unwelcome, come and go. Otherwise, there would be no circulation, no life and no history. Thus it is not the foreign body as such which is the source of trouble, but the way in which it can be received. Freud's analogy with the surgical operation points to exactly this modification: the task of analysis now is to enable the patient (like the bodily environment) to be able to take in and respond to what comes her way.

The *Studies* conclude with the almost painfully modest promise that all analysis can do is to try to transform 'hysterical misery into common unhappiness [*gemeines Unglück*]', enabling patients to 'arm' themselves better against that unhappiness (p. 306). There is also something commonplace about chimney-sweeping. It is a messy job that has to be done regularly in order for life to continue as normal but that, unlike a theatre, public or private, goes on *behind* the scenes. It is a necessary and dirty task – domestic, but semi-external, and usually undertaken by paid outsiders. It is best not seen but unnoticed, showing up only negatively, when it hasn't been done. Dramatic *dénouements* seem to be in another world from the regular household work that is never over because there will always be new experiences to be cleared up and dealt with.

Breuer in particular stresses the way that patients' troubles are often derived from aspects of their domestic role. Of his two typical situations giving rise to hysterical daydreaming, sick-nursing involves, as well as continual anxiety, hard work and repetitiveness. Like chimney-sweeping it also involves working and waking in the dark, having to live according to another rhythm from the natural alternations of day and night. In these connections, Breuer and Freud's regular use of metaphors of wiping away, sweeping up and brushing away to describe their removal of symptoms begins to make the process of therapy sound like a matter of housework. At the other extreme from the dramatic model, this analogy associates the talking cure with routine, daily life, necessary household work. Like all domestic tasks, chimney-sweeping is never finally done. It doesn't vanish, never to return. And no more did the hysteria of the 1890s disappear once and for all, forgotten in the subsequent emergence of new kinds of twentieth-century symptom, and buried like a lost city under the modern developments of later psychoanalytic and psychiatric doctrines, disputes and institutions. Instead, we have found the subject of hysteria returning again and again – to haunt with the shadow of its strangeness, and also with the sense of something remaining from the nineteenth century which will never quite go away.

Rachel Bowlby, 2003

My warm thanks to Kate Flint, Nicola Luckhurst, Adam Phillips and Carl Schorske for their help.

Notes

1. Aristotle's notion of catharsis was the object of extensive debate among classical scholars in the nineteenth century. Closer to home, it was none other than Freud's own uncle by marriage, Jacob Bernays, who had

controversially brought out the bodily and therapeutic connotations of catharsis; whence Breuer and Freud's transposition of the word to actual medical practice. See Jacques Le Rider, *Freud, de l'Acropole au Sinaï: Le retour à l'Antique des Modernes viennois* (Paris: PUF, 2002), pp. 177–89.

2. In fact, Freud calls it not a Sisyphean task but a task of the Danaides, a *Danaidenarbeit*. Both Sisyphus and the Danaides suggest the idea of an interminable, perpetually repeated task, one that is imposed as a permanent punishment in hell. Sisyphus endlessly rolls a boulder up a hill before it drops down and he begins again, while the daughters of Danaus are forever filling leaky containers with water. Presumably the present translator, like James Strachey in the *Standard Edition*, changed the Danaides to Sisyphus as a more familiar figure to English-speaking readers. But the differences are worth attention. The Danaides nicely change the expected gender of the analyst-figure, at a time when women were not yet doing the job in reality. The analogy also blurs the distinction between patients and doctors, by identifying the doctor with a group of women, like all the hysterics described in this volume: patients too faced a potentially endless task.

Further Reading

Appignanesi, Lisa, and John Forrester, *Freud's Women* (1992; 2nd edn, London: Penguin, 2000)

Bollas, Christopher, *Hysteria* (London: Routledge, 2000)

Bronfen, Elisabeth, *The Knotted Subject: Hysteria and its Discontents* (Princeton: Princeton University Press, 1998)

Didi-Huberman, Georges, *Invention de l'hystérie: Charcot et l'iconographie photographique de la Salpêtrière* (Paris: Macula, 1982)

Jones, Ernest, *Sigmund Freud: His Life and Work*, 3 vols (London: Hogarth Press, 1953–7)

Le Rider, Jacques, *Freud, de l'Acropole au Sinaï: Le retour à l'Antique des Modernes viennois* (Paris: PUF, 2002)

Micale, Mark S., *Approaching Hysteria* (Princeton: Princeton University Press, 1994)

Mitchell, Juliet, *Mad Men and Medusas: Reclaiming Hysteria and the Effects of Sibling Relations on the Human Condition* (London: Allen Lane, 2000)

Roudinesco, Élisabeth, *Why Psychoanalysis?* (1999), trans. Rachel Bowlby (New York: Columbia University Press, 2001)

Showalter, Elaine, *Hystories: Hysterical Epidemics and Modern Culture* (London: Picador, 1997)

Veith, Ilza, *Hysteria: The History of a Disease* (Chicago: University of Chicago Press, 1965)

Translator's Preface

Unlike a work of literature, translation finds itself not in the centre of the language forest but on the outside facing the wooded ridge; it calls into it without entering, aiming at that single spot where the echo is able to give, in its own language, the reverberation of the work in the alien one.

Walter Benjamin, 'The Task of the Translator'

Every translation has its agenda. It also has an unconscious agenda, which might be called its place in time. My translation of *Studies in Hysteria*, as part of Penguin's new translation of Freud, had been given an anti-agenda – I was to produce a 'literary' translation. In other words I was on my own with the text, not part of any regulated translation project, not subject to standardization or group politics. But I was also translating with an awareness of the history of Freud's passage into English and of his current retranslation and re-evaluation in English and in other languages. The strength of James Strachey's classic translation is such that when people heard that I was translating Freud they would often ask 'into which language?' – the degree of naturalization means that Freud is felt by many to have written in English. As Joyce Crick notes, 'It has for half a century belonged to that rare category of translations which Goethe described as read not instead of the original, but in their place.'[1] And as regards terminology, Strachey's choices, 'cathexis', 'ego', 'id' and so on, have passed into, if not common usage, then at least common intellectual usage. His agenda involved bringing Freud into English as a consistent, convincing and scientific body of writing and it was achieved by his work as editor and translator in the creation of the *Standard Edition*.[2] Translating Freud today, we, the Penguin translators, are relieved of this agenda – but it has a powerful legacy. It informs both the Institute of Psychoanalysis's project of publishing a revised Strachey – a new 'official Freud' – and its non-institutional French counterpart, a new translation whose manifesto explicitly rejects the idea of a 'Strachey français'.[3] The Institute's English translation has chosen to preserve Strachey's work, albeit making corrections to it; the French have chosen to translate counter-Strachey, whose edition they refer to as the 'vulgate Freud'. This means resisting the urge to 'tame' or 'acclimatize' the text, and instead translating as closely as possible to the original, but according to a highly regulated programme of terms and principles. This manifesto suggests that the principle of truth to the letter of the original is so strong that translation choices will be made – both syntactical and as regards terminology – that will sound unnatural in the French, and indeed the aim is, in part, that the French language will be changed by the translation.

I want to describe this context of translation in order to indicate just how serious the business of translating Freud is for the psychoanalytic community of practitioners and scholars – and to recall that there are other kinds of seriousness informing translation. These have to do, quite simply, with translating a literary text, by which I mean an attention to the writing – to language, register and style. This attention is unencumbered by the need to standardize, which must necessarily skew the translation – there being no one-to-one equivalence between languages, a translator having to find a variety of effects to capture the original. And it is an attention which can, I hope, open up new ways for us to hear Freud – to hear things that are latent in the text and that might otherwise be passed over.

I knew that I wanted to stay close to the text – of course. I wanted to stay with what is at times its roughness and strangeness of style, and with the sense that the writers – Freud and Breuer – were developing a new language, the language of psychoanalysis. In stylistic terms, this closeness might mean translating the historic present tense in German as the historic present in English – not smoothing it into the contours of a past narrative as has been done before. This present-tenseness is, I feel, both that of the thought process in which Freud as writer is thinking through, working with the material; but also that of the showman, whereby the clinician is literally showing his work – his patients – and presenting the reader with this encounter in the most immediate way possible. The immediacy may result in note form, as if we were very close to the material in time. I have retained this form, resisted 'correction' of the text (the insertion of verbs to make complete sentences, for example), because again it seemed important to render the newness of what is being done and how it is being presented to the reader. Which is to say that, rather in the style of Proust's *A la recherche du temps perdu*, Freud is often working and thinking aloud – making the reader party to his intellectual processes. At other times, of course, the style swings back to that of the expert, so that we have a curious and beguiling sense of hesitation between 'work in progress' and intellectual bravura.

There is a similar hesitation between art and science. This is famously the text of which Freud wrote, 'I myself still find it strange that the case histories that I write read like novellas and lack, so to speak, the serious stamp of science.' But Freud's statement sits alongside analogies in which cerebral paths of conduction are represented as telephone wires or as an 'electrical system with many different branches for supplying light and transmitting motor power, a system which is required to make each lamp and machine operate simply by establishing a contact'. The hesitation is felt too at the level of vocabulary. In this early, possibly founding text in the history of psychoanalysis (*Studies in Hysteria* was first published in 1895) the battery of technical terms is not yet developed. Rather, a theoretical language is emerging and there were points at which I found it difficult to assess whether a word was still being used in its full, 'everyday' sense or whether it had been coined as a technical term. The most striking instance of this is the word *Besetzung*, meaning 'charge', 'investment' and 'occupation' – with its latent electrical, economic and military metaphors. This translator's problem, namely that there is no single-word equivalent in English, has been the subject of much discussion, as has Strachey's solution to it.[4] Strachey coined 'cathexis' to deal with this cluster of meanings. He also notes that *Besetzung*-cathexis makes its first appearance in 'the special sense in which Freud used it to denote one of the most fundamental concepts in his psychological theory' in *Studies on Hysteria*.[5] Now this poses a problem for later translators. In a sense Strachey has broken the rules: he has used a neologism to render what is not a neologism in the original. More problematic is that his invented word has caught on – at least among psychoanalytically informed readers. First, I had to ask 'Is Freud's usage here already so firm that we can say *Besetzung* is being used in a precise theoretical sense?' I wasn't sure that it was. My understanding was rather that he was still feeling his way to what the word might mean, that the richness of its different inflections was very much present. Second, I had to think about readership. For those familiar with psychoanalytic literature 'cathexis' would be fine; for other readers, probably the majority, it would need a footnote. The most honest and pragmatic solution – if not entirely satisfactory – seemed to be to incorporate the reaching towards meaning that I felt was present in Freud's usage. In this way I could accept that Strachey's coining of cathexis had passed into the literature, and at the same time use the stylistic trait of working through to provide the reader with the various significations of the German that are encapsulated by this technical term. My translation of the sentence reads as follows: 'I drew on examples from everyday life to show that when an idea is cathected – that is, charged, invested and occupied – with unresolved affect in this way it will always bring with it a certain degree of associative inaccessibility and incompatibility with new cathexes.' I think this is the point at which I have taken most liberties with the text. Other key terms that are contentious in later texts are less so here. '*Das Ich*', which Strachey translates as 'the ego', I render as 'the self' because in this early text Freud is not referring to it as part of a complex model of the mind; rather it is being used in a more ordinary sense. The word choices I have made don't, however, always make things easier for the reader or easier on the ear. '*Affekt*' on the whole remains 'affect' and does not become, say, 'feeling' or 'emotion' in the English, because the German is a difficult, high-register term and because it describes a state that is more acute than 'feeling' or 'emotion'. The English 'affect' is somewhat more unusual than its German counterpart, but better this slight disjunction than a language of feeling which was too everyday and undifferentiated.[6]

The terminology of psychoanalysis is one of the most striking and contentious areas of translation, but Freud's language does, of course, work through metaphors and narratives, as well as key terms. For example, I was struck by the metaphorical language of pregnancy, labour and childbirth that permeates *Studies in Hysteria*: words such as *'erzeugen'*, meaning 'to beget, produce, engender', as in 'the engendering of symptoms', or statements in which pathogenic ideas are 'torn precipitately from [their] context' ('The Psycho-therapy of Hysteria'), as if extracted by caesarean section. Emmy von N. is strikingly described as *'der größten Entbindung von Leiden-schaftlichkeit fähig'*, 'capable of delivering the greatest passion', where the German *'Entbindung'* suggests delivery in childbirth. These metaphors, often neutralized in earlier translations, seem important in that they indicate an unconscious feminine identifica-tion – by which I mean Freud's empathy (or counter-transference) for his patients as women and as mothers. Recovering these meta-phors may allow hysteria to signify differently, as we hear Freud's patients dis-identify with their maternal or pregnant self, and project it into the psychoanalyst.

The physicality of Freud's German at times suggests that he is speaking the language of the hysteric – whether by unconscious identification or by conscious intent, as part of his therapeutic technique. Hysteria is described as creating 'somatic expressions', physical symptoms, to stand for 'affectively marked idea[s]'. Of Frau Cäcilie M. (p. 183) Freud states: 'In taking the verbal expression literally – feeling the "heart bleeding" and the "slap in the face" when spoken to in a wounding way as a real event – she is not practising some kind of witty verbal misuse, but simply reviving the sensations to which the expression owes its justification.' And his conclusion – 'Perhaps [it is] wrong to say that [hysteria] creates these kinds of sensation by symbolization; it may be that it has not taken linguistic usage as its model at all, but that both hysteria and linguistic usage draw from a common source' – suggests that hysteria itself might be considered a form of language. But this is not simply the subject of discussion in *Studies in Hysteria*, rather Freud's language mirrors the bodily language of the hysteric: he uses a physical vocabulary to describe the psychical, just as the hysteric's symptoms are a translation of psychical distress into the physical. More than this, he develops and describes a therapeutic technique in which the hysteric is made to speak as a result of physical pressure. It is as if Freud were trying to give a physical sense of how ideas feel, the pressure that they exert and, in turn, the pressure that the analyst must exert in order to discover what the patient is thinking:[7]

> A psychical force [. . .] had originally pushed the pathogenic idea out of association and was now opposing its return to memory [. . .] the therapist's task consists in overcoming this *resistance to association* through psychical work. This can be accomplished first by means of 'pushing', through the application of psychical compulsion in order to direct the patients' attention to the traces of ideas that are being sought. (p. 271)

But, Freud continues,

> For an unfamiliar doctor who is unacquainted with the matter, 'pushing' will be no match for the 'resistance to association' of a serious hysteria. More powerful means must be devised.
>
> At this point I turn first to a small technical trick. I tell the patient that in a moment I am going to apply pressure to his forehead, assure him that throughout the application of this pressure a memory will appear to him either in the form of an image or as an idea coming to mind, and I make him promise to tell me about this image or idea, whatever it may be. (p. 272)

Only by selecting words which will retain the physicality of the German – 'pushing', for example, rather than 'insisting' – can the translation suggest that Freud is in a sense speaking the language of the hysteric here.

There is a paradox in the translation practice I have adopted, which is that the new Penguin Freuds are meant to be more accessible to the general reader. But sticking with the – in part – roughness and present-tenseness of the text; not pre-theorizing when the language still seems open; attempting to preserve the physicality of a language that wants to involve the body when speaking of the emotions; not allowing the text to dissolve into our contemporary language of 'feeling' – all of this has consequences for readability. It may make the text more difficult, where Strachey's standardization of terms and the more authoritative narrative voice that he gives to Freud may make for a smoother read. My text tends to hesitate, as I feel the original does, between different styles, genres and voices – literally in the sense that the text is co-written by Freud and Breuer, but also because this is a second edition into which later materials have been inserted, and finally because we hear the voices of the patients, rendered with different degrees of directness of quotation. This exuberant heterogeneity of style might be described as modernist. More than that, as the metaphoric traces of pregnancy and childbirth suggest, it is a style which makes us party to the development and birth of psychoanalysis.

Notes

1. Joyce Crick, 'Note on the Translation', in Sigmund Freud, *The Interpretation of Dreams* (Oxford, 1999), p. xli.
2. As Anna Freud describes, 'His ambition went far beyond that of the mere translator. What he set out to do was to conjure up for the English-speaking public the whole conceptual world of psychoanalysis, to widen the existing language where it was unable to accommodate the new notions, and, simultaneously, to hold the right middle line between coining a precise and indispensable technical terminology and expressing complex thoughts in simple words. [...] It is difficult to judge now [...] whether in Strachey's own mind his role as translator had taken precedence over that of editor and commentator, or whether his interest had taken the opposite course.' *The Writings of Anna Freud*, vol. VII (New York, 1971), pp. 278–9.
3. See André Bourguignon, Pierre Cotet, Jean Laplanche and François Robert's *Traduire Freud* (Paris, 1989).

4. Darius Ornston, 'The Invention of "Cathexis" and Strachey's Strategy', *International Review of Psychoanalysis*, 12 (1985), 391–9; John Forrester, *Language and the Origins of Psychoanalysis* (London, 1980), p. 224.

5. Sigmund Freud, *Studies on Hysteria*, translated by J. Strachey (London, 1955), p. 89.

6. On the terminology and semantics of 'affect' see André Green, *The Fabric of Affect in the Psychoanalytic Discourse*, translated by A. Sheridan (London, 1999), pp. xii–xiii, and pp. 4–8.

7. See John Forrester's article, 'The Balance of Power Between Freud and His Early Women Patients', in André Haynal and Ernst Falzeder (eds), *One Hundred Years of Psychoanalysis. Contributions to the History of Psychoanalysis* (Geneva, 1994), pp. 41–54.

Acknowledgements

This translation was completed during my British Academy Fellowship.

I would like to thank Ladislaus Löb for his careful reading of my translation, his constructive and elegant suggestions, and for saving me from a number of errors. I'm also immensely grateful to Stephen Lehmann for his acute and sensitive responses to my queries. Warm thanks are due to friends and colleagues – Louise Adey-Huish, Christopher Bollas, Rachel Bowlby, Susan Budd, Rima Dapous, John Forrester, Annette Haberstock, Pauline von Hellermann, Dorothee von Hellermann, Rupert Reed, Ritchie Robertson, Sarah Wootton, the students of the Psychoanalysis Unit at University College London (2001–2002) – and to my editors, Anna South and Simon Winder at Penguin, my copy editor, Jane Robertson, and Adam Phillips.

Finally I want to thank the person to whom I dedicate this translation, Stephen Grosz.

Preface to the first edition

In a 'Preliminary Statement' of 1893[1] we published our experiences of a new method for investigating and treating hysterical phenomena and attached as succinct an account as possible of the theoretical views at which we had arrived. This 'Preliminary Statement' is reprinted here as the thesis to be illustrated and proven.

We have now appended a series of case histories which, unfortunately, we were unable to select for scientific reasons alone. Our experience was gathered in private practice among an educated and literate social class, and its subject matter touches in many ways on the most intimate life and fortune of our patients. It would be a severe abuse of confidence to publish reports of this kind, with the risk of patients being recognized and facts which had been entrusted to the doctor alone spreading among friends and acquaintances. We have had, therefore, to do without observations which are highly instructive and offer powerful evidence. This, of course, applies above all to those cases in which the sexual and marital relations have an aetiological significance. Thus we have been able to supply only very incomplete proof of our view that sexuality, as the source of psychical traumas and as the motive of 'defence', of the repression of ideas from consciousness, plays a major role in the pathogenesis of hysteria. Precisely these observations of a strongly sexual nature had to be excluded from publication.

The case histories are followed by a series of theoretical discussions, and in a concluding chapter on therapy the technique of the 'cathartic method' is expounded as it developed in the hands of the neurologist.

If at some points various and even contradictory opinions are

1

expressed, this should not be regarded as a fluctuation in our conception; rather, it corresponds to the natural and justifiable differences in opinion of two observers who agree about the facts and fundamental views, but whose interpretations and conjectures do not always coincide.

J. Breuer, S. Freud
April, 1895

Notes

1. 'On the psychical mechanism of hysterical phenomena', *Neurologisches Zentralblatt*, 1893, Nos. 1 and 2.

Preface to the second edition

The interest which is increasingly being directed towards psychoanalysis now seems to be extending to these *Studies in Hysteria*. The publisher wants to bring out a new edition of this book, which is now out of print, hence the publication of this unmodified reprint, despite the fact that the views and methods put forward in the first edition have since undergone a broad and far-reaching development. For my own part, I have not been actively involved with the subject since that time, have no share in the significant development it has made, and would not be in a position to add anything new to what was said in 1895. My only wish is, then, for my two contributions to the book to appear in the new edition unmodified.

Breuer

The only possible decision, as far as my part in this book is concerned, was likewise to reproduce the text of the first edition without modification. The developments and modifications which my views have undergone over the course of thirteen working years are too extensive for it to be feasible to bring them to bear on the exposition that I then made without completely destroying its character. Nor, however, do I have any motive for eliminating this evidence of my initial opinions. Even today I do not regard these as mistakes, but as valuable first approximations to insights which have only been gained in their more complete form after long and sustained effort. In this book, an attentive reader will be able to discover the seeds of all the later components of the theory of catharsis (as, for example, the role of psychosexual factors, infantilism, the meaning of dreams and the symbolism of the unconscious). And I can give no better advice to anyone interested in the way in which catharsis developed into psychoanalysis than to begin with the *Studies in Hysteria* and so to take the path that I myself have travelled.

Freud
Vienna, July 1908

I

On the Psychical Mechanism of Hysterical Phenomena[1]

(Preliminary Statement)
Dr Josef Breuer and
Dr Sigmund Freud, Vienna

1

Prompted by a chance observation, we have for a number of years been searching among the most diverse forms and symptoms of hysteria for their precipitating cause – the event which, often many years earlier, first gave rise to the phenomenon in question. In the great majority of cases it is not possible to ascertain the point of origin by means of simple medical examination, however detailed, in part because it often involves experiences which patients find unpleasant to talk about, but principally because they really cannot remember them, and often have no sense of the causal connection between the precipitating event and the pathological phenomenon. Usually it is necessary to hypnotize the patients and arouse their memories of the time when the symptom first appeared under hypnosis; this enables the clearest and most convincing exposition of the connection to be given.

This method of examination has, in a great number of cases, produced results that seem valuable in both theoretical and practical terms.

In *theoretical* terms because they proved to us that chance factors determine the pathology of hysteria to a far greater degree than is known and acknowledged. It is, of course, self-evident that in 'traumatic' hysteria the accident gives rise to the syndrome, and the causal connection is equally evident in hysterical attacks, when it can be inferred from the patient's statements that they repeatedly hallucinate the same event which gave rise to the first attack. The matter is more obscure in the case of other phenomena.

Our experiences have, however, shown us *that the most diverse symptoms which are held to be spontaneous, so to speak idiopathic products of the hysteria, maintain an equally compelling connection to the precipitating trauma as do those phenomena mentioned above where the connection is quite transparent.* We have been able to trace various symptoms back to precipitating factors of this kind – all kinds of neuralgias and anaesthesias, which have often persisted for many years, contractures and paralyses, hysterical attacks and epileptoid convulsions that all observers had taken for genuine epilepsy, *petit mal* and tic-like affections, persistent vomiting and anorexia to the point of refusing all food, a great variety of visual disturbances, constantly recurring visual hallucinations and so on. The discrepancy between the hysterical symptom of many years' duration and the single precipitating cause is the same as the discrepancy which we are accustomed to see in traumatic neurosis; quite frequently, events from childhood establish a symptom of varying degrees of severity which persists for many years to come.

The connection is often so clear that it is perfectly apparent why the precipitating incident should have engendered this phenomenon rather than any other. The phenomenon has quite clearly been determined by the precipitating cause. A commonplace example of this might be, then, that a painful affect that arises while eating but is suppressed, subsequently engenders nausea and vomiting, which persists for months as hysterical vomiting. A girl, who, tormented by anxiety, is watching over a sick bed, falls into a twilight state and has a terrifying hallucination, while her right arm, which is hanging over the arm of the chair, goes to sleep; this develops into a paresis of the arm with contracture and anaesthesia. She wants to pray and cannot find the words; finally she manages to say a children's prayer in English. Later, when a difficult and highly complex hysteria develops, English is the only language that she can speak, write and understand, while her mother tongue is incomprehensible to her for eighteen months. – A child who is critically ill has at last fallen asleep; the mother exerts all her willpower in an attempt to keep quiet and not wake the child; but precisely as a consequence of this intention ('hysterical spirit of contradiction'!) she makes a clicking noise with her tongue. This noise is later repeated on another occasion when, again, she wants to keep absolutely quiet and it develops into a tic which for many years occurs whenever she is excited. – A highly intelligent man is present when his brother has an ankylosed hip joint stretched under anaesthetic. Just as the joint gives way with a crack he feels a violent pain in his own hip joint which then lasts for almost a year, and so on.

In other cases the connection is not as simple; all that is present is what might be called a symbolic relation between the cause and the pathological phenomenon, a relation such as healthy people form in dreams – so, for example, psychical pain is joined by a neuralgia or the feeling of moral disgust by vomiting. We have studied patients who made very extensive use of this kind of symbolization. In another group of cases this kind of determination is not readily comprehensible, and precisely those symptoms typical of hysteria – hemi-anaesthesia, narrowing of the field of vision, epileptiform convulsions and so on – belong to this category. The exposition of our views on this group will have to be reserved for a fuller discussion of the subject.

Observations of this kind seem to us proof of an analogy between the pathogenesis of common hysteria and that of traumatic neurosis, and to justify an extension of the concept of 'traumatic hysteria'. In the case of traumatic neuroses it is not the minor physical injury which is the effective cause of the illness, but the affect of fright, the *psychical trauma*. In a similar way our investigations revealed immediate causes for many if not most of the hysterical symptoms, which can only be described as psychical traumas. Any experience which gives rise to the distressing affects of fright, anxiety, shame or psychical pain can have this effect and, understandably, it depends on the sensitivity of the person concerned (as well as on a condition that will be mentioned later) whether the experience will take on traumatic value. In common hysteria, it is not unusual to find several partial traumas in the place of one major trauma, a group of immediate causes which could display a traumatic effect only by summation and which belong together in so far as they form, in part, the components of a single story of suffering. In yet another set of cases, what would seem in themselves to be indifferent circumstances coincide with the event that really is effective, or with a point in time of particular sensitivity, and thereby attain a dignity as traumas

9

that would not otherwise have been expected of them, but which they do subsequently retain.

But the causal connection between the precipitating psychical trauma and the hysterical phenomenon is not such that the trauma in its role as *agent provocateur* would release the symptom which would then continue to exist in its independent state. Rather we are bound to assert that the psychical trauma, or more precisely, the memory of it, operates like a foreign body which must still be regarded as a present and effective agent long after it has penetrated, and proof of this can be seen in an extremely curious phenomenon which is also of significant *practical* interest for our findings.

For we found, at first to our great surprise, that the individual hysterical symptoms disappeared immediately and did not recur if we succeeded in wakening the memory of the precipitating event with complete clarity, arousing with it the accompanying affect, and if the patient then depicted the event in the greatest possible detail and put words to the affect. Remembering without affect almost always fails to be effective; the psychical process that had originally taken place has to be repeated in as vivid a way as possible, brought to its *status nascendi*, and then 'talked through'. This makes any phenomena involving stimuli – cramps, neuralgias, hallucinations – appear once more at full intensity and then vanish for ever. Functional failures, paralyses and anaesthesias vanish in the same way, but of course without their momentary heightening being clearly visible.[2]

It seems reasonable to suspect that this is a matter of unintentional suggestion – that the patient is expecting to be freed from his suffering by the procedure, and that this expectation, not the talking through itself, is the operative factor. Yet this is not so: the first observation of this kind – in which an extremely involved case of hysteria was analysed in this way and the symptoms that had been separately caused were also removed separately – dates back to 1881, that is, to the 'pre-suggestion' period, was enabled by the patient's spontaneous autohypnoses and came as a great surprise to the observer.

By reversing the proposition '*cessante causa cessat effectus*' [when the cause ceases the effect ceases] we may conclude from these observations that the precipitating event in some way still continues to exercise an effect years later, not indirectly through a chain of intermediary causal links, but as a directly releasing cause, in something like the same way that a psychical pain remembered in waking consciousness will still produce the secretion of tears later on: *hysterics suffer for the most part from reminiscences.*[3]

2

At first it appears extraordinary that experiences long past should have such an intense effect, that the memories of them should not be subject to the same process of erosion to which, after all, we see all of our memories succumb. The following considerations will perhaps enable us to reach some understanding of these matters.

Whether a memory fades or rids itself of affect depends on several factors. Of the greatest importance is *whether or not there was an energetic reaction to the affecting event*. By reaction we mean here the whole set of voluntary and involuntary reflexes – from tears to acts of revenge – into which, as experience shows, emotions are discharged. If this reaction ensues to a sufficient extent, a large part of the affect will disappear; our language testifies to this fact of daily observation with expressions such as 'to let off steam', 'to cry one's eyes out' and so on. If the reaction is suppressed the affect remains bound up with the memory. An insult which has been repaid, albeit only verbally, will be remembered differently from one that had to be accepted. Language, too, acknowledges this difference in the psychical and physical consequences, and gives a highly characteristic description of precisely what is suffered in silence as 'injury'. – The hurt person's reaction to the trauma really only has a fully '*cathartic*' effect if it is an adequate reaction, like revenge. But language provides a surrogate for action and with its assistance the affect can be '*abreacted*' almost as well. In other cases, talking itself is the adequate reflex, it might be a complaint or the declaration of a tormenting secret (confession!). If a reaction of this kind is not forthcoming in word or deed, or, in the slightest cases, tears, then for the time being the memory of the incident retains its affective emphasis.

'Abreaction' is not, however, the only way of dealing with a psychical trauma available to the normal psychical mechanism of a healthy person. The memory of a trauma, even if it was not abreacted, enters the large complex of association, takes up its place alongside other experiences that may contradict it, is subjected to correction by other ideas. After an accident, for example, the memory of the danger and the (diminished) repetition of the fright are joined by the memory of what happened next, the rescue, the consciousness of being safe again. A memory of a hurtful statement is corrected by putting the facts right, by considering one's own worth and so on, such that, through the work of association, the normal person succeeds in causing the accompanying affect to disappear.

This is accompanied by that general blurring of impressions, that fading of memories which we call 'forgetting' and which erodes all ideas that no longer have an emotional effect.

From our observations it appears then that those memories which have become the precipitating causes of hysterical phenomena have been preserved with an astonishing freshness and retained their full affective emphasis over a long period of time. But mention needs to be made of another conspicuous fact which we shall be able to turn to account later, namely that these memories, unlike others from their past, are not at the patients' disposal. On the contrary, *these experiences are either completely absent from the patient's memory in their usual psychical state or only present in a highly summary form.* Not until one questions the patients under hypnosis are these memories restored with the undiminished vividness of recent events.

Thus, for six months, one of our patients reproduced under hypnosis and with hallucinatory vividness everything that had excited her on the same day of the previous year (during an acute hysteria); her mother's diary, of which she was unaware, testified to the flawless accuracy of the reproduction. Another patient, partly under hypnosis and partly during spontaneous attacks, relived with hallucinatory clarity all the events of a hysterical psychosis which she had gone through ten years previously and of which, for the most part, she had no memory until the moment at which it resurfaced. Even individual memories of aetiological importance which dated back between fifteen and twenty-five years turned out to be astonishingly intact and of remarkable sensory strength, and when they recurred exercised the full affective force of new experiences.

The reason for this can be found only in that these memories hold an exceptional position in all of the relations to erosion discussed above. *It appears, that is to say, that these memories correspond to traumas that have not been sufficiently 'abreacted'*, and on closer investigation of the reasons which have prevented this, it is possible to discover at least two sets of conditions under which the reaction to the trauma has not occurred.

Among the first group we include those cases in which the patients have not reacted to psychical traumas because the nature of the trauma precluded a reaction, as in the seemingly irreplaceable loss of a loved one, or because social circumstances made a reaction impossible, or because things were involved that the patient wanted to forget, that he intentionally repressed, inhibited and suppressed from his conscious thought. Precisely these kinds of distressing things are then, under hypnosis, found to be the foundation of hysterical phenomena (hysterical deliria in saints and nuns, abstinent women and well brought-up children).

The second set of conditions is determined not by the content of the memories, but by the psychical states which coincided with appropriate experiences on the part of the patient. Hysterical symptoms are, as hypnosis reveals, also precipitated by ideas which, although not in themselves meaningful, are preserved by virtue of having arisen in emotional states that were severely paralysing, such as fright, or during positively abnormal psychical states, as in the semi-hypnotic twilight state of daydreaming, in auto-hypnoses, and so on. In the latter, it is the nature of these states that makes a reaction to what is happening impossible.

Both types of condition can, of course, occur simultaneously and in fact often do so. This is the case when a trauma that is in itself operative occurs during a state of severe, paralysing emotion or altered consciousness; but it seems also to happen that in many people the psychical trauma gives rise to one of those abnormal states, which in turn makes the reaction impossible.

Common to both groups of conditions, however, is that the psychical traumas that have not been dealt with by reaction cannot be dealt with either by associative processing. In the first group it is the patient's resolve that wants to forget the distressing experiences, and thus to exclude them as far as possible from association; in the second group this associative processing does not succeed because there is no extensive associative connection between the normal state of consciousness and the pathological states in which these ideas have arisen. We will have immediate occasion for further and more detailed examination of these conditions.

It may therefore be said that ideas that have become pathogenic have been preserved with such freshness and affective strength because they are denied the normal erosion that occurs through abreaction and reproduction in states of uninhibited association.

3

When listing the conditions which, in our experience, are decisive in the development of hysterical phenomena from psychical traumas, it was already necessary to speak about the abnormal states of consciousness in which such pathogenic ideas arise, and to stress the fact that the recollection of the operative psychical trauma is not to be found in the normal memory of the patient but in their memory under hypnosis. The more we were occupied with these phenomena the more convinced we became that *the splitting of consciousness that is so strikingly present in the well-known cases as* double conscience, *exists in a rudimentary form in every hysteria; and that this tendency to dissociation and thereby to the emergence of abnormal states of consciousness, which we will group together under the term 'hypnoid', is the fundamental phenomenon of this neurosis.* In this view we concur with Binet and the two Janets, although we have no experience of their remarkable findings on patients under anaesthetic.

We would then like to set another proposition alongside the often cited, 'Hypnosis is artificial hysteria', namely that the basis and condition of hysteria is the existence of hypnoid states. These hypnoid states, however varied they may be, have one thing in common with each other and with hypnosis, notably that the ideas emerging within them are very intense, but are blocked from associative exchange with the remaining content of consciousness. These hypnoid states are capable of association amongst themselves, and their ideational content may in this way achieve various degrees of psychical organization. Moreover, the nature of these states and the degree to which they are cut off from the remaining conscious processes may vary in a way similar to that seen in hypnosis, ranging from slight somnolence to somnambulism, and from complete recollection to total amnesia.

If hypnoid states of this kind are already present before the manifest illness, they provide the ground in which the affect establishes the pathogenic memory together with its resulting somatic phenomena. This behaviour corresponds to dispositional hysteria. But our observations have shown that a severe trauma (as in traumatic neurosis) or an arduous suppression (say, of the sexual affect) can also implement a splitting-off of groups of ideas in someone who is otherwise not so disposed, and this would be the mechanism of psychically acquired hysteria. Between the extremes of these two forms we have to allow for a series of cases within which the ease of dissociation in the individual concerned and the affective magnitude of the trauma vary in inverse proportion to each other.

We have nothing new to say about the roots of dispositional hypnoid states. Often, it seems, they develop from the 'daydreams', which are so common even in healthy people, and for which women's handiwork, for example, gives such ample opportunity. The question of why the 'pathological associations' which form in such states should be so firm and why they should exercise a far stronger influence on the somatic processes than we would otherwise expect ideas to have, is part of the more general problem of the effectiveness of l.ypnotic suggestion. Our experiences add nothing new to this, but they do throw some light on the contradiction between the proposition that 'hysteria is a psychosis' and the fact that people of the clearest intellect, strongest will, greatest character and highest discrimination are to be found among hysterics. In such cases, this characterization holds good for their waking thoughts; in hypnoid states they are insane, as we all are in our dreams. But whereas our dream psychoses do not influence us when we are awake, the products of the hypnoid states jut over into waking life in the form of hysterical phenomena.

4

Almost exactly the same claims that we made for long-term hysterical symptoms can be repeated for hysterical attacks. Charcot, as is well known, has given us a schematic description of the 'major' hysterical attack according to which a complete attack has four recognizable phases: 1) the epileptoid phase, 2) the phase of large movements, 3) the (hallucinatory) phase of *attitudes passionelles*, 4) the concluding phase of delirium. Charcot derives all those forms of hysterical attack which are in fact more frequently observed in the complete *grande attaque* from the abbreviation, extension, omission or isolation of these individual phases.

The explanation we are attempting takes up from the third phase, that of the *attitudes passionelles*. When this is markedly present, it exposes the hallucinatory reproduction of a memory that was significant for the outbreak of the hysteria, either the memory of a single major trauma, which we find *par excellence* in what is called traumatic hysteria (κατ' ἐξοχὴν) or of a series of closely related partial traumas, such as underlie common hysteria. Or, in the final instance, the attack may bring back events which have been raised to the level of trauma by coinciding with a moment which is so disposed.

But there are also attacks which seem to consist only of motor phenomena and which lack a *phase passionelle*. If one succeeds in establishing a rapport with the patient during such an attack of general spasms or cataleptic rigidity, or during an *attaque de sommeil* [attack of sleep] or, better still, if one manages to bring on the attack in hypnosis, one finds that underlying this too is a memory of the psychical trauma or series of traumas which would otherwise become conspicuous in a hallucinatory phase. A little girl has for years been suffering from attacks of general cramps that could and indeed were thought to be epileptic. She is hypnotized for the purposes of differential diagnosis and immediately has her attack. But when asked, 'What can you see now?' she answers, 'The dog, the dog is coming', and it really does transpire that the first attack of this kind arose after she had been chased by a wild dog. The success of the therapy then confirmed the diagnosis.

A man who has become hysterical as a consequence of being maltreated by his employer suffers from attacks in which he collapses and falls into a raving fit, without saying a word or giving any sign of hallucination. The attack can be provoked in hypnosis, and the patient now states that he is reliving the scene when his master abused him in the street and hit him with a stick. A few days later he returns with the complaint that he had the same attack all over again, and this time, under hypnosis, it turns out that he had relived the scene to which the outbreak of the illness really was attached: the scene in the courtroom when he failed to obtain reparation for the maltreatment etc.

Indeed, in every other respect, too, the memories that emerge or can be wakened in hysterical attacks correspond to the precipitating causes that we have discovered at the root of long-term hysterical symptoms. These memories involve, as do the precipitating causes, psychical traumas that have not been dealt with by abreaction or by the work of associative thought; they are, likewise, completely absent, or their most significant components are absent, from what normal consciousness is capable of remembering, and appear to belong to the ideational content of hypnoid states with restricted association. Finally, these memories can also be tested therapeutically. Our observations have often taught us that a memory of this kind that had formerly provoked attacks becomes incapable of doing so if during hypnosis it is brought to a point of reaction and corrected by association.

The motor phenomena of the hysterical attack may in part be interpreted as general forms of reaction assumed by the affect accompanying the memory (like jiggling one's arms and legs about, which even babies do), in part as movements which are directly expressive of this memory, but in another sense this explanation fails to account for them, just as it fails to account for the hysterical stigmata in the case of long-term symptoms.

We can arrive at a particular appreciation of the hysterical attack by taking into account the theory (indicated above) that in hysteria groups of ideas originating in hypnoid states are present which are excluded from associative exchange with the other ideas, but which, as they can associate amongst themselves, represent the more or less highly organized rudiment of a second consciousness, a *condition seconde*. A long-term hysterical symptom, then, corresponds to a jutting over of this second state into the innervation of the body which is otherwise controlled by normal consciousness; a hysterical attack, on the other hand, is evidence that this second state is more highly organized, and, when the attack appears for the first time, it indicates a moment at which this hypnoid consciousness has taken hold of the subject's entire existence, in other words, an acute hysteria; when, however, the attack is recurrent and contains a memory, it indicates a return of that moment. Charcot has already voiced the thought that hysterical attacks might be the rudiments of a *condition seconde*. During the attack, control of the body's innervation is transferred in its entirety to the hypnoid consciousness. Normal consciousness, as well-known observations have shown, is not always wholly repressed when this occurs; it is even able to perceive the motor phenomena of the attack, although the accompanying psychical processes are beyond its grasp.

The typical course of a severe hysteria is known to be as follows: to begin with an ideational content is formed in hypnoid states; once this content has grown sufficiently it takes control, during a period of 'acute hysteria', of the innervation of the patient's body, and indeed of his entire existence, then creates chronic symptoms and attacks, and finally, save for a few remaining traces, clears up. If a normal person can regain control, then what survives of the hypnoid ideational content returns in hysterical attacks and periodically draws the person into similar states, which are themselves once more susceptible to influence and receptive to traumas. It then frequently happens that a kind of equilibrium is established between the psychical groups that are assembled in the one person; attack and normal life proceed alongside one other, without influencing each other. The attack then occurs spontaneously as memories tend to occur to us, but it can also be provoked, just as every memory can be wakened according to the laws of association. The attack is provoked either through stimulation of the hysterogenic zone, or through a new but similar experience that is reminiscent of the pathogenic experience. We hope to be able to show that there is no significant difference between these two apparently very different conditions, and that in both cases a hyperaesthetic memory is stirred. In other cases this balance is very unstable, and the attack appears as the expression of the remains of the hypnoid consciousness whenever the normal person is exhausted and incapacitated. We cannot dismiss the possibility that in cases such as this the attack, stripped of its original significance, may return as a motor reaction devoid of content.

The conditions which determine whether a hysterical personality is expressed in attacks, or in chronic symptoms, or in a mixture of the two, remain to be investigated.

5

Why the psychotherapeutic method expounded here has a curative effect should now be clear. *The method removes the effectiveness of the idea that had not originally been abreacted by allowing its trapped affect to drain away through speech; it then submits the idea to associative correction by drawing it into normal consciousness (under light hypnosis) or by using the doctor's suggestion to remove it, as occurs in somnambulism with amnesia.*

We believe that the therapeutic advantages of applying this

procedure are considerable. We do not, of course, cure hysteria, in as much as it is inherent in the patient's disposition; we can do nothing to prevent the recurrence of hypnoid states. Nor, during the productive stage of an acute hysteria, can our procedure guard against the possibility of new phenomena immediately replacing those which we have worked so hard to clear away. But once this acute stage has run its course and what is left remains in the form of chronic hysterical symptoms and attacks, then our method, because radical, is frequently able to clear these away for ever, and it is in this that it seems by far to surpass the effectiveness of removal by direct suggestion as is currently practised by psychotherapists.

In uncovering the psychical mechanism of hysterical phenomena we have taken a step further along the path first trodden so successfully by Charcot with his explanation and experimental imitation of hystero-traumatic paralyses, yet we are not blind to the fact that this has brought us nearer to understanding only the mechanism of hysterical symptoms and not the internal causes of hysteria. We have only touched on the aetiology of hysteria and it is really only the causes of acquired forms, that is, the significance of accidental factors for neuroses, that we have been able to illuminate.

Vienna, December 1892

Notes

1. Reprint from the *Neurologisches Zentralblatt*, 1893, Nos. 1 and 2.
2. The possibility of a therapy of this kind was clearly recognized by Delbœuf and Binet, as the following quotations demonstrate; Delbœuf, *Le Magnétisme animal* (Paris 1889): 'We are now able to explain how the hypnotist promotes the cure. He puts the subject back into the state in which his trouble appeared and uses words to fight this same trouble, but in a renascent state.' – Binet, *Les Altérations de la personnalité* [*Personality Changes*] (1892, p. 243): '. . . it will perhaps be seen that by using mental artifice to transport the patient back to that very moment when the symptom appeared for the first time, the patient is made more susceptible to curative suggestion.' – In P. Janet's interesting book *L'Automatisme psychologique*

[*Psychological Automatism*] (Paris 1889) there is a description of how a hysterical girl was cured by the application of a procedure analogous to ours.

3. We cannot distinguish what is new in this preliminary statement from what can be found in other authors such as Möbius and Strümpell, who have advanced similar views on hysteria. We found the closest approximation to our theoretical and therapeutic explanations in a few remarks published occasionally by Benedikt and will deal with these elsewhere.

II

Case Histories

1 Fräulein Anna O. (Breuer)

Fräulein Anna O. fell ill at the age of twenty-one (1880). She appeared to have a moderate neuropathic heredity, as some psychoses had occurred among her more distant family, but her parents were healthy in this respect. Before this time she too had always enjoyed good health, showing no sign of nervous indisposition during her development. Of considerable intelligence, remarkably acute powers of reasoning, and a clear-sighted intuitive sense, her powerful mind could have digested, needed even, more substantial intellectual nourishment, but failed to receive it once she had left school. Her rich poetic and imaginative gifts were controlled by a very sharp and critical common sense. The latter also made her *quite closed to suggestion*. Only arguments had any influence on her, assertions were without effect. Her will was energetic, tenacious and persistent, sometimes heightened to such obstinacy that it would give way only out of kindness and consideration for others.

One of her principal traits was a sympathetic kindness. Even during her illness, she benefited greatly from the care and support she gave to some sick and poor people, for it allowed her to satisfy a strong drive. Her spirits always tended slightly to exaggeration, whether of joyfulness or grief, and as a consequence she was also somewhat moody. The element of sexuality was remarkably undeveloped: the patient, whose life became transparent to me in a way that seldom happens between people, had never been in love, and not once in the mass of hallucinations that occurred during her illness did this element of the inner life emerge.

This girl of an overflowing mental vitality led an extremely monotonous life in her puritanically minded family, a life that she embellished for herself in a way that was probably decisive in the development of her illness. She systematically cultivated the art of daydreaming, calling it her 'private theatre'. While everyone believed her to be present, she was living out fairy tales in her mind, yet was always alert when spoken to so that no one was aware of it. Her domestic duties, which she carried out irreproachably, were almost incessantly accompanied by this mental activity. What I will, in due course, have to report is how seamlessly the habitual daydreaming of the healthy person became an illness.

The course of the illness falls into several distinct phases. They are as follows:

(A) Latent incubation. From mid-July 1880 to approximately 10 December. This case was exceptional because it afforded so complete an insight into a phase that in most cases escapes us, and for this reason alone its pathological interest could not be overestimated. I will expound this part of the history later.

(B) Manifest illness: a peculiar kind of psychosis, paraphasia, *strabismus convergens* [convergent squint], severe visual disturbance, paralysing contractures, complete paralysis in the upper right and both lower extremities, partial paralysis in the upper left extremity, paresis of the neck muscles. A gradual reduction in the contracture of the right extremities. Some improvement, interrupted by a severe psychical trauma (death of the father) in April, after which

(C) a period of continual somnambulism ensues, which then alternates with more normal states; continuation of a series of chronic symptoms until December 1881.

(D) Gradual winding down of mental states and symptoms until June 1882.

In July 1880 the patient's father, for whom she had a passionate affection, fell ill with a peripleuritic abscess that would not heal, and in April 1881 he succumbed. During the first months of this illness Anna devoted her every energy to the care of the patient, and it came as no surprise to anyone that gradually she became severely run down. No one, perhaps not even the patient herself, knew what was going on inside her; but gradually her state of weakness, anaemia and disgust at the thought of eating became so serious that to her great distress she was removed from the care of the patient. The immediate cause of this was an extremely acute cough, which was the reason for my first examining her. It was a typical *tussis nervosa* [nervous cough]. A marked need for rest in the afternoon soon became evident, followed in the evenings by a sleep-like state, which in turn gave way to intense agitation.

At the beginning of December *strabismus convergens* developed. An eye doctor explained it (erroneously) as being due to the paresis of one of the abducent muscles. On 11 December the patient became bed-ridden and remained so until 1 April.

A series of severe disorders that were *apparently* quite new developed in quick succession: pains at the back left of her head; *strabismus convergens* (diplopia or double vision) significantly aggravated by excitement; a complaint that the walls are falling in (affection of the *obliquus* [oblique muscles]); disturbances of vision that were difficult to analyse; paresis of the front neck muscles, such that her head could ultimately be moved only by the patient raising her shoulders and forcing her head back between them, while moving her whole back; contracture and anaesthesia of the right upper extremity and, after some time, of the right lower extremity – the latter was also fully extended, adducted and rotated inwards. The same affection subsequently occurred in the lower left extremity and finally in the left arm, although here the fingers retained partial mobility. Nor were the shoulder joints on either side completely rigid. At its maximum the contracture affected the upper-arm muscles, and later too, when the anaesthesia could be tested more precisely, the area around the elbow proved to be least sensitive. At the outset of the illness it was not possible to make a satisfactory test of the anaesthesia, because of the resistance arising from the patient's feelings of anxiety.

Such was the condition of the patient when I undertook her treatment, and I was soon able to ascertain the severity of the psychical deterioration with which I was presented. There were two quite separate states of consciousness which alternated very frequently and without warning, and which became increasingly distinct over the course of the illness. In one state she recognized her surroundings, was sad and anxious, but relatively normal. In the other she hallucinated, was 'naughty', that is to say, she was abusive; threw pillows at people, as and when the contracture allowed; would pull off the buttons from the bedclothes and linen with whichever fingers were still mobile; and so on. If something in the room was changed during this phase, if someone came in or went out, she would complain that she had lost time and would notice the gap in the course of her conscious thoughts. Since everyone did their best to deny this and tried to soothe the patient when she complained that she was going mad, she would, after her cushion-hurling and the like, make complaints about what was being done to her, what a muddle she was being left in, and so on.

These absences had already been noticed before she took to her bed; she would stop mid-speech and, after a while, repeat the last words she had said before she continued. Gradually this assumed the proportions portrayed above, and at the height of the illness, when the contracture had also taken hold of her left side, there were only very short periods during the day when she was to any degree normal. But even these moments of relatively clear consciousness were invaded by the disturbances: the most rapid and extreme changes of mood; fleeting instances of high spirits; but in general severe feelings of anxiety, stubborn opposition to all therapeutic measures, frightening hallucinations in which her hair, laces and so on would appear as black snakes. And yet at the same time she would always tell herself not to be so stupid, that it was only her hair, etc. In these moments of complete lucidity, she complained of the deep darkness inside her head, of not being able to think, of becoming blind and deaf, of having two selves, her real self and a bad one, that made her do wicked things, etc.

In the afternoons she lay in a somnolent state until an hour or so after sunset, would then wake up and complain that something was tormenting her, or, to be more precise, she would constantly repeat the infinitive: torment, torment.

For as the contractures developed, a deep functional disorganization of speech set in. The first thing that became noticeable was that she could not find words and gradually this became worse. Then her speech lost all grammatical structure, the syntax was missing, as was the conjugation of verbs, so that in the end she was using only infinitives that were incorrectly formed from a weak past participle, and no articles. As the disorder developed she could find almost no words at all, and would painfully piece them together out of four or five different languages, which made her almost incomprehensible. Whenever she attempted to write, she used the same jargon (at least initially, until the contracture prevented it completely). For two weeks she was completely mute, and despite continual strenuous attempts to speak could not utter a sound. Here the psychical mechanism of the disturbance became clear for the first time. As I knew, she had taken great offence at something and had resolved to say nothing about it. When I guessed as much and forced her to talk about it, the inhibition, which had until then made it impossible for her to speak about anything else either, disappeared.

This development occurred in March 1881, coinciding with the restoration of mobility to the left extremities. The paraphasia receded, but now she spoke only in *English*, yet seemed to be unaware of it, and would quarrel with the nurse, who was, of course, unable to understand her. Not until several months later did I manage to convince her that she was speaking English. She herself, however, still understood her German-speaking environment. Only in moments of great anxiety would her speech fail her completely, or she would mix up all kinds of languages. She would speak French or Italian at those times when she was at her best and most free. Between these periods and those in which she spoke English lay complete amnesia. The squint now also improved, eventually recurring only in moments of intense excitement. She was able to support her head again. On 1 April she got up for the first time.

Then, on 5 April, her father whom she idolized died. She had seen him only very rarely and for short periods during her illness. His death was the most severe psychical trauma that she could possibly have encountered. Violent excitement was followed by a deep stupor lasting about two days, from which she emerged in a quite different state of mind. At first she was much calmer and her feeling of anxiety was significantly diminished. The contracture of

29

the right arm and leg persisted, as did the anaesthesia of these limbs, which was not deep. There was high-degree restriction of the field of vision. Looking – with delight – at a bunch of flowers she could only ever see one flower at a time. She complained that she could not recognize people; that she used to be able to recognize faces without having to think about it and work at it. Now she had to go through a laborious process of what she called in English '*recognizing work*', saying to herself 'the nose is like this, and the hair like that, so it has to be so and so'. It was as if everyone was a wax figure bearing no relation to her. The presence of some of her near family was particularly distressing to her, and this 'negative instinct' increased continually. If someone whom she would ordinarily have been pleased to see came into the room, she would recognize them, remain present for a short time, then sink back into her brooding, and the person would fade from her sight. I was the only one whom she always recognized when I went into her room and, as long as I talked to her, she would also always remain present and in good spirits, save for the quite sudden interventions of hallucinatory absence.

Now she was only speaking in English and could not understand what people said to her in German. Those around her had to speak English; even her nurse learnt how to make herself understood like this to some extent. She did read French and Italian and, if she was asked to read them aloud, would sight-read an excellent English translation with astonishing rapidity and fluency.

She began to write again, but in a peculiar fashion: she used her mobile left hand, but wrote in Roman printed script, having gathered together an alphabet from her edition of Shakespeare.

She had previously consumed only very little food, but now she refused to eat anything at all. She would, however, allow herself to be fed by me, and this meant a rapid increase in her nourishment. Bread was the only thing that she constantly refused to eat. She did not once fail to rinse out her mouth after these feedings, and would do so even if for some reason she had not eaten anything: a sign of how absent-minded she was throughout.

The somnolence in the afternoons and deep sopor at sunset

continued. If she then managed to talk things through (I will have to return to this point in more detail later), she was lucid, calm and cheerful.

This relatively tolerable state did not last for long. Some ten days after the death of her father a consultant was brought in; she ignored him completely, as she did all strangers, when I demonstrated all her peculiar characteristics for him. *'That's like an examination,'* she said,[1] laughing, when I got her to read a French text aloud in English. The other doctor tried to intervene in the conversation, to make her notice him, but in vain. It was a genuine case of 'negative hallucination', as has been reproduced experimentally many times since. He finally succeeded in breaking through the hallucination by blowing smoke in her face. Suddenly she saw a stranger, rushed to the door to take out the key, and fell to the ground, unconscious; there followed a short bout of anger, then a bad attack of anxiety, which I had great difficulty in calming down. It was unfortunate that I had to depart that very same evening, and when I returned several days later I found the patient to be much worse. She had maintained total abstinence, was full of feelings of anxiety, and her hallucinatory absences were filled with terrifying figures, skulls and skeletons. Since, as she lived through these things, she would act them out, sometimes speaking aloud, those around her did for the most part know the substance of her hallucinations. Somnolence in the afternoons, at sunset the deep hypnosis for which she had found, in English, the technical term *'clouds'*. If she was then able to recount the hallucinations of the day, she would wake up lucid, calm and serene, would set to work, drawing or writing through the night, and was quite reasonable. At about four o'clock she would go to bed. The next morning the same scenario as the day before would be repeated. There was an extremely strange contrast between the unstable patient who was plagued by hallucinations during the day, and the girl whose mind was completely lucid at night.

In spite of this nocturnal euphoria her psychical condition deteriorated increasingly: powerful suicidal impulses appeared, which made it seem imprudent for her to be living on the third floor. So the patient was moved, against her will, to a country house near Vienna

(7 June 1881). I had never threatened her with this removal from the house, which she regarded with horror, but she herself had secretly expected and feared it. On this occasion, too, the degree to which the intense feeling of anxiety dominated the psychical disturbance again became clear. As in the wake of her father's death a state of calm had set in, so now she quietened down once what she had feared had happened. The transfer itself, however, was immediately followed by three days and nights without any sleep or nourishment whatsoever, a period full of suicide attempts (though these, taking place in the garden, were not dangerous), smashing of windows and so on, and hallucinations without absence, which she was well able to distinguish from the others. Then she quietened down, allowed the nurse to feed her, and even, in the evening, to give her chloral.

Before I describe the further course of the case, I need to go back once more and depict a peculiar characteristic that I have as yet only touched on in passing.

I have already observed that throughout the entire course of the illness until this point the patient was overcome by somnolence in the afternoons, which at sunset turned into a deeper sleep ('*clouds*'). (It seems plausible to read this periodicity simply as the result of the situation during her several months' nursing duty. At night she would watch over the patient or lie awake in bed anxiously listening until the morning; in the afternoon she would lie down to rest for a while, as nurses usually do, and it seems highly probable that this type of night watch and afternoon sleep was carried over into her own illness and continued long after a hypnotic state had replaced sleep.) After an hour or so of the sopor, she would become restless and toss to and fro, crying again and again, 'Torment, torment', all the while keeping her eyes closed. It had also been noticed that during her daytime absences it was quite clear that she was always developing a situation or story of some kind, and the odd word murmured aloud gave a clue to its composition. Now it happened, at first by chance, then intentionally, that someone in the house would let slip one of these key words while the patient was complaining about her 'torment'; she would soon join in, and begin to paint in a situation or recount a story, at first hesitantly in her paraphasic jargon, but becoming more fluent as she went on, until finally she was speaking perfectly correct German. (This was in the first period, before she was speaking nothing but English.) These stories were always sad but sometimes very pretty, in the style of Hans Christian Andersen's *Bilderbuch ohne Bilder* [*Picture-book Without Pictures*] and this was probably her model: the starting or central point was usually the situation of a girl sitting anxiously at an invalid's bedside, but other quite different motifs were also worked into the composition. A few minutes after the story had been completed she would wake up, and was clearly relieved or, as she called it, '*bomfortable*' (comfortable). At night she would again become more restless, and it was clear that by morning, after two hours' sleep, she was once again in a quite different mind-set. If she was ever unable to tell me the story during the evening hypnosis, she would not calm down, and the next day had to tell two stories for this to happen.

The essential factors of this phenomenon as I have described it, namely the accumulation and intensification of her absences up to the evening auto-hypnosis, the effectiveness of the phantastical products as a stimulant to the psyche, and the easing and lifting of the state of stimulation by talking them through during hypnosis, remained constant throughout the entire eighteen months that she was under observation.

The stories naturally became even more tragic after the death of her father. But it was not until her psychical state deteriorated following the violent interruption of her somnambulism described above, that the evening presentations ceased to resemble more or less spontaneous poetic creations and turned instead into a series of dreadful and terrifying hallucinations (which could already be inferred from her behaviour during the day). But I have already described how completely her psyche was relieved once, gripped with fear and horror, she had reproduced and talked through all these nightmarish images.

While the patient was in the country, where I was unable to visit her every day, the situation developed as follows. I came in the evening, when I knew that she would be in her hypnosis, and removed the entire stock of phantasms that she had amassed since my last visit. For this to be successful, there could be no omissions. Then she would become quite calm and on the following day was agreeable, obedient, industrious, and even in good spirits. But on the second day she was increasingly moody, contrary and disagreeable, and this worsened on the third. Once she was in this temper it was not always easy, even in her hypnosis, to get her to talk things through, a procedure for which she had found two names in English, the apt and serious '*talking cure*' and the humorous '*chimney-sweeping*'. She knew that having spoken out she would lose all her contrariness and 'energy'. If, after a comparatively long break, she was already in a bad mood, she would refuse to talk, and I had to wrest it from her, with demands, pleas and a few tricks such as reciting one of the phrases with which she would typically begin her stories. But she would never speak until she had made sure of my identity by carefully feeling my hands. During those nights when talking things through had not calmed her, it was necessary to resort to chloral. I had tried this on a few previous occasions, but found it necessary to give her 5 grams, and sleep was then preceded by a state of intoxication lasting several hours. Whenever I was present, this state was bright and cheerful, but, in my absence, it took the form of an anxious and extremely unpleasant excitement. (It should be noted, in passing, that the contracture was completely unaffected by this state of severe intoxication.) I had been able to avoid the narcotic, because the talking through at the very least calmed her down, even if it did not also allow her to sleep. But while she was living in the country the nights between those in which she was relieved by hypnosis were so unbearable that it was necessary to resort to chloral; gradually, however, she needed to take less of it.

The persisting somnambulism did not return; but the switching between the two modes of consciousness continued. In mid-conversation she would hallucinate, run away, try to climb a tree, and so on. If she was restrained, she would continue the interrupted sentence almost immediately, quite unaware of what had happened in between. All these hallucinations would, however, appear in the presentations she made in her hypnosis.

Her condition on the whole improved. Her nourishment was not problematic: she allowed herself to be spoon-fed by the nurse, the only exception being bread, which she would ask for, then refuse as soon as it touched her lips. There was a significant decrease in the paralytic contracture of the leg. She also regained her power of judgement and became quite attached to the doctor who was then visiting her, my friend Dr B. She drew great benefit from a Newfoundland dog which had been given to her and of which she was passionately fond. And it was splendid to see how when once her darling attacked a cat, this frail girl took a whip in her left hand and beat off the huge animal in order to rescue its victim. Later she looked after some poor, sick people and this too helped her greatly.

It was on my return from several weeks' holiday that I received the clearest evidence both of the pathogenic, stimulating effect of the ideational complex produced during her absences, or '*condition seconde*', and of their being disposed of by being talked through during hypnosis. The 'talking cure' was not implemented during this period, for the patient could not be persuaded to tell her stories to anyone but me – not even to Dr B., to whom she had otherwise become quite devoted. I found her morale to be pitifully low; she was lethargic, disobedient, moody, malicious even. During the evening story-telling it emerged that her phantastical and poetic vein was drying up. Her presentations dealt increasingly with her hallucinations and with what had irritated her over the previous days; they were couched in phantasy but this tended to be expressed merely through the set formulae of phantasy rather than being elaborated into poetic creations. The patient's state only became bearable when I brought her back to town for a week, and evening after evening managed to extract three to five stories from her. By the time I had finished, everything that had accumulated during the weeks that I was away was cleared. Only now was the rhythm of her psychical condition restored, i.e. she was agreeable and in good spirits the day after the talking, more irritable and disagreeable on the next, and on the third quite 'repulsive'. Her morale was, in effect, a function of the time that had lapsed since our last talking session, because every spontaneous product of her imagination and every external event perceived by the sick part of her psyche persisted as a psychical stimulus until it had been recounted in the hypnosis, at which point it ceased to have any effect whatsoever.

When that autumn the patient came back to town (to a different apartment from the one in which she had fallen ill), her condition, both physical and mental, was bearable; for, with the exception of striking experiences, very little was assimilated pathologically as a psychical irritant. I hoped for a steadily increasing improvement, with regular talking sessions preventing her psyche from continually being burdened by new stimuli, but I was, initially, disappointed. In December her psychical condition became significantly worse: she was excited again, dispirited, irritable, and rarely had 'really good days', even when it was impossible to detect anything that was still 'there' inside her. Towards the end of December, at Christmas time, she was particularly agitated and every evening throughout that week, instead of recounting new material, she related phantasms that she had elaborated day by day during the Christmas of 1880 when she was subject to powerful feelings of anxiety. Great relief once this series was over.

A year had now passed since she had been separated from her father and confined to bed, and from this time on her condition became clearer and more systematic in a most peculiar fashion. Characteristically, her two states of consciousness alternated with each other and always in such a way that from the morning on, throughout the day, the absences, i.e. the appearance of the *condition seconde*, became increasingly frequent until by evening only this state remained. Now, however, the difference between the two states was not just, as before, that the patient was normal in the one (the first) and alienated in the second, but rather that in the first she lived – as did we – in the winter of 1881–2, whereas in the second she lived in the winter of 1880–81, and everything that had happened in the meantime was completely forgotten. The only thing of which she remained for the most part conscious was her father's death. She was carried back to the previous year with such intensity that she hallucinated, seeing her old room in the new apartment, and when she tried to approach the door, bumped into the stove which was in the same position relative to the window as was the door to the room in the old apartment. The switch from one state to the other occurred spontaneously, but could very easily be prompted by any sense impression that reminded her vividly of the previous year. Holding up an orange for her to see (she had eaten almost nothing but oranges during the first stage of her illness) was enough to cast her back from 1882 to 1881. This carrying back to a time in the past did not occur in a general, random way; rather the patient relived the previous winter day by day. This would have been merely a hunch on my part were it not for the regular evening hypnosis when she talked through what had troubled her on this particular day in 1881, and for a diary kept secretly by her mother in 1881 which confirmed the unassailable accuracy of the underlying facts. This reliving of the past year continued until the definitive conclusion of the illness in June 1882.

At the same time it was interesting to see how the psychical stimuli that were revived from the second state also had an effect on the first, more normal one. One morning, for example, the patient said laughingly that she didn't know what was wrong with her, but that she was cross with me. Thanks to the diary I knew what this was about and, sure enough, it was then gone through again in the evening hypnosis: I had greatly annoyed the patient on this same evening in 1881. Or she would say that something was wrong with her eyes, that she couldn't see colours properly; she knew that her dress was brown, and yet she saw it as blue. It quickly transpired that she was able to differentiate all the colours of the test papers correctly and clearly, and that the disturbance was attached solely to the fabric of the dress. The reason for this was that over the same days in 1881 she had been very busy making a dressing-gown for her father, for which she had used the same fabric, but in blue. It was often the case too that an effect of these emerging memories was visible in advance, in that the disturbance of the normal condition would already appear at an earlier stage, while the memory for the *condition seconde* was only gradually being awakened.

This was already an ample burden on the evening hypnosis, for we had to talk through not only the fresh products of her imagination, but also the experiences and 'vexations' (as she called them in English) of 1881 (fortunately by this time I had already relieved her of the phantasms of 1881). Yet the workload of both patient and doctor increased enormously as a result of a third series of separate disturbances which also had to be disposed of in this way. These were the psychical *events of the incubation period of the illness* from July to December 1880, events which had produced all the hysterical phenomena, and as they were talked through the *symptoms disappeared*.

The first time that – by chance and quite unprovoked – talking things through during the evening hypnosis caused a long-standing disturbance to disappear, I was very surprised. There had been a period of intense heat during the summer and the patient had suffered from a terrible thirst, for, although she could give no explanation for it, it had suddenly become impossible for her to drink. She would pick up the glass of water she was longing for, but as soon as it touched her lips she would push it away as if she were hydrophobic. At the same time it was clear that during these few seconds she was in an absence. She lived only on fruit, melons, etc., so as to ease her excruciating thirst. This had been going on for about six weeks, when, in her hypnosis, she grumbled about her English lady-companion, whom she did not like, and then, giving every sign of disgust, recounted how she had gone into her companion's room and seen her small dog, the revolting animal, drinking out of a glass. She explained that she did not say anything, for fear of being impolite. Having given vent to the irritation that had been there inside her, she asked for a drink, drank a great quantity of water without any inhibition and woke from the hypnosis with the glass at her lips. At this the disturbance had disappeared forever. Other strange and stubborn quirks disappeared in the same way once the experience that had caused them had been recounted. But a great step forward was taken when the first of the long-term symptoms, the contracture of the right leg, disappeared (which was admittedly already much improved). On the basis of these experiences – namely that in this patient the hysterical phenomena disappeared as soon as the event that had caused the symptom was reproduced in hypnosis – a technical-therapeutic procedure was developed which left nothing to be desired in terms of logical consistency and systematic implementation. Each individual symptom in this complicated clinical picture was dealt with separately: all the occasions on which the symptom had appeared were narrated in reverse order, starting with the days before the patient was confined to bed and working backwards as far as the cause of its first appearance. Once this had been recounted, the symptom was permanently removed.

And so the paralytic contractures and anaesthesias, a number of quite different visual and auditory disturbances, neuralgias, coughing, shaking, etc. and, ultimately, even the speech disorders were 'told away'. The following visual disturbances were, for example, dealt with individually: *strabismus convergens* with double vision; deviation of both eyes to the right, so that when the patient reached for an object her hand was always to the left of it; narrowing of the field of vision; central amblyopia; macropsia; seeing a skull instead of her father; an inability to read. Only a few phenomena eluded this analysis, but they were symptoms that had developed while the patient was confined to bed (as, for example, the spreading of the paralytic contracture to the left side), and it seems most likely that they really did not have any direct psychical cause.

Shortening the process by attempting to evoke in the patient's memory what had first caused the symptom proved quite impractical. She could not find it and became confused, so that the process took longer than if she had been allowed to work calmly and steadily backwards, unwinding the thread of memory that had been taken up. But since this took too long in the evening hypnosis, because the patient was strained and distracted by the 'talking through' of the two other series, and also probably because the memories needed time to become sufficiently vivid, the following procedure was developed instead. I would come to see her in the morning, hypnotize her (using very simple techniques of hypnosis which had been discovered empirically), and, once her thoughts were concentrated on the symptom we were treating, I would ask her about the occasions on which it had appeared. The patient would then use

Studies in Hysteria

captions to describe these external causes in quick succession and I would make a note of them. During the evening hypnosis she would then give a reasonably detailed account of the events, aided by the sequence I had noted. An example will illustrate the exhaustive and exhausting thoroughness with which this occurred. It happened repeatedly that the patient could not hear when people spoke to her. This temporary inability to hear took the following different forms:

(a) Not hearing someone coming into the room. Absent-mindedness. One hundred and eight separate and detailed cases of this, indicating the people, circumstances, and often the date. The first instance was not hearing her father come in.

(b) Not understanding when several people speak at once. Twenty-seven times. The first again involved her father and an acquaintance.

(c) Not hearing when alone and spoken to directly. Fifty times. The origin: her father had asked her in vain for wine.

(d) Becoming deaf through shaking (in the carriage or similar such circumstances). Fifteen times. The origin: her young brother shook her angrily when he caught her listening at the door of the sickroom.

(e) Becoming deaf when frightened by a noise. Thirty-seven times. The origin: her father had a choking fit when swallowing.

(f) Becoming deaf during a deep absence. Twelve times.

(g) Becoming deaf as a result of long periods of listening and eavesdropping so that she would not hear when spoken to. Fifty-four times.

These occurrences are, of course, for the most part identical in that they can all be related to absent-mindedness or *absence*, or to fright. Yet they were so clearly separated in the patient's memory that if she once mistook the sequence it had to be corrected and the right order re-established, otherwise the presentation would be held up. She recounted events devoid of any interest or significance with such precision that there could be no suspicion of their having been invented. As many were purely internal experiences they could not be checked; but some of the other events, or circumstances relating to them, were remembered by those around her.

What happened in this instance was also generally in evidence whenever a symptom was being 'talked away': when the symptom itself was being recounted it would occur with heightened intensity. Thus the patient was so deaf during the analysis of her inability to hear that I had to communicate with her partly in writing. The initial cause of the symptom tended to be a fright of some kind that she had experienced when nursing her father, an oversight on her part, or something of the kind.

The process of remembering was not always easy and sometimes the patient had to make an enormous effort. At one point progress was completely impeded for some time because a memory would not surface. It was one of the patient's most terrible hallucinations: while she was nursing her father she had seen him with a skull. She and those with her at the time remembered how once, when apparently still in good health, she had visited a relative and, on opening the door, immediately collapsed, unconscious. To overcome this obstacle, she now went back there again, and again on entering the room fell unconscious to the floor. In the evening hypnosis the obstacle was then overcome: as she entered the room she had caught sight of her pale face in the mirror opposite the door, but rather than herself, had seen her father with a skull. We observed many times that the fear of a memory, as in this case, inhibits its emergence, and that it has to be forced out by either the doctor or the patient.

The following is just one example among many which demonstrate the high degree of logical consistency of her states. As was mentioned earlier, at night during this period, that is, in 1881, the patient was always in her *condition seconde*. She once woke in the night, claimed that she had been taken away from home again, and became so badly agitated that the whole household was alarmed. The reason was simple. On the previous evening the 'talking cure' had caused her visual disturbance to disappear and this was also the case in the *condition seconde.* When she then woke in the night she found herself in a room that was unfamiliar to her, for her family had moved house in the spring of 1881. These rather unpleasant occurrences were prevented – at her request – by my closing her eyes every evening and making the suggestion that she could not open them until I myself did so the following morning. The commotion recurred only once, when the patient cried during a dream and opened her eyes on waking from it.

Because this laborious analysis of symptoms pertained to the summer months of 1880 during which the illness was developing, I was able to gain a full insight into the *incubation* and *pathogenesis* of this hysteria, of which a brief exposition follows.

In July 1880, when in the country, the patient's father fell seriously ill of a sub-pleural abscess; Anna shared the nursing with her mother. She woke up one night in a state of great anxiety about the patient's high fever and under the strain of expecting the arrival of a surgeon from Vienna for the operation. Her mother had gone away for a while and Anna was sitting at the patient's bedside with her right arm resting over the back of the chair. She fell into a daydreaming state and saw a black snake coming from the wall towards the patient in order to bite him. (It is highly likely that there really were snakes in the field behind the house, that the girl had already been frightened by them before, and that they were now providing the material for the hallucination.) She wanted to fend off the creature, but was as if paralysed. Her right arm hanging over the back of the chair had 'gone to sleep', becoming anaesthetic and paretic, and when she looked at it, her fingers turned into tiny snakes with skulls (her nails). It seems likely that she tried to chase the snakes away with her paralysed right hand, and that through this the anaesthesia and paralysis became associated with the hallucination of the snake. When the snake had disappeared, she tried in her terror to pray, but every language failed her, she could speak none at all until finally she came upon a nursery rhyme in *English* and then found that she could also think and pray in this language.

The spell was broken by the whistle of the train bringing the doctor whom they were expecting. When the next day she had gone to recover a hoop from a bush where it had been thrown during a game, a bent twig revived the snake-hallucination, and at once the arm that she had stretched out froze. This now happened repeatedly, whenever a more or less snake-like object provoked the hallucination. But this, like the contracture, occurred only during the short absences which became increasingly frequent from that night on. (The contracture did not stabilize until December when the patient, having broken down completely, was no longer able to get out of bed.) On another occasion, which I cannot find in my notes and have now forgotten, there was in addition to the contracture of the arm a contracture of the right leg.

The patient's tendency to auto-hypnotic absences was now established. The day after the night described above, she became immersed in a state of such deep absence while waiting for the surgeon that eventually he was standing in front of her without her having heard him enter the room. The constant sense of anxiety interfered with her eating and gradually produced intense nausea. But with this exception every single hysterical symptom arose during the affect. It is not entirely clear that this was always a complete momentary absence but it seems likely because on waking the patient was completely unaware of anything that had happened.

Some of her symptoms seem not to have arisen in her absences but only in an affect when the patient was in a waking state; even so, they recurred subsequently in exactly the same way. All the different visual disturbances could, then, be traced back to a range of more or less clearly determining causes. For example, once when the patient was sitting at her father's bedside, with tears in her eyes, he suddenly asked her the time. She could not see clearly, strained to do so, brought the watch close to her eyes and suddenly the face appeared very large (macropsia and *strabismus conv.*). Or, similarly, when she struggled to suppress her tears so that her patient could not see her crying.

An argument in which she suppressed her response caused a spasm of the glottis, which then recurred on every similar occasion.

She was unable to speak: a) for fear, since first she had hallucinated at night; b) since she had once again stopped herself from saying something (active inhibition); c) since she was once unfairly scolded; d) in every similar circumstance (in which she was offended). Her coughing first occurred when, as she was watching over the sick bed, the sound of dance music drifted over from a neighbouring house, arousing a desire in her to be there, which awakened her self-reproaches. Throughout her entire illness her subsequent reaction to any kind of music with a strong rhythm was a *tussis nervosa*.

I do not overly regret that the incompleteness of my notes prevents my tracing every hysterical symptom back to all the circumstances that caused them. The patient did so for all of them, with the one exception mentioned above, and, as I have illustrated, every symptom disappeared after the recounting of the *first* instance.

It was in this way, too, that the hysteria was resolved in its entirety. The patient herself had made a firm resolution that on the anniversary of her transfer to the country she would have to have finished with everything. At the beginning of June she therefore undertook the 'talking cure' with a great deal of excitement and energy. On the last day, with the help of arranging her room as her father's had been during his illness, she reproduced what had been the root of the whole illness, namely the dreadful hallucinations described above, in which she could think and pray only in English. She spoke German immediately afterwards and was from that moment free of all the countless individual disturbances that she had displayed before. She then left Vienna to travel, but still needed a while longer before fully recovering her psychical equilibrium. Since that time she has enjoyed perfect health.

Although I have suppressed many details which were not without interest, the case history of Anna O. has become more extensive than a hysterical illness which was in itself not unusual would seem to merit. But the account of the case was impossible without going into detail, and its peculiarities seemed to me sufficiently important to justify this extensive presentation. In the same way the eggs of the echinoderm are important for the study of embryology not because the sea urchin is a particularly interesting animal but because the protoplasm of its eggs is transparent, and what can be seen in them allows one to draw conclusions about what may also happen in eggs with cloudy plasma.

The interest of this case seems to me to lie above all in the extensive transparency and intelligibility of its pathogenesis.

Even when the girl was still completely healthy two psychical characteristics predisposed her to hysterical illness:

1) the surplus of psychical liveliness and energy which, unused in her monotonous family life and without any appropriate intellectual work, was discharged in the incessant activity of her imagination and also gave rise to

2) her habitual daydreaming ('private theatre'), thus laying the foundations for the dissociation of her mental personality. Nevertheless, even this remains within the bounds of normal behaviour. Daydreaming, like meditation, during a more or less mechanical activity, does not in itself necessarily produce a pathological splitting of consciousness, for any disturbance, such as someone addressing the dreamer, will reinstate the normal unity of consciousness, and it is unlikely that amnesia will result. Yet in Anna O.'s case the ground was prepared, as has been described, for the affect of anxiety and dread to set in once that affect had transformed her habitual daydreaming into a hallucinatory absence. It is remarkable that from the very first manifestation of this developing illness, its main characteristics appeared already fully formed and then remained unchanged for almost two years. These features were: the existence of a second state of consciousness – initially this took the form of a passing absence, and was later organized as a *double conscience*; the speech impediment, caused by the affect of anxiety, with its chance discharge in the English nursery rhyme; later, paraphasia and loss of her mother tongue, which was replaced by excellent English; finally, the accidental paralysis of her right arm, due to pressure, which later developed into a contractural paresis and anaesthesia of the right side. The mechanism according to which this last affection developed corresponds entirely to Charcot's theory of traumatic hysteria: a hypnotic condition during which a slight trauma occurs.

But whereas the hysterical paralysis that Charcot induced experimentally in his patients was stabilized almost immediately, and whereas paralysis results swiftly in the case of patients suffering from traumatic neuroses who are severely shaken by a traumatic fright, the nervous system of our young girl continued to put up a successful resistance for four months. The contracture, like the other disorders that gradually joined it, occurred only during the momentary absences of the *condition seconde* and left the patient in full possession of her mind and body so that she herself was quite ignorant of it – nor did those around her see anything, since their attention, concentrated on the severely ill father, was distracted.

But as the absences with complete amnesia and accompanying hysterical phenomena grew ever more frequent following the first instance of hallucinatory auto-hypnosis, so the opportunities for the creation of new symptoms multiplied and those that had already been established became further entrenched through frequent repetition. Gradually, too, any sudden, distressing affect came to have exactly the same result as an absence (although it is possible that the affect did actually produce a momentary absence in these instances); chance coincidences produced pathological associations and sensory or motor disturbances which would subsequently always appear together with the affect. But this was still only ever momentary, transitory. Unbeknown to anyone else, the patient had already developed her extensive collection of hysterical phenomena in its entirety before she was confined to her bed. Not until she was extremely debilitated by lack of movement, insomnia and the persistent feeling of anxiety, and had broken down entirely, spending more time in the *condition seconde* than in her normal state of mind, did the hysterical phenomena reach over into the normal state too, turning from the manifestations of an attack into chronic symptoms.

The question that needs to be raised now is that of the extent to which the statements of the patient are reliable and whether the phenomena really were developed and caused as she described. The reliability of the report as regards the more important and fundamental processes does not, in my opinion, come into question. I am not referring here to the disappearance of the phenomena once they had been 'told away'; it would be quite possible to explain this as due to suggestion. But I always found the patient to be completely truthful and reliable; what she recounted was intimately bound up with what was most sacred to her; everything that could be checked by other people was fully corroborated. Even the most gifted girl would probably not have been capable of constructing a system of statements with the degree of logical consistency demonstrated here by the developmental history of her illness. But this does not mean that we can dismiss from the outset the possibility that, following the consistency of this logic, she may (in all good faith) have attributed causes to many of the symptoms that in reality did not exist. But I do not believe this supposition to be correct either. For it is precisely the insignificance of so many of the causes, the irrationality of so many of the connections, that speak for their real existence. It was incomprehensible to the patient that dance music should make her cough. An invention like this is too meaningless to have been intentional, but I, for my part, could see that every scruple of her conscience caused her notorious spasm of the glottis, and that the motor impulses felt by this girl who so loved dancing, turned this spasm of the glottis into a *tussis nervosa*. I therefore believe the statements of the patient to be perfectly reliable and truthful.

To what extent, then, can we justify the supposition that the development of this hysteria is analogous to that of other patients, and that something similar also occurs in cases where no such clearly defined *condition seconde* has been organized? In view of this question, I would like to point out that the entire history of the development of this illness would likewise have remained unknown to both patient and doctor, were it not for the patient's peculiar characteristic, described above, of remembering in hypnosis and recounting what she remembered. On waking she was quite unaware of any of this. It is, then, quite impossible to infer what happens in other cases by carrying out a medical examination of an individual while they are awake, for even with the best will in the world they are unable to give any information. And I have already indicated just how little of all these processes others are able to observe. The experience of other patients could, then, be discerned only by means of a procedure similar to the auto-hypnoses which had simply been presented to us in the case of Anna O. But at this stage we were justified only in the supposition that *similar* processes were probably more frequent than our ignorance of the pathogenic mechanism led us to believe.

When the patient had been confined to her bed, and her consciousness was continually oscillating between the normal and the 'second' state, the army of hysterical symptoms that had arisen individually, and until then been latent, manifested themselves as chronic symptoms. These were then joined by yet another group of phenomena that seemed to be of a different origin, namely the paralytic contracture of the left extremities and the paresis of the muscles supporting her head. I make a distinction between these and the other phenomena because once they had vanished they never reappeared, not even as an attack, or in a mild form, and not even during the concluding and recuperative phase when all the other symptoms were revived from their long slumber. Nor, accordingly, did they ever appear during the hypnotic analysis and were not traced back to affective or imaginative causes. I am therefore inclined to believe that they did not come into being as a result of the same psychical process as the other symptoms, but rather as a result of the secondary extension of that unknown condition which is the somatic foundation of hysterical phenomena.

During the entire course of the illness the two states of consciousness existed alongside one another: the primary state, in which the patient was psychically quite normal, and the 'second' state, which might well be compared with dreams, given its wealth of phantasms and hallucinations, the large gaps in her memory, the lack of inhibition and of control over her thoughts. In this second state the patient was alienated. Now, the fact that the patient's psychical condition was completely dependent on this second state jutting over into the normal one would seem to me to afford a clear insight into the nature of at least one type of hysterical psychosis. Every evening hypnosis supplied proof that the patient was completely clear and well-ordered and that her perceptions and intentions were quite normal so long as none of the products from the second state acted as a stimulus 'in the unconscious'. The spectacular psychosis that occurred whenever a longer break in this process of unburdening was taken proved the extent to which these products influenced the psychical processes of the 'normal' state. It is difficult to express the situation other than by saying that the patient had two personalities, one of which was psychically normal and the other mentally ill. It is my opinion that the sharp division between the two states in the case of our patient simply clarifies behaviour which is the cause of much puzzlement in many other hysterics too. In the case of Anna O. it was particularly striking to see the degree to which the products of the 'bad self', as she herself called it, influenced her moral disposition. Had they not constantly been cleared away she would have become a hysteric of the malicious variety, unruly, lethargic, ill-natured and spiteful; whereas in this way her true character, which was quite the opposite of all these, always came to light immediately after the removal of these stimuli.

But however sharply these two states were separated, the 'second state' did not simply jut over into the first; rather it was frequently the case that, even in very bad states, a keen and quiet observer was, as the patient put it, sitting in some corner of her mind, watching all the mad things going on. The continued existence of such clear thinking when the psychosis was prevalent was expressed in a very peculiar way. When, once the hysterical phenomena had been brought to a close, the patient experienced a temporary depression, she brought up various childish fears and self-accusations, including the claim that she had not been ill at all and that everything had merely been simulated. It is well known that such remarks are not uncommon. When the illness has run its course and the two states of consciousness again merge, the patients see themselves in hindsight as a single undivided personality, who knew what all the nonsense was about, and they believe that they could have prevented it had they so wanted, in other words that they had perpetrated all the mischief on purpose. In any case, the persistence of normal thinking during the second state may have varied enormously in degree and may in large part not even have existed.

I have already described the incredible fact that from the beginning to the conclusion of the illness all the stimuli stemming from the second state and their consequences were permanently removed by being talked through during hypnosis, and nothing needs to be added other than to give the assurance that this was not in any way an invention of mine that I might have suggested to the patient. On the contrary, I was extremely surprised by it, and it was only when a series of symptoms was spontaneously disposed of in this way that I was able to develop a therapeutic technique.

The final stage in the cure of the hysteria deserves a few more words. It ensued, as I have described, with considerable disquiet on the part of the patient and a deterioration of her psychical state. One definitely had the impression that the whole host of products from the second state, which had been slumbering, were now forcing their way into consciousness and being remembered, if initially again in the *condition seconde*, but that they were a burden and disturbance to the normal state of consciousness. It remains to be seen whether the same origin can be attributed to other cases of chronic hysteria which conclude with a psychosis.

Note

1. In English.

2 *Frau Emmy von N., age 40, from Livonia (Freud)*

On *May 1, 1889*, I became the doctor of a lady of about forty years of age, whose affliction and personality alike instilled such a deep interest in me that I devoted a great deal of time to her and made her recovery my responsibility. She was a hysteric who could easily be set into a state of somnambulism. When I became aware of this I decided to apply Breuer's technique of investigation under hypnosis, with which I was familiar from his history of how his first patient was cured. It was my first attempt at implementing this therapeutic method, and I was still far from having mastered it, so that I did, in fact, fail to pursue the analysis either far enough or systematically enough. I can perhaps best illustrate the patient's condition and my medical procedure by reproducing the notes that I made every evening during the first three weeks of the treatment. Wherever subsequent experience has enabled a better understanding of the case, I will incorporate it in footnotes and parenthetical remarks.

May 1, 1889. I find a woman who has distinctive, finely cut features and an appearance that is still youthful lying on the couch with a leather bolster under her neck. Her face bears a tense, pained expression; her eyes are screwed up and cast down; she has a heavy frown and deep naso-labial folds. She speaks as if it were arduous, in a quiet voice that is occasionally interrupted to the point of stuttering by spastic breaks in her speech. When she speaks she keeps her fingers, which exhibit a ceaseless agitation resembling athetosis, tightly interlaced. Numerous tic-like twitches in her face

51

and neck muscles, some of which, in particular the right sterno-cleido-mastoid, protrude quite prominently. In addition, she frequently interrupts herself in order to produce a peculiar clicking noise, which I am unable to reproduce.[1]

What she says is completely coherent and clear evidence of an unusual degree of education and intelligence. This makes it all the more disconcerting that every few minutes she should suddenly break off, contort her face into an expression of horror and revulsion, stretch out her hand towards me with her fingers splayed and crooked, and in an altered, fearful voice call out the words: 'Keep still – don't say anything – don't touch me!' She is probably under the influence of a recurring and horrible hallucination and is using the formula to fend off the interference of this stranger.[2] This interpolation is then concluded with equal suddenness, and the patient continues with what she has been saying, without taking the excitement that has just occurred any further, without explaining or excusing her behaviour, and so, it seems likely, without herself having noticed the interruption.[3]

I discover the following details about her circumstances. Her family is originally from Central Germany, but the last two generations have resided in the Baltic Provinces of Russia where they have extensive estates. There were fourteen children, of which she herself is the thirteenth; only four of them survive. She was brought up with care, but also with a good deal of constraint by her mother, an over-energetic, severe woman. At the age of twenty-three she married a highly gifted and capable man who had achieved an outstanding position as a major industrialist, but who was much older than her. After a short marriage he died suddenly of a heart attack. She describes this event, together with the upbringing of her two daughters (now aged sixteen and fourteen), who were often sickly and suffered from nervous disorders, as having caused her illness. Since the death of her husband, fourteen years ago, she has, with varying degrees of severity, always been ill. Four years ago a course of massage combined with electric baths afforded her temporary relief, but all other attempts to restore her health were unsuccessful. She has travelled a great deal and has numerous lively interests. At present she resides on a country estate by the Baltic not far from a large town. For months she has been seriously ill again, depressed and unable to sleep, tormented by pains; she sought a cure in Abbazia – in vain. For the last six weeks she has been in Vienna, in the care of an excellent doctor.

I suggest that she separate from the two girls (who have their governess) and admit herself to a sanatorium where I can see her daily. She accepts without a word of protest.

On the *evening of May 2* I visit her at the sanatorium. I notice that she is always extremely startled whenever the door opens unexpectedly and so arrange for the house physicians and nurses to knock loudly when they come to visit her, and not to enter until she has called out 'Come in'. Nevertheless, she still grimaces and starts whenever anyone comes into the room.

Today she complains above all of a feeling of coldness and pains in her right leg extending from her back above the iliac crest. I prescribe warm baths and shall massage her whole body twice a day.

She is perfectly suited to hypnosis. I simply hold a finger before her eyes, exclaim 'Sleep!', and she sinks back looking dazed and confused. I suggest that she will sleep, that all her symptoms will be cured etc; she listens with her eyes closed, but with an unmistakably keen attentiveness, and gradually her face softens and takes on a peaceful expression. After this first hypnosis she retains some dim memory of what I said to her; but already after the second, complete somnambulism (amnesia) sets in. I had warned her that I would hypnotize her and she agreed to this without reserve. She has never been hypnotized before, but I can assume that she has read about it, although I don't know what idea of the hypnotic state she may already have.[4]

The treatment of warm baths, twice-daily massage, and hypnotic suggestion was continued over the following days. She slept well, was making a visible recovery, and spent most of the day quietly in her bed. She was not prevented from seeing her children, reading or attending to her correspondence.

On the *morning of May 8* she entertains me, in what seems to be a normal way, with some horrible animal stories. She read in the

Frankfurter Zeitung, which is on the table in front of her, that an apprentice had tied up a boy and put a white mouse in his mouth. The boy died of shock. Dr K. told her, she says, that he had sent a whole case of white rats to Tiflis. As she recounts this, all the signs of horror emerge in the most vivid form. She clenches and unclenches her hand several times in succession. 'Keep still, don't say anything, don't touch me! – If an animal like that were in my bed!' (Shudders.) 'Just think, when it's unpacked! There's a dead rat among them, a rat that has been gn-aw-ed at.'

In the hypnosis I attempt to drive off these animal hallucinations. While she is asleep I pick up the *Frankfurter Zeitung* and indeed find the story of the apprentice-boy's maltreatment, but it involves neither mice nor rats. She must have added these from her delirium when reading.

In the evening I told her of our conversation about the white mice. She knows nothing about it, is quite astonished, and laughs heartily.[5]

In the afternoon she had what she called a 'neck cramp',[6] but 'only for a short while, a couple of hours'.

During the hypnosis of the *evening of May 8* I ask her to speak, which after struggling somewhat she succeeds in doing. She speaks softly and always pauses to think for a moment before giving an answer. Her expression changes according to the subject of her narrative, becoming peaceful as soon as my suggestion has put an end to the impression made by what she is relating. I ask her why she is so easily frightened. She replies, 'These are memories from when I was a very young child.' 'When?' 'First when I was five and my brothers and sisters threw dead animals at me so often, that was the first time I fainted and had convulsions. But my aunt told me that this was dreadful behaviour, one simply couldn't have attacks like that, and so they stopped. Then, when I was seven and suddenly saw my sister in her coffin; then, at the age of eight, when my brother was forever frightening me by dressing up in white sheets as a ghost; then, at the age of nine, when I saw my aunt in her coffin, and – all of a sudden – her jaw dropped open.'

Clearly, this series of traumatic events (her response to my question about why she was so easily frightened) is readily available in her memory. Otherwise it would have been quite impossible for her to assemble these events from the various different periods of her youth with such rapidity, in that brief moment between my question and her answering. At the end of each partial story she has convulsions all over, and her face takes on an expression of fright and horror; at the end of the last she opens her mouth wide and gasps for breath. The words that impart the terrifying substance of her experience are pronounced with difficulty and between gasps: afterwards her features become peaceful.

When asked, she confirms that as she relates these stories the scenes appear to her tangibly and in their true colours. She says that in any case she thinks about these experiences very often and has thought about them again over the last few days. Apparently, as soon as she thinks about it, the scene appears before her eyes as vividly as if it were real.[7] Now I understand why she so often tells me about animal scenes and images of corpses. My therapy consists in erasing these images so that they no longer appear to her. To reinforce this suggestion I brush my hand over her eyes several times.

The *evening of May* 9. She slept very well without my having to renew the suggestion, but had stomach pains in the morning. They had already started yesterday when she spent too much time in the garden with her children. She permits me to restrict her children's visit to two and a half hours; a few days earlier she had reproached herself for leaving the children alone. Today I find her somewhat excited – frowning, clicking and stuttering. During the massage she relates that her children's governess gave her an atlas showing the history of civilizations and that some of the pictures in it, which depicted Indians dressed as animals, gave her a great fright. 'Just think, if they were to come to life!' (Shudders.)

Under hypnosis I ask her why she was so frightened by these pictures, since she is no longer scared of animals. They reminded her, she says, of visions that she had at the time of her brother's death (she was nineteen). I reserve this memory for later. I ask, too, if she has always spoken with this stutter and how long she has had the tic (the peculiar clicking).[8] The stutter, she explains, appeared

55

when she was ill, and she has had the tic for five years, ever since the time when she was sitting at the bedside of her younger daughter, who was very ill, and wanted to stay absolutely *quiet*. I attempt to attenuate the significance of this memory by saying that, after all, nothing did happen to her daughter etc. She says that it comes back to her whenever she is anxious or frightened. I instruct her not to be frightened of the pictures of Indians but instead to laugh heartily at them, to point them out to me even. And this is indeed what happens once she has woken up: she looks for the book, asks if I have ever seen it, opens it at the right page for me, and laughs out loud at the grotesque figures, quite free of anxiety, her features perfectly relaxed. Dr Breuer unexpectedly pays a visit accompanied by the house physician. She takes fright and makes her clicking sound, so that both leave us very quickly. She explains her excitement by saying that she doesn't like the house physician coming in every time as well.

While she was under hypnosis I had also removed the pains in her stomach by stroking it, and told her that although she will expect the pains to return after lunch, they will not appear.

Evening. She is in good spirits and talkative for the first time, displaying a sense of humour that I would not have expected in this serious woman, and, confident of her feeling that she is getting better, she even, among other things, makes fun of the treatment she received from the doctor before me. She had, she tells me, long intended to stop this treatment but couldn't find a polite way of doing so until a chance remark made by Dr Breuer when he was visiting her showed her a way out. When I seem to be surprised by this, she grows frightened and reproaches herself severely for having been so indiscreet, but seems to let me calm her down. – No stomach pains, despite her having expected them.

Under hypnosis I ask about other experiences that have given her a lasting fright. She produces a second series of this kind dating from later in her youth just as promptly as she did the first, and again she assures me that all these scenes appear to her frequently, vividly, and in colour. How, for example, she saw her cousin being taken to a lunatic asylum (when she was fifteen): she wanted to call for help for her, but was unable to, and lost the ability to speak until the evening. Since she talks about asylums so often when she is awake, I interrupt, and ask her if there are any other occasions involving insanity. She tells me that her mother was herself in an asylum for a while. They once had a maid whose mistress had spent a long time in an asylum and who used to tell her horror stories about how the patients there were tied to chairs, beaten and so on. Her hands clench in horror as she talks; she is seeing all of this as if it were happening before her eyes. I try to correct her images of asylums and assure her that she will be able to hear about such institutions without feeling that she herself is implicated; at this her face relaxes.

She continues to enumerate her terrifying memories: how (aged fifteen) she once found her mother lying on the floor – she had suffered a stroke but then lived for another four years; and how, at the age of nineteen, she once returned home to find her mother dead, her face contorted. Attenuating these memories does, of course, present me with considerable difficulties; but after lengthy discussion I assure her that in future even this image will come to seem blurred to her and lacking in strength. – Another memory from when she was nineteen is how she found a toad underneath a stone that she had picked up, and could not speak for hours as a result.[9]

This hypnosis convinces me that she knows everything that occurred in the previous hypnosis, although she knows nothing at all about it when awake.

May 10, morning. She had a bran bath instead of a warm bath for the first time today. I find her frowning and looking annoyed, with her hands wrapped up in a scarf; she complains that she is cold and in pain. When asked what is wrong with her, she says that the bath was uncomfortably short to sit in and that she is now in pain from it. During the massage she starts telling me that she still feels badly about having betrayed Dr Breuer yesterday. I tell a white lie to appease her, saying that I knew about it all along; at this her agitation (clicking, facial contraction) ceases. Thus each time my influence already begins to take effect during the massage: she becomes quieter and more lucid, and even without being questioned under hypnosis is able to discover the reasons for her always being out of sorts. Nor is her conversation during the massage as aimless as it might appear, rather it contains a fairly complete reproduction of the memories and new impressions that have influenced her since our last conversation, and it often opens out quite unexpectedly onto pathogenic reminiscences, which she talks out of herself without being asked. It is as if she had appropriated my procedure and were using our conversation, although it appears to be unconstrained and led by chance, as a supplement to the hypnosis. So today, for example, she happens to talk about her family, and in a very round-about way comes to the story of a cousin, who was a bit simple-minded, and whose parents had had all his teeth pulled out in one sitting. She accompanies this narrative with gestures of horror and keeps repeating her protective formula (Keep still! – Don't say anything! – Don't touch me!). Afterwards, her face relaxes and she is cheerful. Thus her behaviour when awake is governed by the experiences she has had in her somnambulism, despite her belief, when awake, that she knows nothing about them.

Under hypnosis I ask her again what has upset her and receive the same answers but in reverse order: 1) Her indiscreet talk yesterday. 2) The pains from sitting uncomfortably in the bath. Today I ask her what the expression 'Keep still!' etc. means. She explains that when she has frightening thoughts she is anxious that they should not be interrupted in their course, because then everything gets confused and becomes even worse. The 'Keep still' apparently refers to the fact that the animal figures that appear to her when she is in a bad state start to move about and attack her if anyone moves in her presence. And finally, the command 'Don't touch me!' is the result of the following experiences. The time when her brother was very ill from having taken so much morphine and had such dreadful attacks (she was then nineteen) – he would often suddenly grab hold of her; then once an acquaintance who was visiting them suddenly went mad and seized her arm; (there is a third similar case that she cannot remember exactly); and finally, the time when her small daughter was very ill (she was twenty-eight) – she grabbed her so tightly in her delirium that she almost suffocated. Despite the great lapse of time between these four cases, she related them in one sentence and in such swift succession that it was as if they were a single episode in four acts. Incidentally, she begins all the accounts of such groups of traumas with 'the time when', the component traumas being linked by an 'and'. Since I notice that her protective formula is intended to protect her from the recurrence of similar experiences, I use suggestion to remove this fear and really have not heard the formula from her again.

In the *evening* I find her very cheerful. She laughs as she tells me that she was startled by a small dog which barked at her in the garden. Yet her face is a little distorted and there is an inner agitation that is not dispelled until she asks me if I took offence at a remark that she made during the morning massage and I reply that I didn't. Her period has begun again barely a fortnight since the last. I promise her that it will be regulated by hypnotic suggestion and during the hypnosis set the interval at twenty-eight days.[10]

Under hypnosis I ask in addition if she remembers what she last related to me, as I have in mind a task that was left over from yesterday evening. She, however, begins quite correctly with the 'Don't touch me' of this morning's hypnosis. So I take her back to yesterday's theme. I had asked her where her stammer came from and received the answer, 'I don't know'.[11] In response to this I had instructed her to remember it by today's hypnosis. Today, then, without further reflection, but with great excitement and spastic impediments to her speech, she replies: 'The time when the horses bolted with the children in the carriage and another time when I was driving through the wood with the children during a storm, and lightning struck the tree just in front of the horses, and the horses shied, and I thought to myself, "Now you have to keep quite still, otherwise your screaming will frighten the horses even more, and the coachman won't be able to hold them back at all." That's when it started.' This story excited her to an extraordinary degree. I further learn that the stammering first manifested itself immediately after the first of the two incidents, but disappeared soon afterwards, setting in permanently only after the second similar event. I extinguish the vivid memory of these scenes, and ask her to picture them again. She seems to attempt this and remains quiet as she does so; from this point in the hypnosis she speaks without any spastic stammer.[12]

Finding her disposed to open up to me, I ask which other events in her life have frightened her so much that she has retained a vivid memory of them. She replies by giving me a collection of such experiences. – The time when, one year after the death of her mother, she was visiting a Frenchwoman who was a friend of hers, and was sent with another girl into the room next door to fetch a dictionary, and then saw someone sit up in bed who looked exactly like the woman she had just left. She went quite stiff, as if rooted to the spot. She later discovered that it was a dummy that had been rigged up. I tell her that this apparition was a hallucination, appeal to her good sense, and her face relaxes. – The time when she nursed her sick brother and he suffered dreadful attacks because of the morphine, during which he would frighten and grab hold of her. I notice that she has already spoken about the experience this morning, and so, as a test, I ask her when else this 'grabbing' occurred. This time I am pleasantly surprised by her taking a long while to think about the answer, and in the end asking doubtfully, 'My little girl?' She can remember nothing at all about the two other incidents (see above). My banning her memories, extinguishing them, was, then, effective. – Further, the time when she was nursing her brother and suddenly her aunt's pale face appeared over the top of the screen: she had come to convert him to Catholicism.

I notice that I have now arrived at the root of her constant fear of surprises and ask when other surprises have occurred. – The time when they had a friend at home who liked to slip into the room very softly so that all of a sudden he was simply there; the time when following the death of her mother she became very ill and went to a spa, and there a woman who was mentally ill came into her room several times at night by mistake and walked right up to her bed; and, finally, four times during her journey here from Abbazia, when the door of her compartment was suddenly opened by a strange man, who stared at her each time. She was so frightened by this that she called the conductor.

I erase all of these memories, wake her up and, having neglected to give her the appropriate suggestion during the hypnosis, assure her that she will sleep well tonight. Proof of the improvement of her general condition is given by her remark that she read nothing at all today – she is living in such a happy dream, she whose inner restlessness used always to demand constant activity.

May 11, morning. Today is the meeting with the gynaecologist Dr N., who is to examine her eldest daughter because of her menstrual difficulties. I find Frau Emmy rather agitated, but this is expressed through slighter physical signs than before; she cries out from time to time, 'I'm frightened, so frightened, I think I'm going to die.' What is she so frightened of then, I ask, is it Dr N.? She says that she doesn't know, she just is frightened. During the hypnosis, which I carry out before my colleague arrives, she confesses that she is afraid of having offended me by what she thought was an impolite comment of hers during yesterday's massage. She is also afraid of anything new, and thus of the new doctor too. She allows me to soothe her, does start a few times in front of Dr N., but is otherwise well-behaved, and neither the clicking noise nor the speech impediment is in evidence. Once he has gone, I hypnotize her again so as to remove any possible traces of excitement caused by his visit. She herself is very well pleased with her behaviour and places great hope in his treatment. I try to use this example to show her that one need not be frightened of what is new, for good may also come of it.[13]

In the *evening* she is in very good spirits and unburdens herself of a number of apprehensions she has in the conversation before the hypnosis. Under hypnosis I ask which event in her life has had the most lasting effect on her and surfaces most often as a recollection. The death of her husband, she replies. I get her to relate every detail of this experience to me, which she does and appears to be deeply moved, but is free of any clicking and stammering.

The time when they were at a place on the Riviera of which they were both very fond – they crossed a bridge, and suddenly he sank to the ground, in the grip of a heart spasm, lay there for a few minutes, lifeless, but then got up and was quite well. The time when, not long afterwards, she was lying in with her little one and her husband, who was having breakfast at a small table at the end of the bed and reading the newspaper, suddenly got up, looked at her in a very strange way, took a few steps, then fell to the ground, dead. She jumped out of bed; the doctors who had been called in tried to resuscitate him – she heard them from the next room – but it was in vain. She then continues: And the time when the child, who was a few weeks old at the time, became very ill and remained so for six months during which time she herself was confined to bed with a severe fever. – And there now follow, in chronological order, her grievances against this child, which she blurts out with a look of annoyance, as one would when speaking about somebody of whom one has grown tired. She says that for a long time the child was very odd, that she cried all the time and didn't sleep, that she had become lame in her left leg and that they had almost given up hope that it could be cured; when she was four she had visions, she did not begin to walk and talk until a late stage, so that for a long time she was thought to be simple; according to the doctors she had had an inflammation of the brain and spinal cord, and all sorts of other things besides. I interrupt her here and point out that today this same child is normal and flourishing, and I remove her capacity to see all of these sad things again, for not only do I wipe out the vivid recollection, I also remove the entire reminiscence from her memory as if it had never been there. I promise her that this will free her from the expectation of misfortune that is a constant torment to her, and from the pains which for several days had gone unmentioned, but which she has complained of feeling throughout her body while giving this very account.[14]

To my surprise, immediately after this suggestion of mine, she begins to talk about Prince L., whose escape from an asylum was a topic of much conversation at this time: she unearths new anxieties about lunatic asylums, that the people there are treated by having ice-cold showers directed at their heads, that they are placed in an apparatus and turned around inside it until they quieten down. Three days ago when she first complained of her fear of asylums, I had interrupted her after her first story about how the patients there were tied to chairs. I realize that I am getting nowhere with this and that I cannot avoid listening to every point of her story through until the very end. Once we have caught up with this I take this new set of terrifying images away from her too, appeal to her good sense, and point out that she can have more faith in me than in the silly girl who told her the horror stories about how lunatic asylums are run. Since I notice that she still stammers occasionally when making these additional remarks I ask her once again where the stammering comes from. – No answer. – 'Don't you know?' – 'No.' – 'Well, why ever not?' – 'Why? Because I am not allowed to.' (This she blurts out violently and angrily.) I take her statement as evidence of the success of my suggestion, but she demands to be woken from the hypnosis, and I comply.[15]

May 12. Contrary to my expectations she slept little and poorly. I find her in a state of great anxiety, but, incidentally, without the physical signs of distress which usually accompany it. She does not want to say what is wrong with her, save that she has had bad dreams and still keeps seeing the same things. 'How dreadful it would be if they came to life.' During the massage she deals with some things in response to my questions, then becomes cheerful, and talks about her social life in her dower house on the Baltic, about the important men from the neighbouring town whom she entertains and so on.

Hypnosis. She has had terrible dreams: the arms and legs of chairs were all snakes; a monster with a vulture's beak started to eat her, pecking all over her body; other wild animals leapt at her; and so on. From this she moves straight on to other animal-deliria, which, however, she distinguishes by adding, 'That was real (not a dream)'. The time when (a while ago) she was trying to reach for a ball of wool, and it was a mouse and ran away; the time when on a walk a large toad suddenly sprang at her etc. I see that my general ban has done no good, and that I will have to take these fearful impressions away from her one by one.[16] Somehow I then happened to ask her why she had got stomach pains and where they had come from. It is my belief that her stomach pains accompany every attack of zoöpsia. Her fairly grudging answer was that she did not know. I set her the task of remembering by the next morning. At this point she

63

said in a rather sullen tone that I should not always ask her where such and such a thing came from, but should let her tell me what she had to say. I agree to this and, without making any introductory remarks, she continues. 'The time when they carried him out I could not believe that he was dead.' (She is, then, talking about her husband again, and now I understand why she was out of temper, for she has suffered from the remains of this story that had been held back.) And then, for three years afterwards she hated the child, because she said to herself again and again that she could have nursed her husband back to health if only the child had not caused her to be laid up in bed. And then, after the death of her husband, she had had nothing but insults and upsets. She wanted to demand an investigation because his relatives, who were always against the marriage and then angry that they had such a happy life together, had spread the rumour that she herself had poisoned him. They had used some awful crooked journalist to foist all sorts of legal proceedings on her. The scoundrel sent around agents who stirred people up against her; he had libellous articles published in the local newspapers and then sent her cuttings of them. This was at the root of both her fear of people and her hatred of strangers. Once I have spoken some soothing words in response to what she has told me, she says that she feels relieved.

May 13. She slept badly again because of her stomach pains, had no supper yesterday, and is complaining too of pains in her right arm. But her mood is good, she is cheerful, and since yesterday she has treated me with marked respect. She asks my opinion about all sorts of things that seem important to her and becomes disproportionately agitated when, for example, I have to look for the towels needed for the massage. The clicking and facial tic are much in evidence.

Hypnosis: Yesterday evening the reason why the small animals that she sees grow so enormous suddenly occurred to her. It first happened to her at a theatre performance in D., in which an enormously large lizard appeared on the stage. She says that it was this memory that so tormented her yesterday.[17]

The clicking had recurred, she says, because she had pains in her abdomen yesterday and was trying not to let this show by sighing. She is unaware of the actual cause of the clicking [p. 59]. She remembers, too, that I set her the task of finding out where her stomach pains came from. But she says that she does not know, and asks me to help her. I suggest that she might once have forced herself to eat having been very upset. This is the case. For a long time following the death of her husband she had no appetite at all and ate only out of a sense of duty; it was at this time that the stomach pains really began. – I remove the stomach pains now by stroking her a few times across the epigastrium. Then, spontaneously, she begins to talk about what has most affected her, 'I said that I didn't love my little girl. But I must add that nobody would have noticed this from my behaviour. I did everything that had to be done. Yet still I reproach myself for preferring my elder daughter.'

May 14. She is cheerful and well, slept until half-past seven this morning, and her only complaint is of some pain in the radial area of her hand, and in her head and face. Her talking things through prior to the hypnosis is becoming increasingly important. She has scarcely anything dreadful to report today. She complains of pain and loss of feeling in her right leg, and tells of how in 1871 she suffered an abdominal inflammation, then, having barely recovered, nursed her sick brother, and in doing so first experienced the pains that for a time even resulted in the paralysis of her right foot.

Under *hypnosis* I ask her whether she might not already be able to take part in social life again, or if her fear is still predominant. She thinks that she still finds it unpleasant if someone stands behind or close by her, and in connection with this she relates other instances in which she had been unpleasantly surprised by people appearing suddenly. Once, for example, when she was going for a walk with her daughters in Rügen, two suspicious-looking individuals appeared from behind a bush and insulted her. During an evening walk in Abbazia, a beggar suddenly stepped out from behind a rock and knelt down at her feet. He was, it seems, a harmless lunatic. She tells further of how she was very frightened when her isolated country house was broken into one night.

Yet it is easy enough to see that, fundamentally, this fear of people goes back to the persecution to which she was subjected after the death of her husband.[18]

Evening. To all appearances she is in good spirits, but greets me with the exclamation: 'I am frightened to death, oh, I can hardly bear to tell you, I hate myself.' In the end I discover that Dr Breuer paid her a visit and that on seeing him she started. When he noticed this she assured him that it was 'just this once', and she was so very sorry on my behalf that she should have betrayed this remnant of her former fearfulness! I had, in any case, had ample opportunity over the past few days to take note of how hard she is on herself, how quick to reproach herself severely for the smallest oversight – if, for example, the towels for the massage are not in their usual place, or if the newspaper that I read while she sleeps is not visibly ready for me. Once the first, most superficial layer of tormenting reminiscences has been cleared away, her morally hypersensitive personality with its tendency to self-deprecation comes to the fore. Then, whether she is under hypnosis or awake, I recite to her what is in effect a paraphrase of the old legal maxim *'de minimis non curat lex'*, that between good and evil there is a whole class of small, indifferent things for which no one should reproach themselves. She is, I imagine, not much more ready to take in this lesson than some ascetic monk from the Middle Ages who sees the hand of God and the temptation of the devil in the slightest thing that happens to him, and who is not able to imagine that the world might – even for the briefest moment, in some small corner – bear no relation to him.

Under hypnosis she reports more individual instances of frightening images (in Abbazia, for example, bloody heads on every wave). I get her to repeat the lessons that I gave her when she was awake.

May 15. She slept until half-past eight, but towards the morning became restless, and she greets me with a slight tic, clicking, and some impediment to her speech. 'I am frightened to death.' Tells, when questioned, that the pension in which her children are staying is on the fourth floor and reached by a lift. Yesterday she demanded that the children use the lift when they are coming down as well, and now she is reproaching herself for this, as the lift is not wholly reliable. Indeed, the owner of the pension himself told her that it was not. Did I know the story of Countess Sch., who died in just such an accident in Rome? Now, it happens that I am familiar with the pension and know that the lift is the private property of its owner; it would seem to me fairly unlikely that this man, who boasts of the lift in his advertisement, should himself warn people about using it. In my opinion this is a case of anxiety inspiring a false memory; I tell her what I think and have no difficulty in getting her to laugh at the improbability of her fears. It is for this very reason that I cannot believe this to have been the cause of her anxiety, and I resolve to address the question to her hypnotic consciousness. During the massage, which I recommence now after a break of several days, she recounts some loosely connected stories, which may have been true – such as the story of a toad which was found in a cellar, of an eccentric mother who looked after her idiot child in a peculiar way, of a woman who because of her melancholia was confined to a lunatic asylum – thus revealing the sort of reminiscences that pass through her mind when she is overcome by a sense of unease. Once she has rid herself of these stories she becomes very cheerful, talks about life on her estate, about the contacts she has with prominent men in German Russia and North Germany, and I really find it very difficult to reconcile these kinds of activity with the image of such an acutely nervous woman.

Under hypnosis, then, I ask her why she was so put out this morning, and instead of concerns about the lift I am told that she was afraid that her period was going to start again and would once more disrupt the massage.[19]

I also get her to tell me the story of the pains in her leg. The beginning is the same as yesterday, but there then follows a long series of experiences – by turns distressing and wearing – which she had had at the time of the pains in her leg. With each experience the pain increased to the point of paralysis and loss of feeling in both legs. Something similar happened with the pains in her arms, which also began during a period when she was nursing someone, at exactly the same time as the neck cramps. I now discover the following details about her 'neck cramps': these cramps took over from peculiar states of disquiet accompanied by depression that had been present at an earlier stage, and they took the form of an 'icy grip' at the back of the neck, stiffening and a painfully cold sensation in all her extremities, an incapacity to speak, and complete prostration. This lasts from six to twelve hours. My attempts to expose this complex of symptoms as a reminiscence are unsuccessful. I ask some questions with this end in view – when she was nursing her brother, who was delirious, did he ever grab her by the neck? – to which the answer is 'No', she says that she does not know where these attacks come from.[20]

Evening. She is in very good spirits, and generally displays a splendid sense of humour. She says that in fact the matter of the lift was not quite as she had told me. It was, apparently, just a pretext that it should not be used to go down in. A great many questions follow, which have nothing pathological about them. She has had distressingly severe pains in her face, along her hand on the thumb side, and in her leg. When she sits still or stares at a fixed point for any length of time, she feels stiff and her face hurts. Lifting anything heavy gives her pains in her arms. – Examination of her right leg reveals fairly good sensitivity in the thigh, a high level of anaesthesia in the lower part of her leg and foot, and less so in the pelvic and lumbar regions.

In the hypnosis she states that from time to time she still has frightening thoughts, as, for example, that something could happen to her children, they could fall ill or lose their lives; or that her brother, who is now on his honeymoon, could have an accident, his wife might die, because all her siblings had been married such a short time. She will not be drawn on any other fears. I forbid her this need to be afraid when there is no reason for it. She promises to refrain from doing so, 'because you ask me to'. Further suggestions for the pains, leg, etc.

May 16. She slept well, is still complaining of pains in her face, arms and legs, but is in very good spirits. The hypnosis proves quite unproductive. Faradic brush applied to the right, anaesthetic leg.

Evening. She starts as soon as I come into the room. – 'It's good that you have come. I've had such a fright.' – At the same time she gives every indication of horror, the stuttering, the tic. I begin by getting her to tell me what happened while she is awake, at which, stretching out her hands, her fingers crooked, she gives an excellent portrayal of her terror. In the garden an enormous mouse suddenly darted across her hand and then suddenly disappeared. Things were darting to and fro all the time (the illusion of shadows playing on the ground?). There were nothing but mice sitting in the trees. – Can't you hear the hooves of the horses at the circus? – There's a gentleman groaning nearby, I think he is in pain after his operation. – Am I in Rügen then? Did I have that kind of stove there? – She is confused too by the wealth of thoughts criss-crossing inside her and by her attempt to distinguish the present. When asked about recent events, whether, for example, her daughters were there, she is unable to answer.

I try to disentangle this state in the hypnosis.

Hypnosis. What were you afraid of then? – She repeats the mouse story, giving every sign of horror. She says, too, that when she went down the steps a dreadful animal was lying there which disappeared straight away. I explain that these are hallucinations, and forbid her fear of mice, adding that only drunkards (whom she really loathes) are frightened of them. I tell her the story of Bishop Hatto, which she knows too and listens with the keenest horror. – 'How do you happen on the subject of the circus, then?' – She can hear the horses stamping in the nearby stable quite clearly, and getting tangled up in their halters as they do so, which could injure them. Then Johann, she says, would always go out and untie them. – I deny that there are stables nearby or a man groaning. I ask if she knows where she is? – She does know, but a while ago she thought she was in Rügen. – How did she come upon this memory? – In the garden they were talking about it being particularly hot in one spot, and then the terrace in Rügen where there was no shade occurred to her. – What kinds of sad memories did she have of her stay in Rügen then? – She comes out with a series of them. She had got the most awful pains in her arms and legs there; she ran into fog during several excursions and so lost her way; she was twice pursued by a bull when out walking etc. – Why did she come to have this attack today? –

Yes, she had asked herself this too. She had spent three hours writing a great many letters, and her head was quite full of it. – I can assume then that her fatigue brought on this attack of delirium and that its content was determined by echoes in her memory such as the spot without shade in the garden and so on. – I repeat all the lessons that I usually give her, and leave, having sent her to sleep.

May 17. She slept very well. During the bran bath that she took today, she cried aloud several times because she took the bran to be tiny worms. I know this from the nurse; she does not like talking about it, is almost wildly cheerful, but interrupts herself frequently with cries of 'ugh', grimaces to express her horror, and stammers more than she has done over the last few days. She tells of how, during the night, she dreamt that she was walking on masses of leeches. The night before she had horrible dreams in which she had to lay out a great number of dead people and place them in coffins, but did not want to put the lids on. (Clearly a reminiscence of her husband, see above.) She goes on to say that in the course of her life a great many things had happened to her involving animals: the most horrible was that a bat had got caught in her wardrobe, whereupon she ran out of the room without any clothes on. In an attempt to cure her of her fear, her brother gave her a beautiful brooch in the shape of a bat; but she was never able to wear it.

Under hypnosis she explains that her fear of worms comes from having once received a gift of a beautiful pin-cushion. When she wanted to use it the next morning hundreds of tiny worms crept out, because the bran, which had been used as stuffing, was not quite dry. (A hallucination? Perhaps it did actually happen.) I ask her to tell me some more animal stories. When once she and her husband had gone for a walk in a park in St Petersburg the entire pathway to the pond was so covered with toads that they had to turn back. There have also been times, it seems, when she was unable to shake hands with anyone for fear that her hand might change into a frightful animal, as had so often happened before. I try to rid her of this fear by going through the animals one by one and asking her if she is afraid of them. In the case of one she answers 'No', and of the others: 'I mustn't be afraid.'[21] I ask her why she started and stuttered so both today and yesterday, and she tells me that that's what she always does when she is fearful.[22] – But why was she so fearful yesterday? – In the garden she had had all kinds of oppressive thoughts; and, most of all, the question of how she might be able to prevent things from mounting up inside her again once she was discharged from treatment. – I repeat the three reasons for feeling reassured that I had already given when she was awake: 1. that she has in general become much healthier and more resilient; 2. that she will become accustomed to talking things through with someone else she is close to; 3. that she will become indifferent to all sorts of things that used to burden her. – She replies that she had also been burdened by the thought that she had not thanked me for coming late in the day and by the fear that I would lose patience with her because of her latest relapse. She had been deeply moved and worried when the house physician asked a gentleman in the garden if he now felt up to the operation. The man's wife was sitting there too, and she herself could not help wondering if this would be the poor man's last evening. Having made this last point her depression seems to have lifted.[23]

Evening. She is in very good spirits and contented. The hypnosis produces no result at all. I deal with the treatment of her muscular pains and with restoring the feeling to her right leg, which is very easily done in hypnosis, but the restored sensitivity is in part lost again once the patient has woken up. Before I leave she expresses her astonishment at having gone for so long without the neck cramps that always used to come on before a thunderstorm.

May 18. Last night she slept as she has not done for years, but after her bath complains that she is cold in the neck, and has contractions and pains in her face, hands and feet: her features are strained, her hands clenched. Hypnosis does not indicate that this condition of 'neck cramp' has any psychical content and, once she is awake, I use massage to improve it.[24]

I hope that the above extract from the chronicle of the first three weeks will suffice to give a clear picture of the patient's state, the nature of my therapeutic endeavour, and the degree of its success. I will now proceed to complete the case history.

The last hysterical delirium described above was also the last serious disturbance in Frau Emmy v. N.'s condition. As I was not making an independent inquiry into symptoms and the grounds for them, but instead waiting until something appeared or until she confessed a troubling thought to me, the hypnoses soon ceased to be productive and were mostly used by me to impart precepts which were meant to remain forever present in her thoughts and protect her from lapsing into a similar condition once she was back home again. I had, at that time, quite fallen under the spell of Bernheim's book on suggestion and expected to achieve more from exercising such a didactic influence than I would today. My patient's condition was so much improved in such a short space of time that she assured me that she had not felt as well as this since the death of her husband. After a total of seven weeks' treatment I discharged her and she returned to her home on the Baltic.

It was not I, but Dr Breuer who received news of her about seven months later. She had remained well for several months, but had then given way under a further psychical blow. The eldest daughter, who had already started to imitate her mother's neck cramps and milder hysterical states during her first stay in Vienna, but who suffered mostly when walking because of a *retroflexio uteri* [retroverted uterus], had, at my advice, been treated by Dr N., one of our most distinguished gynaecologists; using massage he put right her uterus and she was then free of her complaint for several months. When, back home, her complaint recurred her mother consulted the gynaecologist from the university town nearby. He provided her daughter with a combination of local and general therapy, but this caused her to develop a severe nervous illness. It seems likely that this was the first sign of the girl's pathological disposition (she was seventeen at the time), which was to manifest itself a year later in a personality change. The mother, who had entrusted her child to the doctors with her usual mixture of submission and suspicion, reproached herself most severely when the outcome of this cure proved unsuccessful and, following a train of thought that I have not pursued further, she concluded that both of us, that is, both Dr N. and I, were to blame for her child's having fallen ill, because we had made light of her serious condition. By an act of will, as it were, she then reversed the effect of my treatment and straightaway lapsed back into the very condition of which I had relieved her. An excellent local doctor, whom she approached, and Dr Breuer, who corresponded with her, managed to persuade her of the innocence of both the accused parties; but even once this had been cleared up the aversion to me which she had developed during this period persisted as a hysterical residue, and she declared that it would be impossible for her to place herself in my care again. Following the advice of the same medical authority she sought help in a sanatorium in North Germany, and I informed the physician in charge which modifications to the hypnotic therapy had proved effective in her case.

The attempted transfer was a thorough failure. She seems not to have got along with the doctor from the very beginning, she exhausted herself by resisting whatever was done to her, became run down, lost her appetite, could not sleep, and did not recover until a friend who was visiting her at the sanatorium in effect secretly abducted her and nursed her in her house. Not long afterwards, exactly a year after her first meeting with me, she was back in Vienna and again put herself in my hands.

I found her to be far better than the reports given in the correspondence had led me to imagine. She was mobile, free of anxiety, in fact, much of what I had set right the previous year had lasted. Her chief complaint was that she was often confused, 'storm in the head' as she called it. Other than this she had insomnia, often could not stop crying for hours on end, and became sad at a certain time of day (5 o'clock). This was in fact the time at which, in the winter, she was allowed to visit her daughter, who was staying in the sanatorium. She stuttered and clicked a great deal, often rubbed her hands together furiously, and when I asked her if she could see many animals her only reply was: 'Oh keep still!'

At the first attempt to put her under hypnosis, she clenched her fists and cried: 'I don't want any antipyrin injections, I would rather keep my pains. I don't like Dr R., he is repugnant to me.' I realized that she was caught in a reminiscence of being hypnotized at the sanatorium, and she calmed down once I brought her back to the present situation.

At the very beginning of the treatment I made an instructive discovery. I had asked her how long it had been since her stuttering had recurred, and (in the hypnosis) she answered hesitantly: since the fright that she had had during the winter in D. A waiter at the guest house in which she was staying had hidden in her room; in the darkness she thought the thing was a greatcoat, reached over to it, and then suddenly the man 'shot up in the air'. I remove this memory image and thenceforward, whether she is under hypnosis or awake, her stuttering really is barely noticeable. I cannot remember what moved me to try to test my success here, but on my return that evening I asked her a seemingly harmless question as to how I should go about securing the door so that when I went away and left her asleep no one could slip in. To my astonishment she gave a violent start, began to grind her teeth and rub her hands again, and intimated that she had had a violent fright of precisely this kind in D., but could not be persuaded to tell the story. I noticed that she meant the same story that she had told that morning in hypnosis and that I thought I had wiped away. In the next hypnosis she then gave a far more detailed and truthful version of the story. That evening she had in her excitement walked up and down the passage, found the door to her chambermaid's room open, and wanted to go in to sit down there. The chambermaid blocked her way, but she would not be kept out, went in regardless, and then noticed this dark thing on the wall, which turned out to be a man. Clearly it had been the erotic factor of this little adventure that had caused her to depict it untruthfully. But I had discovered that an incomplete story given under hypnosis does not effect a cure: I became accustomed to judging a story as incomplete when it was of no benefit, and gradually I learnt to see from the patients' expressions whether or not they had withheld a significant part of the confession.

The work that I had to do with her this time consisted of using hypnosis to remove unpleasant impressions that she had absorbed during her daughter's treatment and during her own stay at the sanatorium. She was full of suppressed rage at the doctor who had forced her under hypnosis to spell t . . . o . . . a . . . d, and made me promise never to ask this word of her. It was at this point that I allowed myself what was the only – and in any case fairly harmless – abuse of the hypnosis of which I am guilty in the case of this patient: I used suggestion to play a trick on her. I reassured her that her stay in —tal would seem so very far removed and distant from her that she would not even be able to think of the name of the place, and that whenever she wanted to mention it she would hesitate between —berg, —tal, —wald, and so on. This did then occur, and soon her uncertainty about the name was her only noticeable speech defect, until a remark of Dr Breuer's led me to release her from this compulsive paramnesia.

I had a far longer struggle with the state that she called 'storm in the head' than with the residues of these experiences. When I first saw her in this condition she was lying on the divan, her features distorted and her entire body in ceaseless agitation; she kept pressing her hands to her forehead and crying out as if in longing and desperation the name 'Emmy', which was her own as well as that of her elder daughter. Under hypnosis she informed me that this condition was a recurrence of the many fits of despair that would come over her during her daughter's treatment, when she had spent hours thinking about how the negative results of the treatment might be set right, without finding a solution. At this point, feeling that her thoughts were becoming confused, she had got into the habit of calling her daughter's name aloud to help her to regain some clarity. For at that time, when her daughter's illness was making new demands on her and she felt that her nervous condition was again gaining power over her, she had resolved that everything to do with the child had to be kept clear of confusion, even if everything else in her head went to pieces.

After a few weeks, these reminiscences too were overcome, and for a while longer Frau Emmy remained under my supervision in perfect health. Right at the end of her stay something happened that I want to relate in detail, because this episode sheds the clearest light on the character of the patient and the way in which her states developed.

I once paid her a visit at lunchtime and caught her throwing something wrapped in paper into the garden, where it was caught by the porter's children. When questioned, she admitted that it was her (dry) pudding and that it tended to go the same way every day. This gave me cause to look around for the remains of the other courses, and I found more left on the plates than she could have consumed. When taken to task about why she ate so little, she replied that she was not used to eating more, that it would do her harm if she did, and that she had the same constitution as her late father who was also a poor eater. In answer to my question about what she drank, she said that she could tolerate only thick fluids, such as milk, coffee, cocoa, and so on; whenever she drank spring or mineral water it upset her stomach. Now this bore all the hallmarks of a nervous selection. I took a urine sample and found it to be very concentrated and carrying a surfeit of salts of uric acid.

I therefore considered it advisable that she drink more plentifully and I also undertook to increase her nutritional intake. She was by no means strikingly thin, but it did seem worthwhile to try to feed her up somewhat. When, on my next visit, I recommended an alkaline water to her and forbade her usual way of dealing with her pudding, her agitation was not inconsiderable. 'I'll do it because *you* ask me to, but I'm telling you now, it will come to no good, because it goes against my constitution, and my father was just the same.' When asked in hypnosis why she could no longer eat anything or drink water, she answered rather sullenly, 'I don't know.' The next day, the nurse confirmed that Frau Emmy had managed her whole portion and drunk a glass of alkaline water. But I found the patient herself lying down, deeply depressed, and in a most ungracious mood. She complained of extremely violent stomach pains, 'I told you so. Now we've again lost everything that we struggled for so long to achieve. I have upset my stomach as I always do if I eat more or drink water, and I'll have to starve myself again completely for five to eight days until I am able to tolerate anything.' I assured her that she would not have to starve herself and that it was quite impossible to upset one's stomach in this way; her pains were simply a result of her anxiety when eating and drinking. It was obvious that my explanation had not made the slightest impression on her, for when soon after this I tried to send her to sleep, the hypnosis went wrong for the first time, and from the furious glance that she flung at me, I recognized that she was in the process of utter rebellion and that the situation was very serious. I dispensed with the hypnosis and announced that I was giving her twenty-four hours to think things over and come round to the view that her stomach pains were simply the result of her fear; after this period I would ask her if she was still of the opinion that one could upset one's stomach for a whole week with a glass of mineral water and a modest meal, and if she said yes, I would ask her to leave. This little scene was in extremely sharp contrast to our normal relations, which had been very friendly.

Twenty-four hours later I found her humble and worn down. In answer to the question of what she thought about the origin of her stomach pains, she replied, for she is incapable of pretence, 'I believe that they are due to my anxiety, but only because that's what you say.' I then set her under hypnosis and asked her once again, 'Why can't you eat more?'

A prompt answer ensued which again took the form of her giving a chronologically ordered series of motives from her memory. 'When I was little it often happened that, out of naughtiness, I didn't want to eat my meat. Then mother was always very strict, and under the threat of severe punishment I had to eat up the leftover meat on the same plate two hours later. The meat had become quite cold and the fat so hard (she shows her disgust) . . . and I can still see the fork in front of me . . . one of the prongs was a little bent. Whenever I sit down to eat now, I see the plate in front of me with the cold meat and the fat; and the time when many years later I was living with my brother, who was an officer, and had the nasty illness; – I knew that it was infectious and was so horribly frightened that I would mix up the cutlery and take his knife and fork (shuddering) . . . and yet I did eat my meals with him, so that no one would notice that he was ill; and the time soon after that when I nursed my other brother, who was so very ill with lung disease, and then we would sit at his bedside, and the spittoon was always on the table and uncovered (shuddering, again) ... and he had a habit of spitting across the plates into the bowl, and then I would always feel sick, but I couldn't let it show for fear of hurting his feelings. And these spittoons are still on the table now when I eat and it still makes me feel sick.' Of course, I made a thorough job of clearing away this whole apparatus of disgust, and then asked her why she couldn't drink water. When she was seventeen the family spent a few months in Munich, and almost all of them contracted gastritis from the poor drinking water. Everyone else's illness was quickly relieved by following doctor's orders, but in her case it persisted; even the mineral water that she was advised to drink did nothing to improve matters. As soon as the doctor gave her this prescription, she thought to herself, 'that's bound to do no good either'. This intolerance of spring and mineral water had since recurred countless times.

The therapeutic effect of this investigation under hypnosis was immediate and lasting. She did not fast for a week, but on the very next day was already eating and drinking without any difficulty whatsoever. Two months later she wrote in a letter: 'I am eating very well and have put on a lot of weight. I have already drunk forty bottles of the water. Do you think that I should continue with this?'

I next saw Frau v. N. the following spring on her estate at D. Her elder daughter, whose name she tended to call out during her 'storms in the head', was at this time entering a phase of abnormal development; she exhibited immense ambitions which were out of all proportion to her meagre talent, became unruly and even violent towards her mother. I still enjoyed the mother's confidence and was summoned to deliver my judgement on the young girl's condition. My impression of the psychical change that she had undergone was not favourable and in making the prognosis I had also to take into account the fact that all of the patient's step-brothers and -sisters (children of Herr v. N. from the first marriage) had succumbed to paranoia. Nor was there any lack of neuropathic inheritance on the mother's side, although none of her immediate family had deteriorated to the point of chronic psychosis. I imparted the information requested by Frau Emmy v. N. without reservation, and her response was calm and comprehending. She had gained strength and seemed to be in flourishing health; during the eight months that had elapsed since the end of the last treatment she had enjoyed relatively good health, only slightly disturbed by neck cramps and other minor complaints. I learnt of the full extent of her duties, occupations and intellectual interests for the first time over these several days spent at her house. I also met the family doctor, who did not find that the lady gave him too much cause for complaint; she had, then, to an extent made her peace with the 'profession'.

The woman had become much healthier and fitter, but despite all my instructive suggestions there was little change in the fundamental traits of her character. She seemed to me not to have acknowledged the category of 'indifferent things'; her tendency to torment herself was hardly any less than at the time of the treatment. Nor had the hysterical disposition been idle during this good period; she complained, for example, that over the last few months she had become unable to take lengthy railway journeys, and a necessarily hurried attempt to release her from this impediment produced only a variety of slight unpleasant impressions that she had caught on her last journeys to D. and in the region. She seemed unwilling to communicate under hypnosis and even then I was already suspicious that she was on the point of withdrawing from my influence once more, and that the secret intention of her railway inhibition was to prevent a further visit to Vienna.

Over these several days she also reiterated her complaint about gaps in her memory, 'especially about the most important events', from which I concluded that my work of two years ago had exercised a sufficiently deep and lasting effect. – When one day she took me along an avenue that led from the house to a seaside cove, I risked asking her if this avenue was often covered with toads. By way of a reply, I was met with a reproachful glance, although this was not accompanied by any sign of horror, and then in addition came the remark, 'But there are real ones here.' – During the hypnosis that I carried out in order to remove the railway inhibition, she herself seemed dissatisfied with the answers that she gave, and she voiced the fear that now she probably would no longer obey the hypnosis as she had done before. I determined to convince her that the opposite was true. I wrote down a few words on a piece of paper that I handed to her, and said, 'At midday today you will pour me a glass of red wine as you did yesterday. As I raise the glass to my lips you will say, "Oh please, pour me a glass too", and then when I reach for the bottle, you will call out, "No, thank you, I would rather not after all." At this, you will reach into your pocket and pull out the piece of paper on which these same words appear.' That was in the morning; a few hours later this little scene was executed exactly as I had arranged, and it proceeded so naturally that it went unnoticed by any of the numerous people present. She seemed visibly in conflict with herself when she asked me for the wine – for she never drank wine – and once she had refused the drink, with evident relief, she reached into her pocket, pulled out the piece of paper on which the words she had last spoken were written, shook her head, and looked at me with astonishment.

Since this visit in May 1890 my news of Frau Emmy gradually became sparser. I discovered, in a roundabout way, that the regrettable condition of her daughter, which caused her all manner of upset and agitation, had in the end undermined her good health. The last I heard of her (summer 1893) was a short note in which she asked me to permit another doctor to hypnotize her, as she was ill again and not able to come to Vienna. At first I did not understand why this needed my consent; then the memory came to me that in the year 1890 I had, at her own request, protected her from being hypnotized by anyone else, so that she would not risk the distress of again coming under the control of a doctor whom she found unsympathetic, as she had done during the time at —berg (—tal, —wald). And so I relinquished my exclusive prerogative in writing.

CRITICAL ANALYSIS

Unless we first reach a thorough agreement regarding the value and meaning of terms, deciding whether an illness should count as a case of hysteria or as one of the other (not purely neurasthenic) neuroses is no simple matter, and in the area of the commonly occurring mixed neuroses we are still waiting for a guiding hand to set the boundaries and mark out the features which are essential for its characterization. If, therefore, we have until now been accustomed to diagnose hysteria in the narrower sense according to its resemblance to familiar and typical cases, then the definition of hysteria in the case of Frau Emmy v. N. can hardly be open to dispute. The ease with which deliria and hallucinations occurred while her mental activity was otherwise intact, the change in both personality and memory when in a state of artificial somnambulism, the anaesthesia of the painful extremity, certain data from the anamnesis, the ovarian neuralgia, and so on, leave no doubt as to the hysterical nature of the illness or at least of the patient. That the question might be raised at all is due to a specific characteristic of this case, which offers, too, an opportunity for making an observation of general validity. As is made clear in the 'Preliminary Communication', which appears at the beginning of this volume, we view hysterical symptoms as the effects and remains of excitations that had influenced the nervous system as traumas. Remains of this kind are not left over if the original excitation is drawn off by abreaction or by thought-work. Here we can no longer avoid taking quantities into account (even if these are not measurable), conceiving of the process as if a sum total of excitation entering the nervous system were converted into chronic symptoms in so far as it had not been expended in external action proportionate to its amount. We are now accustomed to find in hysteria that a considerable part of the trauma's 'sum total of excitation' is transformed into purely physical symptoms. It is this trait of hysteria that has for so long prevented it from being thought of as a psychical affection.

If, for the sake of brevity, we adopt the term 'conversion' to designate the transformation of psychical excitation into chronic physical symptoms which distinguishes hysteria, then we might say that the case of Frau Emmy v. N. displays a small amount of conversion: the excitation, which was psychical in origin, also tends to remain in the psychical domain, and it is easy to see how in this way it comes to resemble those other, non-hysterical neuroses. There are cases of hysteria in which the conversion affects the entire surplus of stimulus, so that the physical symptoms of the hysteria jut over into what seems to be a completely normal consciousness. More usual, however, is an incomplete transformation, so that at least one part of the affect accompanying the trauma remains as a mood-component in consciousness.

The psychical symptoms in our case of hysteria with only slight conversion may be divided into alterations of mood (anxiety, melancholic depression), phobias and abulias (inhibitions of will). The second and third types of psychical disturbance, which are regarded by psychiatrists of the French school as stigmata of nervous degeneracy, prove in our case to be adequately determined by traumatic experiences: they are, for the most part, traumatic phobias and abulias, as I will set out in detail below.

It is true that some of the phobias (in particular those of the neuropath) correspond to primary human phobias, in particular the fear of animals (snakes and toads, as well as all the vermin whose proud ruler is Mephistopheles), fear of storms, and so on. Yet even these phobias have been fortified by traumatic experiences, as was the fear of toads, by the impression made early in her youth when her brother threw a dead toad at her, upon which she had the attack of hysterical convulsions; the fear of storms by that shock that caused her clicking to develop; and the fear of fog by that walk in Rügen; at any rate, in this group the primary, or as it were, instinctive fear, regarded as a psychical stigma, takes the leading part.

The other, more specific phobias are also accounted for by particular experiences. Her fear of a sudden, unexpected fright is the result of the terrible impression made on her when she saw her husband, who was in the prime of health, pass away from a heart attack. Her fear of strangers, and fear of people in general, proves to be left over from the time when she was exposed to the persecutions of her family, was inclined to see every stranger as an agent acting on behalf of the relatives, and suspected that strangers knew about the spoken and written rumours that had been spread about her. Her dread of lunatic asylums and their inmates goes back to a whole series of unhappy experiences in her family, and to stories that she had lapped up from a stupid maid when she was a child. Apart from this, her phobia is on the one hand supported by the healthy person's primary, instinctive horror of madness, and on the other by the concern common to her as to every person with a nervous condition that she herself might succumb to madness. A highly specialized fear, such as that someone might be standing behind her, is motivated by several frightening impressions from her youth and from later in her life. Since an experience in a hotel that was – because of its erotic connection – particularly distressing for her, her fear that a stranger might steal into the room has been particularly prominent. And finally, a phobia which is often characteristic of neuropaths, the fear of being buried alive, is fully explained by the belief that her husband was not dead when his corpse was taken away, a belief which so movingly expresses her inability to reconcile herself to the fact that her life with the man she loved had come to a sudden end. I believe, in any case, that all of these *psychical* factors can explain the selection, but not the persistence of the phobias. For the latter, I will have to adduce a *neurotic* factor, namely the fact of the patient's having for years been in a state of sexual abstinence, which in itself is one of the most frequent causes of a *tendency to anxiety*.

Our patient's abulias (inhibitions of the will, incapacity), still less than her phobias, may be interpreted as psychical stigmas resulting from a general restriction of capacity. Rather, the hypnotic analysis of the case shows clearly that here the abulias are determined by a twofold psychical mechanism which is basically just a single mechanism. The first kind of abulia is simply the consequence of a phobia, namely in all those cases in which the phobia is attached to an action of the subject's own rather than to an expectation (going out, calling on people – the other kind being the expectation that someone might creep in etc.), and what causes the inhibition of the will is the anxiety linked to the successful completion of this action. It would be wrong to list these types of abulias together with their corresponding phobias as particular symptoms, yet it must be conceded that if they are not too extreme phobias of this kind can exist without leading to abulias. The other sort of abulia is based on the existence of unresolved associations which are affectively marked and which oppose the attachment of new associations, in particular those that they find incompatible. The most striking example of an abulia of this kind is provided by our patient's anorexia. She eats only very little because she doesn't like the taste, and she cannot acquire any taste for food, because for her the act of eating has for a very long time been attached to memories of revulsion, whose sum of affect has not yet decreased. It is, however, impossible to eat with revulsion and pleasure at the same time. The revulsion which had long been associated with meals failed to diminish because she had each time to suppress it instead of freeing herself from it by reaction. As a child, fear of punishment compelled her to eat – with revulsion – the cold meal, and in later years it was concern for her brothers that prevented her from expressing the intense feelings to which she was exposed during their meals together.

At this point I may perhaps recall a short study in which I have tried to give a psychological explanation of hysterical paralyses. In this study, I arrived at the hypothesis that the cause of such paralyses lay in the inaccessibility of the group of ideas connected with, say, one extremity, to new associations; this associative inaccessibility itself stems from the fact that the idea of the paralysed limb is included in the memory of the trauma, which is encumbered with unresolved affect. I drew on examples from everyday life to show that when an idea is cathected – that is, charged, invested and occupied – with unresolved affect in this way it will always bring with it a certain degree of associative inaccessibility and incompatibility with new cathexes.[25]

To this day I have not managed to prove, by means of hypnotic analysis, this theory about cases of motor paralysis, but I can refer to Frau v. N.'s anorexia as proof that this mechanism is true of certain abulias, and abulias are, after all, nothing other than very specialized – or, according to the French expression, 'systematized' – psychical paralyses.

The principal characteristics of Frau v. N.'s psychical situation can be given by emphasizing two points. 1. The distressing affects from her traumatic experiences have remained unresolved, notably, depression, pain (about her husband's death), resentment (at being persecuted by her relatives), revulsion (at the forced meals), fear (about her many frightening experiences), etc. 2. Her memory displays a lively activity which sometimes spontaneously, sometimes awoken by contemporary stimuli (e.g. at the news of the revolution in San Domingo), summons the traumas together with their accompanying affects bit by bit to her present-day consciousness. My therapy followed the course of this activity of the memory and tried day by day to resolve and dispose of what the day had brought to the surface until the accessible reserve of pathological memories seemed to be exhausted.

Working from these two psychical characteristics, which I believe to be generally present in hysterical paroxysms, I was able to make a number of important observations. I want, however, to defer these until I have brought some attention to bear on the mechanism of the physical symptoms.

It is not possible to say that all the patient's physical symptoms are derived in the same way; rather one discovers – even in this case in which few such symptoms were displayed – that the physical symptoms of a hysteria arise in various ways. I will for the moment take the liberty of counting pain as a physical symptom. As far as I can see, some of the pains were certainly organically determined by those slight (rheumatic) modifications to the muscles, tendons and fascia, which cause so much more pain to those who have a nervous condition than to healthy people; another set of pains was in all probability a memory of pain, a memory-symbol of the periods of agitation and nursing which had taken up so much of the patient's life. Even these may originally have been legitimate organic pains, but they had subsequently been adapted for the purposes of the neurosis. I base these claims relating to Frau v. N.'s pains on observations made elsewhere which I will relate at a later point in this study; little explanation was to be gathered from the patient herself on this particular matter.

A number of the striking motor symptoms displayed by Frau v. N. were simply the expression of emotion and easily recognizable as such, as, for example, holding out her hands with her fingers splayed and crooked as the expression of horror, the facial expressions, and so on. In any case, there was a more vivid and less inhibited expression of emotion than would be in keeping with her normal facial and body language, her education and breeding; when not in a hysterical state she was measured and almost stiff in her expressive movements. Other of these motor symptoms were, according to the patient, directly related to her pains: she played restlessly with her fingers (1888) or rubbed her hands together (1889) so as not to cry aloud, and this motivation brings vividly to mind one of Darwin's principles in explanation of the expression of emotions, namely the principle of 'the overflow of excitation', by which he explains, for example, why dogs wag their tails. Indeed, all of us use other kinds of motor innervation as a substitute for crying out when we experience painful stimulation. Anyone who is at the dentist's and has resolved to keep their head and mouth still and not to put their hands in the way, will at the very least drum their feet.

A more complex process of conversion can be identified in the tic-like movements of Frau v. N., the tongue-clicking and stuttering, the calling out of her name 'Emmy' in fits of confusion, the composite protective formula – 'Keep still – don't say anything – don't touch me!' (1888). Of these motor utterances the stuttering and clicking are explicable in terms of a mechanism that I have described in a short paper published in the *Journal on Hypnotism* [*Zeitschrift für Hypnotismus*] vol. 1, 1893[26] as the 'objectification of contrasting ideas'. The process involved would, in the light of this very same example, be the following: the hysteric, exhausted by worrying and keeping watch, is sitting at the bedside of her sick child who has, *at long last*, fallen asleep. She says to herself, now you have to keep quite still, so that you don't wake the little one. It is likely that this intention awakens a contrasting idea, the fear that she will after all make a noise and wake the little one from the sleep that she has so longed for. Contrasting ideas of this kind, which work against a firm intention, can also be seen to emerge markedly in us when we do not feel confident of carrying out an important resolution.

Neurotics, whose self-consciousness is seldom lacking a strain of depression and of anxious expectation, form a greater number of these contrasting ideas, or rather are more readily aware of them and also regard them as more meaningful. In a state of exhaustion, such as that of our patient, the contrasting idea, which in other circumstances was rejected, proves the stronger; this is the idea which is now objectified and which, to the horror of the patient, really does produce the noise she feared. In explanation of the whole process I assume too that the exhaustion is partial; it affects, according to the terminology of Janet and his followers, only the primary self of the patient, and it does not result in a weakening of the contrasting idea as well.

I further assume that the horror at the noise produced against the patient's will is what gives the moment its traumatic effect and fixes this noise itself as the corporeal memory-symptom of the scene as a whole. Indeed, in the very character of this tic, which consists of the spastic gasping-out of several sounds, separated by pauses in such a way as to resemble a kind of clicking more than anything else, I believe that I can distinguish the traces of the process to which it owes its origin. It seems that a battle between the intention and the contrasting idea, the 'counter-will', has taken place here, giving the tic its discontinuous character and limiting the contrasting idea to paths other than the usual ones for innervating the speech musculature.

The spastic speech impediment, the peculiar stuttering, was left behind from an occasion that was in essence similar, save that this time it was not the outcome of the final innervation, the cry, but the innervation process itself, the attempt at a convulsive repression of the organs of speech, that was installed as the symbol of the event in her memory.

The association of these two symptoms, the clicking and stuttering, which were closely related by virtue of their genesis, was prolonged and they became chronic as they were repeated under similar circumstances. But they were then put to a further use. Having arisen during violent fright, they were subsequently attached to every scare (according to the mechanism of monosymptomatic hysteria, which I will demonstrate in case V), even when this scare could give no cause for the objectification of a contrasting idea.

They were, ultimately, connected with so many traumas and had such ample reason to be reproduced in the patient's memory that they took the form of a meaningless tic, constantly interrupting speech without needing any particular cause. What the hypnotic analysis could then show is how much significance lay hidden behind this apparent tic, and the failure of the Breuer method in this instance to make both symptoms vanish completely, and at a single stroke, was due to the fact that the catharsis extended only to the three main traumas and not to those secondarily associated with them.[27]

According to the laws of hysteria, the crying out of the name 'Emmy' during her attacks of confusion reproduced her frequent state of helplessness during the treatment of her daughter. It was connected with the content of the attack by a complicated train of thought and, roughly speaking, corresponded to a protective formula on the part of the patient against this attack. Had a freer use been made of its meaning, this cry would probably also have been liable to degenerate into a tic, indeed the complex protective formula 'Don't touch me' etc. was already used in this way, but in both cases the hypnotic therapy checked further development of these symptoms. I came upon the cry 'Emmy' when it was newly arisen and still limited to its native soil, the attack of confusion.

Now, regardless of how these motor symptoms arose – the clicking from the objectification of a contrasting idea; the stutter from the simple conversion of psychical excitation into motor activity; the cry of 'Emmy' and the longer formula as protective measures from the voluntary action of the patient during a hysterical paroxysm – one thing is common to all of them, namely that either originally or persistently they have a demonstrable connection with traumas, representing them as symptoms in the activities of the memory.

Other of the patient's physical symptoms are not at all hysterical in nature, as for example the neck cramps, which I take to be a modified form of migraine and which, as such, are certainly not to be classed as a neurosis, but rather as an organic affection. Hysterical symptoms do, however, frequently become attached to these affections; in the case of Frau v. N. the neck cramps were used for hysterical attacks, whereas the typical manifestations of the hysterical attack were not at her disposal.

I would like to complete this characterization of Frau v. N.'s psychical condition by turning to the demonstrably pathological changes in her consciousness. As was the case for the neck cramps, unpleasant impressions in the present (compare the last instance of delirium in the garden) or powerful echoes of any of her traumas transport her into a state of delirium. Given the few observations that I made on this subject it is impossible for me to conclude other than that in this state there prevails a restriction of consciousness, a compulsion to association similar to that experienced in dreams; hallucinations and illusions are greatly facilitated, and feeble-minded and even nonsensical conclusions are drawn. This state, which is comparable to mental alienation, is likely to stand in for her attack, the equivalent being something like an acute psychosis, which one would classify as 'hallucinatory confusion'. It bears a further similarity to the typical hysterical attack in that a section of the old traumatic memories can usually be detected as the foundation of the delirium. The transition from the normal state to this state of delirium frequently occurs quite imperceptibly; she might only just have spoken in a perfectly proper manner of things which have little affective content, and as the conversation continues and leads her to distressing ideas, I would notice from her exaggerated gestures, from the appearance of her speech formulas and so on, that she was delirious. At the beginning of the treatment the delirium extended throughout the entire day, which made it difficult to say with any certainty whether the individual symptoms – and gestures – pertained to the psychical state merely as symptoms of an attack, or whether, as was the case with the clicking and stuttering, they had become genuine chronic symptoms. Often hindsight alone enabled one to differentiate between what had happened in the state of delirium and what had happened in the normal state. For the two states were separated by her memory and she would then be most astonished to hear of the things that the delirium had brought piecemeal into her normal conversation. My first conversation with her was the most remarkable example of the way in which the two states were entangled yet unaware of each other. In the course of this psychic see-sawing there was only one instance of an influence on her normal consciousness which was connected with the present, namely when she told me that she was a woman from the last century, a reply originating in her delirium.

The main reason why this analysis of Frau v. N.'s delirium was not carried out exhaustively enough is that her condition straightaway improved to such an extent that the deliria were sharply distinguished from her normal life and were restricted to those times when she had neck cramp. I did, however, gather a great deal more material concerning the patient's behaviour in a third psychical state, that of artificial somnambulism. Whereas in her normal state she did not know what she had experienced psychically in her deliria or in her somnambulism, during her somnambulism she had memories from all three states at her disposal, and it was then that she was really at her most normal. If I discount the fact that as a somnambulist she was far less reserved towards me than she was at the best of times in her normal life, i.e. that as a somnambulist she told me things about her family and so on, but would otherwise treat me as if I were a stranger; if, in addition, I disregard the fact that she displayed the somnambulist's complete openness to suggestion, then I really have to say that as a somnambulist she was in a completely normal state. It was, on the other hand, interesting to observe that there was no trace of this somnambulism being over-normal, that it bore all the psychical failings which we attribute to the normal state of consciousness. The way in which somnambulistic memory operates may be illustrated by the following examples. During one of our conversations she expressed her delight at a pretty ornamental pot-plant in the entrance hall of the sanatorium. 'But whatever is its name, Doctor? Don't you know it? I used to know the German and Latin names and I've forgotten both.' She was extremely knowledgeable about plants, whereas I, on this occasion, admitted my ignorance in matters botanical. Under hypnosis, only a few minutes later, I asked her, 'Do you know the name of the plant in the stairway now?' The answer came without the slightest pause for thought. 'Its German name is *"Türkenlilie"* [Turk's-cap lily], but I really have forgotten the Latin.' On another occasion when she was in good health she told me about a visit to the catacombs in Rome and was unable to bring to mind two of the terms used to describe them, a matter in which I was also unable to assist her. In the hypnosis immediately afterwards I asked which words she meant. She didn't know in the hypnosis either. At this I said, 'Don't think about it any more, tomorrow in the garden between five and six o'clock in the afternoon – nearer six than five – they will suddenly come to you.'

The next evening during a conversation which had nothing at all to do with the catacombs, she suddenly burst out with 'Crypt, Doctor, and columbarium'. 'Ah, so those are the words that you couldn't find yesterday. When did they occur to you?' 'This afternoon in the garden, just before I went up to my room.' I noticed that this was her way of showing me that she had kept exactly to the given time, as she used to leave the garden at about six o'clock. So even in somnambulism she did not have access to the full range of her knowledge; there was an actual and a potential consciousness in this state too. It also happened fairly frequently that in somnambulism she would respond to my question about where this or that phenomenon came from by frowning and, after a moment's pause, answering sheepishly, 'I don't know'. I had then become accustomed to saying, 'Think about it, you'll find out in a minute', and having reflected a little, she was able to give me the information I had asked for. But it sometimes happened that nothing occurred to her and then I would have to leave her with the task of remembering by the morning, which she would do without fail. This woman went to extreme lengths in her everyday life to avoid any kind of untruthfulness, nor did she lie under hypnosis, but there were instances of her making incomplete statements, in which she held back some part of her report until I forced her to complete it a second time around. As in the example given on p. 74 it was mostly the aversion instilled in her by the topic which closed her mouth, in both somnambulism and everyday life. In spite of these restrictive traits the impression made by the behaviour of her psyche in somnambulism was still on the whole that the powers of her mind were unfolding without inhibition and that she had complete access to her stock of memories.

Although undeniably open to suggestion in somnambulism she

was far from manifesting a pathological lack of resistance. I have to say that on the whole I made no greater impression on her than I might have expected of an investigation of this kind into the psychical mechanism of any person who listened to me with great trust and in complete clarity of mind, the only difference being that in her so-called normal state Frau v. N. was unable to present me with such a favourable psychical disposition. Whenever I failed to produce convincing reasons (as with her fear of animals), or chose to use the effects of authoritative suggestion rather than going into the psychical history of the origins of a symptom, I was always aware of the tense, dissatisfied expression on the face of the somnambulist; and if I then asked in conclusion, 'So, are you still going to be afraid of this animal?' the answer was, 'No – since *you* ask me not to be.' But this kind of promise, whose only basis was her submissiveness towards me, was never really successful, in fact it had as little success as the many general lessons that I gave her, in place of which I might just as well have repeated the one suggestion: Be healthy.

This same person, who clung so stubbornly to the symptoms of her illness in the face of suggestion, and would let go of them only in response to psychical analysis or personal conviction, was, on the other hand, as compliant as the best medium in any hospital when the suggestions were trivial, that is, things unrelated to her illness. I have provided examples of this kind of post-hypnotic obedience in the case history. I do not find this behaviour contradictory. The stronger idea was bound to claim its due here too. On investigating the mechanism of pathological *idées fixes*, one finds that they are based upon and supported by experiences so numerous and of such an intense effect, that one can hardly be surprised to find them capable of putting up a successful resistance to suggested counter-ideas, which, in turn, have been furnished with only limited powers. Only if one were dealing with a brain that was truly pathological would it be possible to use suggestion to dispel such legitimate products of intense psychical processes.[28]

It was while I was studying the somnambulistic state of Frau v. N. that I first experienced substantial doubts about the validity of Bernheim's proposition '*Tout est dans la suggestion*' [Suggestion is everything] and his astute friend Delbœuf's conclusion '*Comme quoi il n'y a pas d'hypnotisme*' [It follows, then, that there is no such thing as hypnotism]. Even today I cannot understand how holding my finger before her eyes and once saying 'Sleep' should have created the patient's particular psychical state, in which her memory encompassed all her psychical experiences. I may have called forth the state, but I did not create it by my use of suggestion, since its characteristics, which, incidentally, are universally valid, were so great a surprise to me.

The way in which therapy was practised during somnambulism in this instance has been made sufficiently clear in the case history. As is usual in hypnotic psychotherapy I used reassurances, prohibitions and the introduction of all kinds of counter-ideas to combat the pathological ideas present in the patient, but, not content with this, I also pursued the genesis of individual symptoms, so as to be able to combat the premises on which the pathological ideas were founded. It then happened regularly during these analyses that the patient would display violent excitement and talk through things whose accompanying affect had previously only been discharged as an expression of emotion. I cannot say how many of the therapeutic successes of this period came down to suggesting the symptom away *in statu nascendi*, how many to resolving the affect through abreaction, since I combined these two therapeutic factors. This case could not, then, be taken as strictly proving that the cathartic method is inherently effective as a therapy, but I have to say that the only symptoms which were permanently removed were those to which I applied a psychical analysis.

The therapeutic success was on the whole considerable, but not lasting; the patient's tendency to fall ill in the same way on encountering further traumas was not removed. If anyone wanted to undertake the definitive cure of a hysteria such as this, they would have to account for the connections between the phenomena more thoroughly than I myself attempted at that time. Frau v. N. was undoubtedly a person with a severe neuropathic heredity. To accomplish hysteria without a disposition of this kind would most likely be impossible. But the disposition alone does not make the hysteria –

there are reasons for it, and indeed, as I maintain, reasons which will adequately determine an aetiology. I mentioned previously that in the case of Frau v. N. the affects from a great many traumatic experiences seemed to have been retained and that the lively activity of her memory brought now one, now another trauma to the surface of her psyche. I would now like to venture an explanation for the retention of affects in Frau v. N. There is, it is true, a connection with her hereditary disposition – which is to say that, on the one hand, her feelings were extremely intense, she was of a vehement nature, and capable of delivering the greatest passion, but that, on the other, she had been living in utter spiritual isolation since the death of her husband, the persecution of her relatives had made her mistrustful of friends, and she guarded jealously against anyone gaining too much influence over her actions. Her duties were wide-ranging and she attended to all the psychical work demanded of her on her own, without a friend or *confidant*, almost completely isolated from her family, and further impeded by her conscientiousness, her tendency to harsh self-criticism, and often too by her natural helplessness as a woman. In short, the mechanism of the *retention of large sums of excitation* is, in itself, unmistakable here. It was supported partly by the circumstances of her life, partly by her natural disposition; her shyness at talking about herself, for example, was so great that none of the daily visitors to the house, as I noted with astonishment in 1891, knew that she was ill, or that I was her doctor.

Have I now exhausted the aetiology of this case of hysteria? I do not think so, for at the time of both treatments I was not yet asking myself the questions which need to be answered if I am to arrive at an exhaustive elucidation. I now think that something else must have happened to provoke an outbreak of the affliction in precisely those last few years, when the operative aetiological conditions had for so many years remained unchanged. It also struck me that among all the intimate information which the patient communicated to me, the sexual element, which is after all more liable than any other to give rise to traumas, was completely absent. It is highly unlikely that the excitations left no trace at all in this area; I was probably being given an *editio in usum Delphini*, a bowdlerized version of her life-story. The patient behaved with a great and, to all appearances, unaffected sense of propriety, without prudishness. Yet, thinking of the reluctance with which under hypnosis she told me of the little adventure of her chambermaid in the hotel, I am led to suspect that this intense woman, who was capable of such strong feelings, had not conquered her sexual needs without a hard fight, and had sometimes reached a point of severe exhaustion in her attempt to suppress this most powerful of all drives. She once confessed to me that she had not remarried because her large fortune prevented her from believing in the disinterestedness of her suitors and because she would have reproached herself for having harmed the interests of her two children by marrying again.

I must add one more observation before concluding the case history of Frau v. N. Both Dr Breuer and I knew her fairly well, and over a fairly long period of time, and we used to smile when we compared her character with the depiction of the hysterical psyche, which can be traced through the writings and opinions of doctors since ancient times. If our observations of Frau Cäcilie M. had allowed us to see that hysteria of the severest kind is compatible with the richest and most original gifts – a fact that is self-evident in the light of the biographies of women who were eminent in history and literature – then the case of Frau Emmy v. N. demonstrated that hysteria does not preclude a flawless development of character and a purposeful way of life. We had made the acquaintance of an outstanding woman whose moral seriousness in the execution of her duties, virtually masculine intelligence and energy, high degree of education and love of truth impressed us both, while her benevolent care of all those in her service, her personal modesty and the refinement of her manners also distinguished her as a true lady. To call such a woman 'degenerate' one would have to distort the meaning of the word beyond recognition. We would do well to make the conceptual distinction between 'disposition' and 'degeneracy', lest we be forced to confess that humanity owes a large proportion of its great achievements to the efforts of 'degenerate' individuals.

I must also confess that I can find nothing of the 'psychical insufficiency' from which P. Janet sees hysteria as originating. The hysterical disposition would, in his view, involve an abnormal restriction of the field of consciousness (as a consequence of hereditary degeneration), which in turn causes the neglect of a great number of perceptions and, as a further consequence, the disintegration of the self and the organization of secondary personalities. It follows that what remains of the self once the psychical groups organized by the hysteria have been removed would necessarily be less capable than the normal self, and in fact, according to Janet, in cases of hysteria the self is afflicted by psychical stigmata, condemned to mono-ideism, and incapable of those exertions of the will required by daily life. Janet has, I think, wrongly elevated those states resulting from changes in consciousness due to hysteria to the rank of primary conditions of hysteria. This subject would be worth pursuing in more detail elsewhere; in the case of Frau v. N., however, there was no evidence of such 'insufficiency'. At those times when her states were most severe, she was and remained capable of attending to her share in the direction of a large industrial enterprise, keeping a constant eye on her children's education, continuing her correspondence with intellectually distinguished persons, in short, fulfilling all her duties well enough for her illness to remain hidden. I am inclined to think, though, that this would involve a considerable excess of psychical efficiency, that could perhaps not be maintained indefinitely and would necessarily lead to exhaustion, to the secondary '*misère psychologique*'. It seems likely that her capacity had already begun to be disrupted in this way at the time when I first saw her, but in any case severe hysteria had been present for many years before these symptoms of exhaustion.[29]

Notes

1. This clicking proceeded at a number of tempi. On hearing it, colleagues of mine who knew something about hunting compared the final notes with the mating cry of the capercaillie.

2. The words did in fact correspond to a *protective formula*, as will be

explained later. I have since observed similar protective formulas in a melancholic woman who used them in an attempt to control the thoughts that tormented her (wishing that something dreadful would happen to her husband and her mother, blasphemies, etc.).

3. This was a case of hysterical delirium alternating with the normal state of consciousness, rather as a genuine tic will insert itself into a voluntary movement without disturbing or merging with it.

4. On waking from the hypnosis she would always look around for a moment as though confused; her gaze would then come to rest on me, she would seem to have come to her senses, would put on her glasses, which she had removed before falling asleep, and then be cheerful and quite herself. Although we spoke to each other about all manner of things and although I put her to sleep twice a day almost every day during the course of the treatment (which lasted seven weeks in this first year and eight in the second), she never questioned me about the hypnosis or commented on it at all, and in her waking state she seemed, so far as possible, to ignore the fact that she was being hypnotized.

5. A sudden intrusion like this of a delirium into a waking state was not uncommon for her and recurred frequently while she was under my observation. She used to complain that she often gave such absurd answers that her staff could not understand her. During my first visit I asked her how old she was, and she answered quite seriously, 'I am a woman from the last century.' Weeks later she explained to me that in her delirium at that time she had been thinking of a beautiful old cupboard that she had acquired when travelling, for she loved antique furniture. She was referring to this cupboard, when my question about her age prompted her to speak about dates.

6. A form of migraine.

7. Many other hysterics have reported this kind of remembering in vivid, visual images and stressed that it was particularly true of pathogenic memories.

8. When she was awake I had received the following answer to my question about the origin of the tic, 'I don't know; oh, a very long time now.'

9. A particular kind of symbolism must have been connected with the toad but unfortunately I did not attempt to get to the bottom of it.

10. This did then happen.

11. It is possible that the answer, 'I don't know', was right, but it could equally signal her reluctance to talk about the causes. Subsequent experience with other patients showed that, even under hypnosis, the greater the effort they had made to repress something from their consciousness, the harder it was for them to remember the event in question.

Studies in Hysteria

12. As can be seen here, the patient's tic-like clicking and spastic stammer are two symptoms that can be traced back to similar causes and an analogous mechanism. I have considered this mechanism in a short paper entitled, 'A case of hypnotic healing together with some observations on hysterical counter-will' (*Zeitschrift für Hypnotismus*, vol. 1) [1892–3] [*Standard Edition*, vol. I] and shall also come back to it below.

13. Didactic suggestions of this kind always misfired with Frau Emmy, as the outcome of the case has shown.

14. This time I was probably too vigorous and went too far. Even after eighteen months, when I saw Frau Emmy again and found her to be in a relatively good state of health, she complained to me that it was curious that she had only an extremely vague recollection of certain very important moments in her life. While she took this as evidence of the decline of her memory, I had to guard against giving her the explanation for this special kind of amnesia. The striking success of the therapy in this area probably came from my having got her to recount these recollections to me in such detail (in far greater detail than has been kept in the notes), whereas at other times I was too often satisfied simply with passing references.

15. It was not until the following day that I understood this little scene. Her unruly nature, which rebelled against any form of constraint whether she was awake or in artificial sleep, had made her angry with me for thinking that her story was finished and interrupting her with my concluding suggestion. There are many other such instances which prove that in her hypnotic consciousness she was keeping a critical eye on my work. She probably wanted to reproach me for interrupting her narrative today as I had done before with the horror stories about the asylum, but did not venture to do so, and instead seemed to produce these supplementary remarks without making any transition and without revealing the connecting train of thought. The following day a rebuke made my mistake clear to me.

16. Unfortunately, in this case I failed to research the significance of this 'zoöpsia', or, for example, to think about distinguishing what in this fear of animals was symbolic and what was expressive of a primitive horror (as is characteristic of many neuropaths from childhood onwards).

17. The visual memory of the big lizard had clearly become important only in that it coincided temporally with an intense emotion that she must have undergone during this performance. But in treating this patient it happened frequently – as I have already admitted – that I was content to make extremely superficial inquiries, and in this instance, too, did not push my investigation any further. Incidentally, I would also like to indicate the

98

possibility of hysterical macropsia. Frau Emmy was extremely short-sighted and astigmatic, and her hallucinations may often have been provoked by the indistinctness of her visual perceptions.

18. At this time I tended to attribute a *psychical* origin to all the symptoms of hysteria. Today, I would explain the tendency to anxiety of this woman who lived in abstinence as *neurotic* (anxiety neurosis).

19. The course of events was, then, as follows: When she woke up that morning she felt anxious and seized on the anxious idea that was nearest to mind as an explanation. A conversation had occurred on the previous afternoon about the lift in the building where the children were staying. Always concerned about her children, she had asked the governess if the elder daughter, who could not walk much because of the ovarian neuralgia on her right side and pains in her right leg, was using the lift to go down as well as up. A slip of her memory then allowed her to connect her anxiety, of which she was conscious, with the idea of this lift. She could not find the real reason for her anxiety among her conscious thoughts; not until I questioned her in the hypnosis did this come to light, and then it did so unhesitatingly. The process was the same as that studied by Bernheim and others after him in individuals who follow instructions given during the hypnosis when in a post-hypnotic state. So, for example, Bernheim suggested to a patient ('Suggestion' [*De la suggestion et de ses applications à la thérapeutique*, 1886, p. 29]) that on waking up he should put both thumbs in his mouth. This he then does, and excuses himself by saying that his tongue has been hurting since he bit it the day before during an attack resembling an epileptic fit. In another such instance of obedience to a suggestion, a girl attempts to murder a law-court official who is a complete stranger to her. When seized and questioned about the motives of her action, she invents a story about having suffered an insult which demands revenge. There seems, then, to be a need to draw psychical phenomena of which one becomes conscious into causal connection with other conscious matter. Whenever the true causation eludes conscious perception, one does not hesitate to make another connection which one believes oneself, despite its being false. It is clear that there is a split in the content of consciousness which is of the greatest importance in advancing such *'false connections'*. I would like to spend a little more time considering the example of a false connection mentioned above because it may be described as exemplary in more than one respect. Exemplary in the first instance of the behaviour of this patient who, over the course of the treatment, repeatedly gave me the opportunity to use hypnotic elucidation to resolve such false connections and remove the effects which result from them. I will describe one such case in detail, because it illuminates the psychological fact in question with sufficient clarity. I had suggested to Frau Emmy von N. that in place of her usual lukewarm bath, she try a cool hip-bath, which I promised her would be more refreshing. She always observed doctor's orders with the utmost obedience but followed them on each occasion with the keenest suspicion. As I have already reported, medical treatment had almost always failed to afford her relief. My suggestion that she take cool baths was not given in so authoritative a manner that she could not have plucked up the courage to express her concerns to me. 'Whenever I have had a cool bath, I have been melancholy for the rest of the day. But I will try it again, if you *want*; please don't think that I would fail to do something that you tell me to do.' I pretended to give up my suggestion, but, in the next hypnosis, I put it to her that she herself should propose taking cool baths – having thought it over, she might after all want to risk trying again, and so on. And so it happened that on the following day she herself returned to the idea of taking cool hip-baths, and used all the arguments with which I had presented her, in an attempt to win me over. I gave in without much protest. But the day after the hip-bath I really did find her in a deep depression. 'Why are you like this today?' – 'I knew this would happen. It always happens with cold baths.' – 'But you yourself requested it. Now we know that you can't tolerate it, we'll go back to the lukewarm baths.' – During the hypnosis I then asked her, 'Was it really the cool bath that made you so depressed?' – 'Oh, the cool bath had nothing to do with it,' was her reply, 'what happened was that I was reading in the paper this morning that a revolution has broken out in San Domingo. When there is unrest there, the whites are always the ones who suffer, and I have a brother in San Domingo who has already given us much cause for concern, and now I'm worried that something might happen to him.' And at that the matter between us was settled. The next morning she took a cool hip-bath as if it were perfectly natural, and carried on doing so for several weeks, without once identifying it as the cause of a depression.

It will be agreed that this example is also typical of the behaviour of a great many neuropaths towards the therapy recommended by their doctor. Whether there is unrest in San Domingo or anywhere else that might on a particular day give rise to a specific symptom, the patient will always be inclined to attribute this symptom to the doctor's last intervention. Of the two conditions necessary to produce this kind of false connection, the one, mistrust, seems always to be present; the other, the splitting of consciousness, may be substituted, as most neuropaths either have no knowledge of the real causes (or at least the circumstantial causes) of their suffering, or have no intention of acknowledging them, because they are reluctant to be reminded of the share of the blame that they themselves bear.

It would be possible to take the view that the psychical conditions of ignorance or intentional neglect which we have distinguished as character-istic of neuropaths not suffering from hysteria, would necessarily be more favourable to the development of a false connection than would be the presence of a split in consciousness, which, after all, removes from con-sciousness the substance necessary to causal connections. Yet this split is seldom clear-cut; as a rule, parts of the subconscious complex of ideas jut over into normal consciousness, and it is precisely this which gives rise to such disturbances. What is usually perceived consciously, as in the above example, is the general feeling – the mood of anxiety or of mourning – which is linked with this complex, and this feeling, through some kind of 'compulsion to associate', demands to be connected with another complex of ideas which is present in consciousness. (This may be compared with the mechanism of 'obsessional ideas' which I describe in a paper published in the *Neurolog. Zentralblatt*, nos. 10 and 11, 1894. See also 'Obsessions et phobies', *Revue neurologique*, no. 2, 1895. [*Standard Edition*, vol. III])

I was able to ascertain the power of this compulsion to associate on the basis of some recent observations in another field. For several weeks, I had to give up my usual bed for a harder one, in which I probably dreamt more, or had livelier dreams, or perhaps I simply could not reach my normal depth of sleep. In the quarter of an hour immediately after I woke up I remembered every dream I had had that night, and went to the trouble of writing them down, and attempting to find a solution to them. I succeeded in tracing all of these dreams back to two factors: 1. to the necessity of working out such thoughts as were of only fleeting concern to me during the day, and had only been touched on and not resolved, and 2. to the compulsion to make a connection between things that are present in the same state of consciousness. The senseless and contradictory nature of the dreams could be traced back to the free reign of the second factor.

It is regularly the case that the mood relating to an experience and the subject matter of that experience may appear in a quite different relationship to that held in primary consciousness. This I had occasion to observe in a different patient, Frau Cäcilie M., with whom I became far more thoroughly acquainted than with any other patient referred to here. This lady's case afforded me a collection of numerous and highly convincing proofs for the type of psychical mechanism of hysterical phenomena which we have represented in this study. Unfortunately, personal circumstances prevent me from giving a detailed account of this case history, although I shall have occasion to refer to it from time to time. Frau Cäcilie M. had latterly been in a peculiar hysterical condition and, while I am sure that it was not an isolated instance, I do not know if it has ever been formally recognized. It could be described as a 'hysterical psychosis for the quitting of debts'. The patient had experienced countless psychical traumas and spent many years in a state of chronic hysteria which took a variety of different forms. Neither she nor anyone else knew the grounds for any of these conditions. Striking gaps showed up in her remarkably well-stocked memory, and she herself complained that it was as if her life were dismembered. One day she was suddenly overcome by an old reminiscence which stood out vividly and so freshly that it was as if she were feeling it for the first time, and from this moment on, for almost three years, she relived all of her life's traumas – which she had believed to be long forgotten and some of which she had never really remembered at all – with the most terrible outlay of suffering and the return of all the symptoms that she had ever had. This 'quitting of old debts' encompassed a period of thirty-three years and allowed the often very complex way in which each of her conditions was determined to be identified. The only means of bringing her any relief was to give her the opportunity in the hypnosis to talk away whichever reminiscence was tormenting her at that time, together with all its attendant outlay of mood and physical expression; and when I was prevented from being there, so that she had to speak in front of someone else, of whom she felt shy, it did then happen on a few occasions that she would tell her story quite quietly, and belatedly, in the hypnosis, present me with all the tears and expressions of desperation with which she had really wanted to accompany what she had to relate. For a few hours after a purging of this kind in the hypnosis she would be quite well and remain present. After a short time the next reminiscence in the series would break in. This reminiscence would, however, send on the mood associated with it some hours in advance. She would become very irritable, or fearful, or despairing, without ever sensing that this mood did not belong to the present but to the condition that would next befall her. During this transitional period she would regularly make false connections and cling to them stubbornly until the hypnosis. So, for example, she once greeted me with the question: 'I'm no good, am I? Isn't what I told you yesterday a sign that I'm no good?' What she had said the day before did not seem to me to justify her damning verdict; after a short discussion, she was quite ready to recognize this, but in the next hypnosis there came to light a reminiscence of an event which, twelve years ago, had caused her to reproach herself severely – though, incidentally, in the present she no longer held to these self-reproaches in the least.

20. On subsequent reflection I cannot help thinking that these 'neck cramps' may have been an organically determined condition analogous to a migraine. In medical practice one sees a number of conditions of this kind which are not described, but which bear such a striking similarity to classic cases of hemicrania that one is tempted to broaden the definition of the latter and attach only secondary importance to the localization of the pain. As is well known, many neuropathic women tend to combine hysterical attacks (spasms and deliria) with migraines. Whenever I saw Frau Emmy with neck cramp, it was always accompanied by an attack of delirium.

As far as the arm and leg pains are concerned, I think that they were determined by chance coincidence – a case of little interest, but one which is all the more common for that. She had pains of this kind during the period of agitation and nursing and, as a consequence of her exhaustion, had felt them more acutely than usual. These pains, which were at first only coincidentally associated with what she had experienced, were later repeated in her memory as the physical symbol of the complex of association. I shall be able to cite several more examples which demonstrate this process below. The pains were likely to have been rheumatic in origin, that is, to give this often misused term a specific meaning, pains which are located principally in the muscles and in which a marked sensitivity to pressure and a change in the consistency of the muscles can be detected; which are felt most acutely after a substantial period of rest or immobility of the extremities, as in the morning; which may be improved by repeating the movement which causes pain and removed entirely by massage. These myogenic pains, although common in all sorts of people, take on great significance in neuropaths, who believe them to be nervous in origin, and are often supported in this by doctors who are not used to checking the muscles by pressing them with their fingers, thus providing the substance of countless hysterical neuralgias, so-called sciatica, and so on. I will make only brief reference here to the relationship between this kind of pain and the disposition to gout. My patient's mother and two of her sisters had suffered severely from gout (or chronic rheumatism). It is possible that some of the pains of which she complained at the time may also have been current. I do not know, as I then had no experience of judging this muscular condition.

21. The method I followed here could hardly be regarded as a good one. None of this was carried out exhaustively enough.

22. Tracing the stuttering and clicking back to the two initial traumas did not fully remove them, although there was, from that point on, a striking improvement in both symptoms. The explanation for this being only partially successful was given by the patient herself (see pp. 55–6). She had become accustomed to clicking and stuttering whenever she took fright, so that ultimately these symptoms were dependent not only on the initial traumas, but also on a long chain of associated memories that I had neglected to clear away. This is a common enough case and one which always impairs the elegance and completeness of the therapeutic results of the cathartic method.

23. This was my first experience of something that I have subsequently been able to verify countless times, namely, that when hypnosis is being used to treat a new hysterical delirium the patient will give their account in reverse chronological order, beginning with the most recent and less important impressions and thought connections, and only in conclusion reaching the primary impression, which is, in all likelihood, the most important one causally.

24. Her astonishment the evening before at not having had neck cramp for such a long time was, then, a presentiment of an approaching condition, which was already forming at the time and was noticed in the unconscious. This curious form of presentiment was an altogether common experience in the case, mentioned above, of Frau Cäcilie M. Every time that she was in good health and said something like 'It's been such a long time since I've been frightened of witches at night', or 'I'm so pleased that I haven't had the pain in my eyes for so long', I could be quite certain that the following night the nurse would have extra work dealing with a severe onset of her fear of witches, or that her next attack of the dreaded pains in the eyes would begin. On each occasion the vague outlines of what was already fully formed in the unconscious showed through, and the unsuspecting 'official' consciousness (as Charcot describes it) reworked this representation, which surfaced as an idea that had suddenly come to mind, into an expression of satisfaction, which swiftly and unfailingly proved ill-founded. Frau Cäcilie, a highly intelligent lady, to whom I am also indebted for having greatly assisted me in my understanding of hysterical symptoms, herself drew my attention to the fact that such occurrences may have given rise to the well-known superstition that boasting or 'talking of the devil' is likely to tempt fate. One should not boast about one's good fortune, but nor should one imagine the worst, or it will come about. In fact, one does not boast about one's happiness until unhappiness is already just around the corner, and one expresses the presentiment in the form of a boast because the content of the reminiscence emerges here before what we feel about it, in other words, because a pleasing contrast is present in consciousness.

25. 'Quelques considérations pour une étude comparative des paralysies motrices, organiques et hystériques', *Archives de Neurologie*, Nr. 77, 1893

['Some points for a comparative study of organic and hysterical motor paralyses', *Standard Edition*, vol. I].

26. ['A Case of Successful Treatment by Hypnotism', *Standard Edition*, vol. I.]

27. I may give the impression here of attributing too much importance to the details of the symptoms and of becoming lost in unnecessarily petty sign-interpretation. Yet what I have learnt is that the determination of hysterical symptoms really extends to the finest detail of their execution and that it is difficult to attribute too much meaning to them. I would like to cite an example that will justify my argument. Some months ago I was treating an eighteen-year-old girl from a family with a bad heredity; hysteria contributed its fair share to her complex neurosis. The first thing that I learnt from her was that she complained of attacks of despair and that these took on two different forms. In the one, she sensed a pulling and prickling in the lower part of her face, from her cheeks down towards her mouth; in the other, the toes of both feet were stretched out convulsively and moved restlessly to and fro. At the outset I myself had little inclination to attribute much significance to these details, and it certainly would have occurred to my predecessors in the study of hysteria to see these phenomena as proof of the stimulation of the cortical centres during attacks of hysteria. While it is true that we are unaware of the location of the centres for such paraesthesias, it is known that paraesthesias of this kind induce partial epilepsy and constitute what Charcot terms sensory epilepsy. The close proximity of the symmetrical cortical areas to the median fissure would have been held responsible for the movement of the toes. Yet the explanation proved to be different. Once I had got to know the girl better, I asked her directly what sort of thoughts came to her during these attacks, adding that she shouldn't be embarrassed, she must surely be able to give an explanation for the two phenomena. The patient blushed with shame and was in the end persuaded, without hypnosis, to give the following explanation, the truth of which was fully confirmed by her companion who was present at the time. Since the onset of menstruation she had for years suffered from *Cephalalgia adolescentium*, which made any sustained occupation impossible and interrupted her education. When at last she was free of this impediment, the ambitious and somewhat simple child decided to set to work on herself with all her might, so as to catch up with her sisters and other girls of her age. She exerted herself beyond all measure and an endeavour of this kind usually ended with an outburst of despair at having overestimated her powers. Of course, she also tended to compare herself physically with other girls and to be unhappy whenever she discovered that she was physically at a disadvantage. She began to feel upset about her prognathism (which was quite apparent) and came upon the idea of correcting it by repeatedly pulling her top lip down over her protruding teeth for a quarter of an hour at a time. The lack of success of this childish endeavour once led to an outbreak of despair, and from then on the pulling and prickling running down the cheek was established as the form of one type of attack. The determination of the other attacks – with the motor symptoms of stretching out and wriggling of the toes – was no less obvious. I was informed that the first such attack occurred after an excursion on the Schafberg near Ischl, and her relatives were, naturally, inclined to attribute it to over-exertion. The girl, however, gave the following report: she and her siblings loved to tease one another by pointing out each other's (undeniably) big feet. Our patient, who had long been unhappy about this blemish, tried to force her feet into the tightest boots, but her attentive father would not tolerate this and saw to it that she wore only comfortable footwear. She was most unhappy with this regulation, thought about it all the time, and got into the habit of playing with her toes inside her shoes as one does when one wants to measure if the shoe is much too big, how much smaller a shoe one could bear, and so on. During the outing up the Schafberg, which she did not find at all tiring, the shortened skirts which they were wearing of course provided a renewed opportunity for her attention to be drawn to her shoes. As they were walking one of her sisters said to her, 'You really have put on especially big shoes today.' She tried to play with her toes and had the same impression. She could not rid herself of her distress at the unfortunate size of her feet and on her return home she had the first attack in which the memory-symbol for the entirety of this distressing chain of thoughts was the action of the toes curling and moving involuntarily.

I want to note that this was not a question of persistent symptoms, but of the symptoms of an attack, and, in addition, that after this confession the attacks of the first type ceased and those of the second with the toe-movement continued. Something then must have been left over that had not been confessed.

Postscript: Later I also discovered the following: the foolish girl was working at her beautification with such excessive enthusiasm because she wanted to please a young cousin of hers. (*Addition 1924*:) A number of years later her neurosis turned into a *dementia praecox*.

28. I was deeply impressed by another case of this interesting opposition between the most far-reaching obedience during somnambulism in all matters unrelated to the symptoms of the illness and the stubborn resistance of those symptoms, because they are deep-rooted and inaccessible to analysis. The patient was a lively and gifted young girl who for eighteen months had experienced severe difficulties in walking; I had treated her for more than five months, without being able to help. The girl was analgesic, had painful areas on both legs and rapid tremors in the hands; she walked leaning forwards, dragging her legs and taking small steps; she staggered as if her cerebellum were impaired and, in fact, often fell over. Her mood was strikingly cheerful. One of our leading authorities in Vienna at the time had misguidedly diagnosed this complex of symptoms as multiple sclerosis; another expert identified hysteria, a view supported by the complicated form of the clinical picture at the beginning of the illness (pains, fainting, amaurosis), and referred the patient to me for treatment. I tried to improve her walking by hypnotic suggestion, treatment of the legs under hypnosis, and so on, but without the slightest success, although she was an excellent somnambulist. One day, as she came staggering into the room again, one arm on that of her father, the other supported by an umbrella, whose spike was already greatly worn down, I became impatient and during the hypnosis shouted at her 'This has been going on for too long now. By tomorrow morning that umbrella will break in your hand, you'll have to walk home without it, and from then on you won't need an umbrella any more.' I don't know how I came upon the foolish idea of directing a suggestion at an umbrella. Afterwards I was ashamed and did not suspect that my clever patient would undertake to rescue me from her father, who was a doctor and present during her hypnoses. The next day her father said to me: 'Do you know what she did yesterday? We were out walking on the Ringstraße; suddenly she became wildly happy and – in the middle of the street – began to sing "We live a free life" [Ein freies Leben führen wir], beat time with the umbrella against the pavement, and broke it to pieces.' Of course she had no notion that she herself had so wittily transformed a nonsensical suggestion into a spectacularly successful one. When the reassurance, commands and treatment given during hypnosis failed to improve her condition, I turned to psychical analysis and asked her to tell me what emotion had preceded the outbreak of her affliction. She then told me (during hypnosis, but without any agitation), that shortly beforehand a young relative of hers, to whom she had for many years considered herself betrothed, had died. But this communication changed nothing whatsoever in her condition, and so in the next hypnosis I told her that I was quite convinced that the death of her cousin had nothing at all to do with her condition and that something else must have happened that she had not mentioned. At this she let slip a single hint, but had hardly uttered a word before she fell silent and her old father, who was sitting behind her, began to sob bitterly. I did not, of course, press my investigation of the patient any further, but nor did I ever see her again.

29. (*Addition 1924*:) I am aware that no analyst can read this case history today without a smile of pity. But it should be borne in mind that this was the first case in which I made extensive use of the cathartic procedure. For this same reason, I want to leave the report in its original form, advancing none of the criticisms which can so easily be made today, and making no attempt to fill in the numerous gaps retrospectively. I want to add only two things: the insight that I later gained into the immediate aetiology of the illness and information about how it later developed.

When, as mentioned, I spent a few days as a guest in her country house, a stranger was present at one of the meals who was obviously making efforts to please. After his departure she asked me if I liked him and added, as if in passing, 'Just imagine, the man wants to marry me'. From this, together with other statements, which I had failed to take into consideration, I could only conclude that she longed to remarry at this time, but that the existence of her two daughters, the inheritors of the paternal fortune, presented an obstacle to the realization of her intention.

At a scientific meeting a few years later, I met a distinguished physician from Frau Emmy's part of the country. I asked him if he was acquainted with the lady and knew anything of her condition. Yes, he did know her and had himself treated her with hypnosis: she had gone through the same performance with him – and with many other doctors – as she had with me. She had come in a wretched state, repaid the hypnotic treatment by making an extraordinary improvement, only to take against the doctor all of a sudden, dismiss him, and reactivate her illness to its full extent. This was a genuine case of the 'compulsion to repeat'.

It was twenty-five years before I received news of Frau Emmy again. Her elder daughter, the same one of whom I had once made such an unfavourable prognosis, approached me with a request for a report on her mother's mental condition on the grounds of my former treatment of her. She intended to take legal proceedings against her mother whom she portrayed as a cruel and ruthless tyrant. She had disowned both children and refused to support them in their financial difficulties. The correspondent herself had gained a doctorate and was married.

3 Miss Lucy R., age 30 (Freud)

At the end of 1892 a colleague and friend of mine referred a young lady to me whom he was treating for chronically recurrent suppurative rhinitis. As it later transpired, the persistence of her complaint was due to caries of the ethmoid. Finally the patient had approached my colleague with new symptoms which he, a knowledgeable doctor, could no longer put down to a local affection. She had completely lost her sense of smell and was almost incessantly pursued by one or two subjective smell-sensations. She found these most distressing and was, besides, in low spirits, tired and complaining of a muzzy head, together with loss of appetite and stamina.

The young lady, who was living as a governess in the house of the managing director of a factory in the outskirts of Vienna, visited me from time to time during my surgery hours. She was an English-woman of a delicate constitution, with poor pigmentation and, save for the nasal affection, healthy. Her first statements confirmed what the doctor had told me. She was suffering from low spirits and fatigue, and was tormented by subjective sensations of smell. In terms of hysterical symptoms there was fairly clear evidence of general analgesia, although her sense of touch was unimpaired and a rough test (by hand) revealed that her field of vision was not restricted. The inside of her nose was completely insensitive and incapable of reflex action. She could feel it being touched, but the organ's sense perception was absent, whether for specific stimuli or other irritants (ammonia, vinegar). The suppurative nasal catarrh was just then going through a period of improvement.

On first attempting to make sense of this illness, it was necessary to interpret the subjective smell-sensations, which were recurrent hallucinations, as chronic hysterical symptoms. Her low spirits were perhaps the affect pertaining to the trauma, and it ought to have been possible to find an experience in which the smells that had now become subjective had been objective; this experience must have been the trauma, which the recurring sensations of smell symbolized in her memory. It was perhaps more accurate to view the recurrent hallucinatory smells, together with the accompanying low spirits, as the equivalent of a hysterical attack – in fact, recurrent hallucinations are, by their very nature, not suited to the role of chronic symptom. But in any case this was irrelevant given the rudimentary nature of this case. It was, however, absolutely necessary that the subjective sensations of smell were specialized to a degree that would correspond to their originating in a real and quite specific object.

This expectation was immediately fulfilled. In response to my question about what kind of smell she was most often pursued by, I received the answer: a smell like burnt pudding. So I needed only to assume that the smell of burnt pudding really had occurred in the experience that had operated as a trauma. While it is, admittedly, very unusual indeed for smell-sensations to be selected as the memory-symbols of traumas, it was not difficult to find a reason for this choice. The patient was suffering from suppurative rhinitis, so the nose and its perceptions were in the forefront of her attention. As regards the patient's living conditions, I knew only that the family whose two children she looked after had no mother, for she had died of a serious and acute illness some years ago.

I therefore decided to make the smell of 'burnt pudding' the starting point of the analysis. I want to recount the history of this analysis as it might have occurred under favourable circumstances: in fact what should have been a single sitting extended to several, as the patient could visit me only during surgery hours, when I could devote little time to her, and just one of these conversations dragged on for over a week, as her duties also prevented her from making the long journey from the factory very frequently. We would then break off in the middle of the discussion and take up the thread in the same place the next time.

Miss Lucy R. did not become somnambulistic when I tried to hypnotize her. And so I did without the somnambulism and carried out the entire analysis while she was in a state which may have differed very little at all from her normal one.

I ought to go into this point of my technical procedure in more detail. When, in 1889, I visited the clinics in Nancy, I heard the doyen of hypnosis, Dr Liébeault, say: 'Yes, if only we had the means to make everyone somnambulistic, then hypnotic therapy would be the most powerful of all cures.' At Bernheim's clinic it was almost as if such an art really did exist, and as if it could be learnt from Bernheim. But as soon as I tried to practise it on my own patients, I noticed that *my* powers at least were severely restricted in this respect and that, if I could not make a patient somnambulistic in the first three attempts, I had no means of doing so at all. In my experience, however, the percentage of somnambulists was far lower than the figure given by Bernheim.

So I was presented with a choice: either I could refrain from practising the cathartic method in most of the cases which might have been suited to it, or I could experiment by using the method without somnambulism in those cases where the degree of hypnotic influence was slight or even doubtful. The degree of hypnosis reached by this non-somnambulistic state (as measured according to one of the scales drawn up for this purpose) seemed to me a matter of indifference, since the various lines along which suggestibility may develop are in any case independent of each other, and the bringing about of catalepsy, automatic movements and so on counted neither for nor against what I required, which was to facilitate the awakening of forgotten memories. I soon gave up the practice of carrying out tests to ascertain the degree of hypnosis, since in quite a number of cases this roused the patients' resistance, shaking the confidence that they had in me and that I needed to carry out the more important psychical work. In addition I soon tired of giving the reassuring command, 'You are going to sleep. Sleep!' and hearing the objection whenever the degree of hypnosis was slight, 'But Doctor, I'm not sleeping at all', only then to have to propose the all too delicate distinction, 'Of course I don't mean normal sleep, I mean hypnosis.

You see, you're hypnotized, you can't open your eyes etc. In any case I don't need you to sleep,' and so on. Personally I am sure that many of my colleagues in psychotherapy know how to extract themselves from such difficulties far more skilfully than I; they may well proceed differently. But I do find that if one can count on being embarrassed by a word with such frequency, then one does better to avoid both the word and the embarrassment. So when the first attempt did not produce somnambulism or a degree of hypnosis involving marked physical changes, I pretended to give up the hypnosis, demanded only 'concentration' and ordered the patient to lie back and deliberately close their eyes as the means of attaining this 'concentration'. In this way I may with only a slight effort have achieved the deepest level of hypnosis that it was at all possible to reach.

But in doing without somnambulism, it was possible that I was depriving myself of a precondition without which the cathartic method seemed impracticable. The basis of the method was, of course, that in an altered state of consciousness patients could access memories and recognize connections of a kind which they claimed were not present in their normal state of consciousness. If there was no expansion of consciousness under somnambulism nor was there the possibility of establishing any causal connections other than those which the patient presents to the doctor as already familiar to him, and it is, of course, precisely the pathogenic memories 'which are lacking or, at most, present in a highly summary fashion in the patient's memory in its normal psychic state' ('Preliminary Statement').

I was spared this new embarrassment by the memory that I had seen Bernheim himself demonstrating that the memories of somnambulism are only seemingly forgotten when the patient is awake and can be called forth again by a gentle summons together with a pressure of the hand intended to indicate another state of consciousness. He had, for example, given one woman in a state of somnambulism the negative hallucination that he was no longer present, and had then tried all kinds of ways and assailed her quite mercilessly in an attempt to make her notice him. He did not succeed. After the patient had been woken, he asked her what he had done to her while she thought he was not there. Her astonished answer was that she knew nothing, but he would not let it go at that, claimed that she would remember everything, put his hand on her forehead so that she would think back and, lo and behold, she did finally relate everything that she claimed not to have perceived in her somnambulistic state and not to have been cognizant of in her waking state.

This astonishing and instructive experiment was my model. I decided to work on the assumption that my patients knew everything that was of any pathogenic significance and that it was simply a question of making them communicate this. When, therefore, I had reached the point at which my question 'How long have you had this symptom?' or 'Where does it come from?' was answered with 'I really don't know', I proceeded as follows: I laid my hand on the patient's forehead or took the patient's head in my hands and said, 'Now it will come to you under the pressure of my hand. At that moment when I remove the pressure something will appear to you or suddenly come to mind, and you will pick up on it. It will be what we're looking for. – Now, what have you seen, or what has come to mind?'

The first few times that I applied this procedure (it was not with Miss Lucy R.) even I was astonished that it provided me with exactly what I needed, and I can safely say that since then it has hardly ever let me down: it has always shown me the way that my investigation had to go and enabled me to bring every analysis of this kind to a conclusion without using somnambulism. Eventually I became so bold that when patients answered 'I can't see anything' or 'Nothing came to mind', I would explain to them that this was an impossibility, that they were sure to have discovered the right thing, it was just that they didn't think that they had, and had dismissed it. I could, I told them, repeat the procedure as often as they liked, and they would see the same thing every time. And I was, in fact, right every time: the patients had not yet learnt to relax their critical faculty, had dismissed the emerging memory or idea because they thought it was of no use, just something that had come up, a disruption, and after they had told me about it, it proved to be the right one every time. Occasionally, having after the third or fourth pressure extracted the information from the patient, they would also respond by saying: 'Yes, I already knew that the first time, but it was exactly what I didn't want to say,' or 'I hoped that it wouldn't be that.'

Enlarging a supposedly narrowed consciousness in this way was certainly a good deal more laborious than investigating under somnambulism, but it did allow me to become independent of the somnambulistic method, and gave me an insight into the motives which are often decisive in the 'forgetting' of memories. I can safely say that this procedure is often an intentional and desired one. Its success is never more than apparent.

What seemed to me perhaps stranger still was that numbers and dates which were apparently long forgotten could be recovered by means of a similar procedure, so proving that memory is more accurate than one would expect.

The limited choice available when we search for numbers and dates enables us to resort to a proposition familiar from the scholarship on aphasia, namely that recognizing something is a lesser achievement of the memory than thinking of it spontaneously.

So, with a patient who cannot remember the year, month and day on which a certain event occurred, one lists the numbers of the years which might be involved, the names of the twelve months, and the thirty-one numbers of the days of the month, and assures him that at the right number or name his eyes will open of their own accord or that he will feel which number is correct. In almost all cases the patients really do decide on a certain date and often enough (as in the case of Frau Cäcilie M.) we have records from the time which prove that the date was identified correctly. On other occasions and with other patients it transpired from the interrelation of what was remembered that the date which had been found in this way was irrefutable. Having been shown the date that had been obtained by 'counting out', the patient would for example remark, 'But that's Father's birthday', and then proceed to say, 'Yes, of course, because it was Father's birthday I'd been expecting the event (that we were talking about).'

I can only touch on this theme here. The conclusion that I drew from all these observations was that experiences which are significant in the pathogenesis, together with all the secondary factors related to them, are faithfully preserved by the memory, even in those cases where they seemed to have been forgotten and where the patient was incapable of recalling them.[1]

After this long but unavoidable digression I will return to the case of Miss Lucy R. She did not, then, become somnambulistic when I attempted to hypnotize her, but simply lay there quietly under some mild degree of influence, her eyes closed all the time, her face somewhat stiff, without stirring at all. I asked her if she could remember the occasion on which she first had the smell of the burnt pudding. – 'Oh yes, I know exactly when that was. It was about two months ago, two days before my birthday. I was in the schoolroom with the children and was playing cooking with them (the two girls), then a letter was brought in that the postman had just delivered. I recognized from the postmark and handwriting that the letter was from my mother in Glasgow and wanted to open it and read it. Then the children came rushing up to me, tore the letter out of my hand and cried out, "No, you can't read it now, it's sure to be for your birthday, we'll look after it for you." The children were playing around me like this, when suddenly an intense smell filled the air. They had abandoned the pudding that they were cooking and it had burnt. Since then the smell has been pursuing me; actually it's always there and it gets stronger if I am agitated.'

'Does this scene appear clearly to you?' – 'Yes, palpably so, it's just as I experienced it.' – 'What could there be about it that was so agitating?' – 'I was moved by how affectionate the children were towards me.' – 'Weren't they always like that?' – 'Yes, but just then when I received the letter from my mother.' – 'I don't understand why there should be a contrast between the little ones' affection and the letter from your mother, and yet this is what you seem to be intimating.' – 'It was because I had intended to travel home to see my mother, and then I didn't have the heart to leave these dear children.' – 'What is wrong with your mother? Did she send for you because she is living on her own? Or was it that she was ill at this time and that you were expecting to hear from her?' – 'No, her health isn't good, but nor is she ill exactly, and she has a companion with her.' – 'So why did you have to leave the children?' – 'I couldn't stand it in the house any more. The housekeeper, the cook and the French governess seem to have thought that I was putting on airs above my station; they joined forces in getting up some little conspiracy against me, told the grandfather (of the children) all sorts of things about me behind my back, and neither of the gentlemen would give me the support I had expected when I made a complaint to them. At this, I asked the director (the father of the children) to be relieved of my duties. He replied in a very friendly way that I really should think about it for a couple of weeks before I gave him my final decision. It was at that time that I was in this state of indecision; I thought I would leave the house. Since then I have stayed.' – 'And was there a particular bond between you and the children, apart from their affection towards you?' – 'Yes, their mother was a distant relative of my mother's and I had promised her on her deathbed that I would do everything within my power to take care of the little ones, that I would never leave them, and that I would take the place of their mother. I broke this promise when I gave in my notice.'

At this the analysis of the subjective sensation of smell seemed to be complete. The smell had in fact once been objective, and indeed intimately associated with an experience, a small scene, in which competing affects had come up against each other – her regret at leaving the children, and the slights which had driven her to this decision. Her mother's letter had understandably reminded her of the motives for her decision, as she had intended to go to her mother's on leaving here. The conflict between her affects had elevated the moment into a trauma, and the smell connected with it had remained with her as a symbol of the trauma. What remained to be explained was why, among all the sensory perceptions which made up that scene, this one smell in particular had been selected as symbolic. But I was already prepared to explain this in terms of the chronic nasal affliction. Indeed, when questioned directly she did also admit that it was at precisely this time that she had again suffered from such a heavy cold that she could hardly smell anything. But in her distress the smell of burnt pudding was perceptible to her, it broke through the organically determined anosmia.

But I was not content with the explanation reached in this way. Everything did of course sound quite plausible, but there was something I was missing, namely an acceptable reason why all these agitations and this conflict of affects should have led to hysteria rather than anything else. Why didn't the whole thing remain grounded in the normal life of the psyche? In other words, where was the justification for the conversion that had taken place here? Why didn't she constantly think back to the scene itself, instead of the sensation connected with it, which she singled out as a symbol for the recollection? Questions such as these might be over-curious and superfluous in the case of a hysteric of long standing, in whom the conversion mechanism was habitual. But it was not until this trauma, or at least until this little tale of suffering, that the girl had acquired hysteria.

Now, I already knew from the analysis of similar cases that before hysteria can be acquired for the first time one essential condition has to be fulfilled, namely that an idea must be *intentionally repressed from consciousness* and excluded from associative processing.

In my view this intentional repression is also the basis for the conversion, whether total or partial, of the sum of excitation. This sum of excitation, which is not allowed to enter into psychical association, is all the more prompt in finding the wrong path to a physical innervation. The basis for the repression itself can simply be a feeling of reluctance: the one idea that is to be repressed cannot be tolerated by the mass of ideas dominant in the self. Yet the repressed idea takes its revenge by becoming pathogenic.

The fact that Miss Lucy R. had at that moment succumbed to the hysterical conversion led me to conclude that of the preconditions for the trauma there had to be *one* that she deliberately wanted to leave in the dark and that she was struggling to forget. If I took both her affection for the children *and* her sensitivity towards all the other members of the household into account, there could be only *one* possible explanation for the entire situation. I was bold enough to impart this interpretation to the patient. I said to her, 'I don't believe that these are all the reasons for your feelings towards the two children. What I suspect is that you are in love with your master, the director, perhaps without being aware of it yourself, and that secretly you are nursing the hope that you really will take the place of the mother. What is more, you have become sensitive towards the servants after having lived peacefully with them for years. You are afraid that they will spot your hope and make fun of you.'

She answered in her characteristically laconic style, 'Yes, I think that's how it is.' – 'But if you knew that you loved the director why didn't you tell me?' – 'But I didn't know, or rather, I didn't want to know. I wanted to put it out of my mind, not think about it any more, and I believe that recently I have actually managed to do this.'[2]

'Why don't you want to admit to this inclination? Were you ashamed to love a man?' – 'Oh no, I'm not unreasonably prudish, after all, you can't be held responsible for what you feel. It was only embarrassing for me because he is the master and I'm in his service and live in his house; I feel that I'm not completely independent from him as I would be from someone else. And then I'm a poor girl and he is a rich man from a distinguished family. People would laugh at me if they had any idea of it.'

I discover that she is no longer at all resistant to illuminating the development of this inclination. She tells of how she lived in the house quite innocently for the first few years and carried out her duties without coming across any wishes that could not be fulfilled. Once, however, the master, a serious, overworked man, who had otherwise always been reserved towards her, began a conversation with her about the demands of bringing up children. He softened and became warmer than usual, told her how much he counted on her for the care of his orphaned children, and as he said this looked at her in a particular way . . . It was at this moment that she began to love him and was happily preoccupied with the gratifying hope that she had drawn from the conversation. Only then, after she had waited in keen anticipation and in vain for a second hour's intimate conversation and when nothing further ensued, did she resolve to put the thing out of her mind. She is in complete agreement with me that the way he looked at her in the context of the conversation was in memory of his late wife and also recognizes quite clearly that her inclination is quite without hope.

I expected a fundamental change in her condition to result from this conversation, but for the time being this did not occur. She continued to be dejected and depressed; a hydropathic cure that I had her follow at this time freshened her up a little in the mornings, the smell of burnt pudding had not disappeared completely but had become less frequent and weaker; it came, as she said, only when she was very upset.

The persistence of this memory-symbol led me to suspect that it did not only represent the main scene but had also taken on the representation of the many small secondary traumas, and so we then searched for anything that could have some other connection with the smell of the burnt pudding, went through the various themes, the friction in the household, the behaviour of the grandfather, and so on. As we did so her perception of the burning smell faded more and more. During this period there was a considerable interruption due to the return of her nasal disorder, which then led to the discovery of the caries of the ethmoid.

On her return she reported that at Christmas she had received numerous presents from both gentlemen and even from the domestic staff, as if they were all doing their utmost to make it up with her and to dispel her memory of the conflicts of the last few months. She said, however, that these conciliatory gestures failed to make any impression on her.

When on another occasion I asked her again about the smell of burnt pudding, I was informed that it had in fact disappeared completely, but that in its place she was being tormented by another similar smell, like cigar smoke. This smell had probably been there before, but had, as it were, been covered by the smell of the pudding. Now it had emerged clearly.

I was not very satisfied with the success of my therapy. Purely symptomatic therapy is always being accused of removing one symptom only for another to take its place, and this is what had happened here. Despite this, I was eager to get down to removing this next memory-symbol by analysis.

But this time she did not know where the subjective sensation of smell came from, that is, on which important occasion it had been objective. 'People smoke every day at our house,' she said, 'I really don't know if the smell that I am aware of signifies any particular occasion.' I then insisted that she try to remember under the pressure of my hand. I have already mentioned that her memories were tangibly vivid, that she was a 'visual' type. And indeed, at my insistence a picture did emerge in her, at first only hesitantly and piece by piece. It was the dining room of the house, where she waits with the children until the gentlemen come back from the factory for lunch. – 'Now we are all sitting around the table: the gentlemen, the Frenchwoman, the housekeeper, the children, and I. But that's what happens every day.' – 'Just have another look at the picture, it will develop and become more specific.' – 'Yes, there is a guest there, the head book-keeper, an elderly gentleman who loves the children as if they were his own grandchildren; but he comes to lunch so often, that's nothing special either.' – 'Just be patient and carry on looking at the picture, something is bound to happen.' – 'Nothing's happening. We are getting up from the table, the children are to say goodbye and then come upstairs with us as they do every day.' – 'Well?' – 'It *is* a special occasion after all; now I recognize the scene. As the children are saying goodbye the head book-keeper goes to kiss them. The master flares up and actually shouts at him, "Don't kiss the children!" At this, I feel a stab at my heart, and since the gentlemen are already smoking, the cigar smoke stays in my memory.'

This, then, was the second, deeper-lying scene, which had the traumatic effect and left behind a memory-symbol. But what was the effectiveness of this scene due to? – 'Which came earlier,' I asked, 'this scene or the one with the burnt pudding?' – 'This is the earlier, by almost two months in fact.' – 'So why did you feel this stab when the father warded off the old man? After all, the rebuke wasn't directed at you, was it?' – 'But all the same, it wasn't right to let off like that at an old gentleman who is a dear friend and a guest too. Things can be said quietly too.' – 'So it was just the violence of your master's manner that wounded you? Perhaps you were embarrassed on his behalf? Or did you think, "If such a trifle can make him as violent as that towards an old friend and a guest, how much more so might he be with me if I were his wife?"' – 'No, it isn't that.' – 'But it was because of the violence, wasn't it?' – 'Yes, because of the children being kissed, he never did like that.' – And now, under the pressure of my hand, the memory of an even older scene surfaces; this was the trauma that really was operative here and it also lent the scene with the head book-keeper its traumatic effectiveness.

It had happened a few months earlier still that a lady who was a friend of the family came to visit and kissed both children goodbye on the lips. The father, who was present at this scene, managed to stop himself from saying anything to the lady, but once she had gone his rage was vented on the unfortunate governess. He explained to her that he was making this her responsibility – that if anyone kissed the children on the lips it was her duty not to tolerate it and that she would be held neglectful of her duty if she permitted it. If it happened one more time he would put the upbringing of his children in someone else's hands. It was the time when she still thought that she was loved and was waiting for a recurrence of that first friendly conversation. This scene crushed her hopes. 'If he can set on me and threaten me like that over something so slight,' she said to herself, 'when I am, in any case, quite innocent, then I have made a mistake. He can't ever have had any warm feelings for me, otherwise he would have treated me with more consideration.' – Obviously it was the memory of this painful scene that came to her when the head book-keeper wanted to kiss the children and was reprimanded for it by the father.

When Miss Lucy came to see me again two days after this last analysis, I had to ask her what her happy news was.

She was as if transformed, smiling, her head held high. For a moment I thought that I might have judged the relations wrongly after all and that the children's governess had turned into the director's fiancée. But she dismissed my supposition, 'Nothing at all has happened. It's just that you don't know me. You've only ever seen me ill and out of sorts. I'm usually always in high spirits. When I woke up yesterday morning the pressure on me had been lifted and since then I've been well.' – 'And what are your thoughts about your prospects in the house?' – 'I'm quite clear about that. I know that I have none and won't be unhappy about it.' – 'And will you get on with the other staff now?' – 'I think that my sensitivity was most to blame for that.' – 'And do you still love the director?' – 'Of course I do, but that doesn't matter any more. After all, you can have your own thoughts and feelings to yourself.'

I now examined her nose and found that the sensitivity to pain and the reflex excitability had almost completely returned; she could also distinguish smells, although with some uncertainty and only when they were intense. But the question of how far the nasal affliction may have played a part in this anosmia has to be left open.

The treatment had in all lasted for over nine weeks. Four months later I happened to meet the patient at one of our summer resorts. She was in good spirits and assured me that her good health had been maintained.

CRITICAL ANALYSIS

I would not wish to underestimate the medical case related here, despite the fact that it represents a small and slight hysteria, involving only a few symptoms. On the contrary, it seems to me instructive that even an illness such as this, which is paltry when regarded as a neurosis, requires so many psychical preconditions. And on closer examination of this case history I am tempted to describe it as exemplary of one type of hysteria, namely that form that can even be acquired by someone who does not have a hereditary disposition to it but who has had appropriate experiences. Mark that I am not talking about a hysteria that would be independent of any disposition; it is doubtful that such a hysteria exists, but we cannot begin to talk about this type of disposition until the person has become hysterical, there having been no previous evidence of it. A neuropathic disposition, as it is generally understood, is something different; it is already determined before the illness by the degree of negative hereditary factors or by the sum of individual psychical abnormalities. As far as my information goes, neither of these two factors could be detected in the case of Miss Lucy R. Her hysteria may then be termed 'acquired' and presupposes nothing more than what is, in all probability, a very widespread aptitude to acquire hysteria, an aptitude whose characteristics we have as yet hardly begun to track down. In cases such as these the main emphasis falls on the nature of the trauma in connection with, of course, the reaction of the person to that trauma. What proves to be an essential condition for the acquisition of hysteria is the development of a relationship of incompatibility between the self and an idea which is presented to it. I hope to be able to show elsewhere how different neurotic disturbances result from the different procedures which the 'self' pursues in order to free itself from this incompatibility. The hysterical style of defence – for which, precisely, a particular aptitude is required – lies in the *conversion* of the excitation into a physical innervation, and what is gained by this is that the intolerable idea is forced out of the self's consciousness. In its place, the self's consciousness now contains the physical reminiscence that has arisen through conversion – in this case the subjective sensations of smell – and suffers from the affect which more or less clearly connects with precisely these reminiscences. The situation that is created in this way then becomes impervious to change, since repression and conversion have removed the contradiction which would require that the affect be disposed of. Thus the mechanism which engenders the hysteria corresponds on the one hand to an act of moral timidity and, on the other, represents a protective device which is at the disposal of the self. There are cases enough in which it must be admitted that fending off the growth of excitation by producing hysteria is the most expedient thing to do at the time; more frequently, of course, one will conclude that a greater degree of moral courage would have been advantageous to the individual.

The actual traumatic moment, then, occurs when the contradiction forces itself on the self and the self resolves to expel the contradictory idea. The idea will not be destroyed by an expulsion of this kind, but simply forced into the unconscious; if this process is occurring for the first time it will provide a nucleus and central point of crystallization for the formation of a psychical group that is separated from the self, and around which everything that would presuppose an acceptance of the contradictory idea proceeds to gather. The splitting of consciousness in these cases of acquired hysteria is, therefore, deliberate and intentional, or at least it is often initiated by an act of volition, for what in fact happens is different from what was intended by the individual. He may wish to do away with an idea, as if he had never come upon it, but all that he manages to do is isolate it psychically.

In the history of our patient, the traumatic moment corresponds to the scene that the director made with her about the children being kissed. For a while, however, this scene had no visible effect; perhaps it was then that the low spirits and sensitivity began, but I cannot be certain. The hysterical symptoms did not arise until later, and then at moments which might be termed 'auxiliary'; characteristic of these moments is that the two separated psychical groups temporarily flow together, as in the enlarged consciousness which occurs in somnambulism. The first of these moments in which the conversion took place was, in the case of Miss Lucy R., the scene at table, when the head book-keeper went to kiss the children. In this instance the traumatic memory entered into play, and she behaved as if she had not rid herself of everything relating to her affection for her master. In other case histories these different moments coincide, the conversion occurring as an immediate effect of the trauma.

The second auxiliary moment duplicates the mechanism of the first fairly exactly. A strong impression momentarily restores the unity of consciousness and the conversion takes the same path that had opened up to it the first time. It is interesting to note that the second symptom to develop covers the first, so that the first cannot be clearly perceived until the second is cleared away. Noteworthy, too, is the reversal of the sequence, a reversal which the analysis also has to follow. I have had the same experience in a whole number of cases: symptoms that had developed later covered those that had arisen first and only the last symptom reached by the analysis held the key to the whole.

The therapy here consisted in compelling the psychical group that had split off to reunite with the self's consciousness. Curiously, the success did not come about in parallel with the amount of work done; only when the last piece was dealt with did the cure suddenly take effect.

Notes

1. As an example of the technique depicted above of investigation in a non-somnambulistic state, that is when consciousness has not been expanded, I would like to relate a case which I have analysed over just the last few days. I have been treating a thirty-eight-year-old woman who is suffering from anxiety neurosis (agoraphobia, attacks in which she is frightened of dying, etc). As is the case with so many of these patients, she has an aversion to admitting that she acquired this affliction during her married life, and would like to push it back to her early youth. Thus she informed me that she had her first attack of dizziness together with feelings of anxiety and faintness as a seventeen-year-old in the streets of her small home town, and that these attacks recurred periodically until in the past few years they gave way to her current affliction. My suspicion was that these initial attacks of dizziness in which her anxiety faded increasingly into the background were hysterical and I decided to undertake an analysis of them. At first she knew only that this first attack came over her while she was out shopping in the high street. – 'What did you want to buy then?' – 'Various things, I think, for a ball that I had been invited to.' – 'When was this ball to have taken place?' – 'Two days later, I think.' – 'Then something must have happened a few days beforehand to upset you, or make an impression on you.' – 'But I wouldn't know, it was twenty-one years ago.' – 'That makes no difference, you will be able to remember. I will press on your head, and when I release the pressure, you will think of something or see something. This you will then tell me . . .' I carried out this procedure; but she remained silent. – 'Well, has nothing occurred to you?' – 'I have thought of something, but it

can't possibly be in any way connected.' – 'Just tell me what it is.' – 'I thought of a friend, a young girl, who died; but she died when I was eighteen years old, so a year later.' – 'We'll see, let's stick with this. What was wrong with this friend of yours?' – 'Her death came as an enormous shock to me, because I spent a great deal of time with her. A few weeks previously another young girl had died, which caused a great stir in the town. So I must have been seventeen at the time after all.' – 'You see, I told you that you can rely on the things that come to you under the pressure of my hand. Now do you remember what you were thinking about when you had the attack of dizziness in the street?' – 'There weren't any thoughts, just dizziness.' – 'That isn't possible, states like that never occur without an accompanying idea. I will press again, and the thought from that time will come back to you.' – 'So, what came to you?' – 'Now I'm the third. That's what came to me.' – 'What does that mean?' – 'During the attack of dizziness, I must have thought: Now I'm dying too, like the two other young girls.' – 'So that was the idea; you were thinking of your friend during the attack. Her death must have made a great impression on you then.' – 'Yes, of course. I remember now that when I heard of the death I felt awful about going to a ball, when she was dead. But I was so much looking forward to the ball and so preoccupied with the invitation; I didn't want to think about the sad occurrence at all.' (To be noted here is the intentional repression from consciousness which makes the memory of the friend pathogenic.)

The attack was now to a certain extent elucidated. But I did still need to know of some contingent factor that had provoked the memory at precisely that time, and I developed what proved to be a happy conjecture. – 'Do you remember exactly which street you were in at the time?' – 'Yes, of course, it was the high street with all the old houses, I can see it before me now.' – 'Well then, where did your friend live?' – 'In the same street; I had just gone past, and two houses further on I had the attack.' – 'Then, as you were passing it, the house must have reminded you of your dead friend and you were once more struck by the contrast that at the time you wanted to ignore.'

I was still not satisfied. Perhaps something else was at work that had aroused or strengthened the hysterical disposition in this girl who had been normal until then. My suspicions turned to her periodic indisposition as a possible factor, and I asked her: 'Do you know when you had your period that month?' At this she grew indignant, 'Am I supposed to know that too? All that I know is that at about this time it was very infrequent and very irregular. When I was seventeen years old I only had it once.' – 'All right then, we'll count out so as to find when this one time was.' During the counting out, she made a definite decision in favour of one month, then hesitated between two days immediately preceding the date of a public holiday. – 'Does that fit in with the time of the ball?' She answered in a tiny voice, 'The ball was – on the holiday. And now I remember too what an impression it made on me, that the only period I had that year had to come just before the ball. It was the first one that I had been invited to.'

There is no difficulty now in reconstructing the interconnection of the events and we can now see into the mechanism of this hysterical attack. It cannot be denied that this result was the fruit of great labour and required an absolute trust in the technique on my part, together with a few key insights, before it was possible to reawaken, twenty-one years later, these kinds of details from an experience that had been forgotten in a sceptical patient who was, in fact, awake. But after that everything came together.

2. I have never managed to arrive at a better depiction of this curious condition, in which one simultaneously knows and does not know something. It is clearly impossible to understand it unless one has been in such a state oneself. I have one very striking memory of this kind, which is still vivid to me. But if I attempt to remember what was happening inside me at the time, I can come up with very little. On this occasion, then, I had seen something which did not fit in with my expectations at all, and I did not allow what I had seen to divert me in the slightest from the firm intention I had formed, despite the fact that this perception should have made me abandon it. I did not become conscious of this contradiction and was equally unaware of the strong feeling of repulsion which was undoubtedly responsible for the fact that this perception produced no psychical effect whatsoever. With my eyes wide open I was struck by the astonishing blindness that mothers have towards their daughters, husbands towards their wives, rulers towards their favourites.

4 *Katharina . . . (Freud)*

During the summer holidays of 189– I went walking in the Hohe Tauern, so as to forget for a while about medicine and, in particular, about neuroses. I had almost succeeded in doing so when one day I turned off the main road to climb a mountain which was off the beaten track and renowned for its views and well-kept walkers' hut. Having reached the top after a strenuous climb, invigorated and rested, I was sitting immersed in contemplation of a delightful view that stretched into the far distance, so lost in thought that on first hearing the question – 'Are you a doctor, sir?' – I did not wish to connect it with myself. But the question was addressed to me and came from the rather sullen-looking girl of eighteen years or so who had served my meal and who had been called 'Katharina' by the landlady. To judge by her dress and manner she could not be a maid, but was more than likely a daughter or relative of the landlady.

Coming to myself, I answered, 'Yes, I am a doctor. How do you know that?'

'You signed in the visitors' book, sir, and then I thought to myself, perhaps the doctor would have a little bit of time now – my nerves are bad, you see, and I've already been once to a doctor in L—, who did give me something, but I haven't got better yet.'

And so I was back with the neuroses again, for nothing else was likely to be the matter with this big, strong girl with her sorrowful look. I found it interesting that neuroses should flourish so well at a height of over 2000 metres and so I questioned her further.

I will reproduce the discussion that followed between us as it was impressed upon my memory, leaving the patient's dialect intact.

'What are you suffering from then?'

'I get so out of breath. Not always, but sometimes it catches me so that I think I'm suffocating.'

Now at first this didn't sound like a nervous symptom, but soon afterwards I thought it likely that it was simply a description standing in for an anxiety attack. She was unduly singling out the one factor of restricted breathing from the whole complex of anxious feelings.

'Do sit down. Tell me what it's like then, this state of "breathlessness"?'

'It comes over me all of a sudden. First of all it comes down like a pressure on my eyes, then my head gets so heavy and it makes this roaring sound, it's unbearable, and I'm dizzy so that I think I'm going to fall over, and then it presses against my chest so that I can't get my breath.'

'And you don't feel anything in your throat?'

'My throat is all knotted up, as if I were going to suffocate!'

'And is anything else going on inside your head?'

'Yes, there's this hammering as if it were going to burst.'

'Yes, and while this is going on aren't you at all frightened?'

'I always think I'm going to die, and usually I'm so brave, I go about everywhere on my own, into the cellar and down over the whole mountain, but when it's one of those days, when I've got that, then I don't dare to go anywhere, I always think there's someone standing behind me who's going to grab hold of me all of a sudden.'

So it really was an anxiety attack, and what is more, the first sign of its beginning was the hysterical aura, or rather, it was a hysterical attack the content of which was anxiety. But was this all that it contained?

'Do you think something, always the same thing, or do you see something before you when you have the attack?'

'Yes, I always see a really horrible face, and it gives me such a terrible look, that's what I'm afraid of then.'

Perhaps this was a way of advancing swiftly to the heart of the matter.

'Do you recognize the face, I mean, is it a face that you once really did see?' – 'No.'

'Do you know where you get the attacks from?' – 'No.' – 'Well, when did you first get them?' – 'The first was two years ago, when I was still with my auntie on the other mountain, she used to keep the walkers' hut there. We've been here for one and a half years now, but it keeps coming back.'

Was I to attempt an analysis here? Naturally, I did not dare to transplant the technique of hypnosis to these heights, but perhaps a simple conversation would prove successful. I had to try a lucky guess. I had so often seen anxiety in young girls as a consequence of the horror that overcomes virginal minds when they are first faced with the world of sexuality.[1]

So I said, 'If you don't know what it is, then I'll tell you where I think your attacks come from. Once during that time two years ago you saw or heard something that embarrassed you very much, that you would rather not have seen.'

'Heavens, yes,' was her reply, 'I caught my uncle with the girl, with Franziska, my cousin!'

'What was going on there with the girl? Wouldn't you like to tell me about it?'

'Well, I guess you can tell a doctor anything. You see, at that time my uncle – he was the husband of my auntie, the one you saw there – he and my auntie used to have the inn on the —kogel, now they are divorced, and I'm to blame for them being divorced, because it was through me that it came out that he was carrying on with Franziska.'

'I see, and how did you make this discovery?'

'It was like this. Once, two years ago, a couple of gentlemen came up here and wanted to have something to eat. Auntie wasn't at home, and Franziska was nowhere to be found – she was the one who always did the cooking. Uncle wasn't to be found either. We go looking for her everywhere, then the boy, Alois, my cousin, says, "Perhaps Franziska is in Father's room." We both laughed at this, but we weren't thinking anything bad. So we go to the room where Uncle slept and it's locked. This I did find strange, though. And Alois says, "There's a window in the passage, you can look into the room there." We go into the passage. But Alois doesn't want to go up to the window, he says that he's afraid. So I say, "You silly boy,

I'll go, I'm not afraid at all." And I really didn't have anything wicked in mind. I look in, the room was fairly dark, but then I see Uncle and Franziska, and he's lying on top of her.'

'Well?'

'I get away from the window like a shot. I leant against the wall, got the breathlessness that I've had since then, everything went blank, my eyes were forced shut and there was this hammering and roaring inside my head.'

'Did you tell your aunt straightaway that day?'

'Oh no, I didn't say anything.'

'Why were you so frightened then, when you found the two of them together? Did you understand it? Did you make something of what was happening there?'

'Oh no, I didn't understand anything at all then, I was only sixteen years old. I don't know what I was so frightened by.'

'Fräulein Katharin', if you could remember now what was going on inside you when you had your first attack and what you were thinking when it happened, it would be the end of your troubles.'

'Yes, if I only could, but I was so frightened that I've forgotten everything.'

(Which, when translated into the language of our 'Preliminary Statement', means: The affect itself creates the hypnoid state and the products of this state are then excluded from associative relations with the self's consciousness.)

'Tell me then, Fräulein, is the head that you always see when you are breathless perhaps Franziska's head, as you saw it that time?'

'Oh no, hers wasn't as horrible, and in any case it was a man's head.'

'Or was it perhaps your uncle's?'

'I didn't see his face anything like as clearly, it was too dark in the room, and why should he have been making such a terrible face then anyway?'

'You're right.' (Now, suddenly, the path seemed to be blocked. Perhaps something would turn up in the rest of her story.)

'And what else happened then?'

'Well, the two of them must have heard a noise. They soon came out. I felt really ill the whole time, I couldn't stop thinking about it, then two days later it was a Sunday, so there was a lot to do, I worked the whole day, and then, on Monday morning, I got dizzy again and was sick, and stayed in bed, and was sick again and again for three days.'

We had frequently compared the hysterical symptomatology with a pictographic script, which we were able to read once we had discovered a few cases of bilingualism. In this alphabet being sick signifies disgust. So I said to her, 'If you were sick for three days, then I think that back then, when you looked into the room, you were disgusted.'

'Yes, I'm sure I was disgusted,' she says, thoughtfully. 'But by what?'

'Perhaps you saw something naked? How were the two people in the room then?'

'It was too dark to see anything, and the two of them were dressed. Yes, if only I knew what I was disgusted by then.'

Well, I didn't know that either. But I asked her to carry on telling me whatever occurred to her, confident in the expectation that she would come upon exactly what I needed to elucidate the case.

Now she relates that eventually, because her aunt thought that she seemed different and suspected that she was hiding something, she told her what she had discovered; that there followed some very disagreeable scenes between her uncle and aunt; and that the children's eyes were opened to a great deal by the things they heard and would have done better not to have heard; that eventually the aunt made up her mind to take over the other local inn with her children and niece, and to leave the uncle alone with Franziska who was now pregnant. But then, to my astonishment, she drops this thread and begins to tell two sets of older stories, which go back about two to three years prior to the traumatic moment. The first set comprises occasions on which this same uncle made sexual advances to *her* when she was only fourteen years old. One winter she had made a trip with him into the valley and stayed overnight at the inn there. He stayed in the bar, drinking and playing cards; she started to feel sleepy and went on early to the room that they were sharing upstairs. She was not sound asleep when he came up, but then she fell asleep again and suddenly woke up and 'felt his body' in the bed. She jumped up and reproached him. 'What are you up to, Uncle? Why don't you stay in your bed?' He tried to talk her into it, 'Go on, you silly girl, keep quiet, you don't know how good it is.' – 'I don't much like your idea of good, not even letting a person sleep.' She stayed by the door, ready to escape out onto the landing, until he left off and fell asleep himself. Then she got back into her bed and slept until morning. From the way in which she reported having fended him off, it would seem to follow that she did not clearly recognize the attack as sexual. When asked subsequently if she did know what he wanted of her, she replied 'Not at the time', it had only become clear to her much later. She had resisted because she didn't like having her sleep disturbed, and 'because it just wasn't nice'.

I have had to give a detailed account of this event because of its great significance for understanding everything that ensued. – She went on to tell still more experiences from a slightly later time, when at an inn she had once again to fend him off when he was completely drunk, and other such stories. In answer to my question whether on these occasions she sensed anything like the breathlessness she had had later, she answers with complete certainty that on each occasion she had the pressure on her eyes and chest, but nothing like as strongly as during the scene of discovery.

As soon as she has brought this set of memories to a close, she begins to recount a second set, involving occasions on which she became aware of something between her uncle and Franziska. Once the whole family spent the night in a hayloft, fully dressed, and she was suddenly woken by a noise. She thought that she noticed that her uncle, who was lying between her and Franziska, turned away and that Franziska was just setting herself straight. On another occasion they were staying the night at an inn in the village N—, she and her uncle in the one room, and Franziska in another, next door. During the night she woke up suddenly and saw a tall white figure at the door, about to push down the handle. 'Heavens, Uncle, is that you? What are you doing at the door?' – 'Be quiet. I was just

looking for something.' – 'But the way out is through the other door.'
– 'Well, I must have made a mistake,' and so on.

I ask her if she was at all suspicious at this time. 'No, I didn't think
anything of it at all, it just always struck me, but I didn't make
anything more of it.' – And did she get frightened on these occasions
too? – She thinks so, but this time isn't so sure.

On completing these two sets of stories, she pauses. She is as if
transformed: the sullen, suffering face has come to life, her eyes are
bright, she is relieved, exalted. And in the meantime the meaning
of her case has become apparent to me; the last thing she told
me, apparently at random, provides a perfect explanation of her
behaviour at the scene of discovery. At the time she was carrying
two sets of experiences, which she remembered but did not understand, and could not use to draw any conclusion. On catching sight
of the couple in sexual intercourse, she immediately made the
connection between the new impression and these two sets of
reminiscences, and began simultaneously to understand them and
to fend them off. There then followed a short period of working-out,
of 'incubation', and after that the symptoms of the conversion –
vomiting as a substitute for moral and psychical disgust – set in. At
this the puzzle was solved: she had not been disgusted by the sight
of the couple, but by a memory that the sight had awoken in her
and, all things considered, this could only be the memory of the
nocturnal assault, when she 'felt the body of her uncle'.

And so, once she had finished her confession, I said to her, 'I
know now what you were thinking to yourself when you looked into
the room. You were thinking: Now he's doing with her what he
wanted to do with me on that night and on the other occasions.
That's why you were disgusted, because you remembered the
sensation when you woke up in the night and felt his body.'

She answers, 'That may well be, that that was what I was disgusted
by and that that was what I thought.'

'Just tell me one thing, though, after all you're a grown-up girl
now and know all sorts of things –'

'Yes, I do now, of course.'

'Just tell me, what did you really feel of his body that night?'

She does not give a more definite answer, only an embarrassed smile as if she has been found guilty, like someone who has to admit that the heart of the matter has now been reached and that little remains to be said. I can imagine what the tactile sensation was that she later learnt to interpret; her facial expression too seems to be telling me that she assumes that I am thinking of the right thing, but I cannot penetrate any further. In any case I am indebted to her for being so much easier to talk to than the prudish ladies in my town practice, for whom all *naturalia* are *turpia* [all natural things are shameful].

At this the case seemed to have become clear. But wait! What of the hallucination of the head that recurred during her attacks and so terrified her. Where did that come from? I ask her about this now. As if she too had broadened her understanding during this conversation, she answers promptly, 'Yes, I know that now: the head is my uncle's. I recognize it now, but not from *that* time. Later, when all the quarrels got going, Uncle got into a furious rage with me. He always said that I was to blame for everything; if I hadn't've let on then it would never have come to a divorce. He always threatened to do something to me. If he saw me from a distance his face would become distorted with rage and he would set after me with his hand raised. I always ran away from him and was always terrified that he would catch me somewhere unawares. The face that I always see now is his face when he was in a rage.'

This information reminded me that her first hysterical symptom, the vomiting, had passed; the anxiety attack remained and took on a new content. This was, therefore, a case in which the hysteria had in good part been abreacted. And she had in fact informed her aunt of the discovery soon afterwards.

'Did you tell your aunt the other stories too, how he pursued you?'

'Yes, not straightaway, but later, when divorce was already being discussed. Then my aunt said, "We'll keep that to ourselves. If he causes trouble in court, then we'll say that too."'

I can well understand that the memory-symbol was left over from precisely this most recent period – a period of accumulation and retention, when there were ever more upsetting scenes at home and when her condition ceased to arouse the interest of her aunt, who was fully preoccupied by the dispute.

I hope that talking things through with me in some way benefited this girl whose sexual sensibility had been wounded at such a young age; I did not see her again.

CRITICAL ANALYSIS

If someone wished to see in this medical history a case of hysteria solved more by guesswork than analysis I would have no grounds for objection. The patient acknowledged everything that I interpolated into her report as likely to be true; but she was not in a position to recognize it as something that she had experienced. This would, in my opinion, have required hypnosis. If I assume that I guessed correctly and now try to reduce this case to the schema of an acquired hysteria, like that produced in Case 3, then it seems reasonable to compare the two sets of erotic experiences with traumatic moments and the scene in which the couple are discovered with an auxiliary moment. The similarity lies in the fact that in the former experiences a content in consciousness was created and preserved but excluded from the mental activity of the self, whereas in the latter scene a new impression forced this outlying group to unite associatively with the self. On the other hand, there are also differences which cannot be ignored. The cause of the isolation is not, as in Case 3, the volition of the self, but the ignorance of the self, which does not yet know what to make of sexual experiences. In this respect the case of Katharina is typical; in the analysis of every hysteria based on sexual traumas one finds that impressions from the pre-sexual period, by which the child remained unaffected, take on traumatic power later as memories when the virgin or married woman has acquired an understanding of sexual life. The splitting-off of psychical groups is, as it were, a normal process in adolescent development and it is understandable that psychical disturbances are caused with reasonable frequency by the later admission of these groups into the self. I would, in addition, like to express doubt at this point, as to whether the splitting of consciousness due to ignorance can really be differentiated from the splitting due to conscious rejection, and whether adolescents too might not possess sexual knowledge far more frequently than one supposes and than they themselves believe.

A further difference in the psychical mechanism of this case is that the scene of discovery which we have described as 'auxiliary' deserves equally to be called 'traumatic'. It is effective by virtue of its own content, rather than just as something that awakens previous traumatic experiences; it unites the characteristics of an 'auxiliary' and of a traumatic moment. But I do not see this coincidence as grounds for giving up a conceptual separation which in other cases also corresponds to a temporal separation. Another peculiarity displayed by Katharina's case, and which has, incidentally, long been known, is that the conversion, the engendering of hysterical phenomena, does not occur immediately after the trauma but after an interval of incubation. Charcot liked to call this interval the 'time of psychical working out'.

The anxiety from which Katharina suffered in her attacks is hysterical, meaning that it reproduces the anxiety that arose during every one of the sexual traumas. I will on this occasion refrain from elucidating the process which I have identified as occurring regularly in an extraordinarily large number of cases, namely that for virgins the mere hint of sexual relations gives rise to the affect of anxiety.[2]

Notes

1. At this point I want to cite the case in which I first recognized this causal relationship. I was treating a young woman for a complicated neurosis and, once again, she did not want to admit that her married life had been the source of her suffering. Her objection was that even as a girl she had suffered from attacks of anxiety that resulted in her fainting. I stood firm on this. One day, when we had got to know one another better, she suddenly said to me, 'Now I'll tell you where the anxious states I had as a young girl came from. At the time I used to sleep in a room next to my parents', the

door was wide open and a nightlight was burning on the table. So a few times I saw how my father went to my mother in bed and I heard something that excited me greatly. After that I had my attacks.'

2. (*Addition 1924:*) I venture now, after a great many years, to lift the veil of discretion that I observed at that time, and to state that Katharina was not the niece, but the daughter of the landlady. The girl had then fallen ill as a result of sexual temptations that came from her own father. A distortion such as I have undertaken in this instance should be avoided at all costs in a case history. Clearly, in terms of our understanding of the case, this kind of distortion is less trivial than, say, shifting the scene from one mountain to another.

5 *Fräulein Elisabeth von R. (Freud)*

In autumn 1892 a colleague and friend of mine asked me to examine a young lady who had suffered from pains in her legs for more than two years and had difficulties walking. On making this request he added that he thought that this was a case of hysteria, even though none of the usual signs of neurosis could be found. He had a slight acquaintance with the family and knew that recent years had brought them a good deal of misfortune and little joy. First, the patient's father died, then the mother had to undergo a serious operation on her eyes, and soon after that a married sister of the patient had succumbed to a long-standing heart complaint after giving birth. The greatest share of all this grief and nursing had fallen to our patient.

I did not get much further in understanding this case after having seen this young woman of twenty-four years for the first time. She seemed intelligent and psychically normal, and bore the affliction which had caused her social life and pleasures to waste away with a cheerful countenance – the *belle indifférence* of the hysteric, I couldn't help thinking. She walked with her upper body bent forward, but without using any support, in a manner that did not correspond to any of those recognized as pathological and which, in any case, was by no means strikingly bad. All that was apparent was that she complained of great pains when walking, of very quickly becoming tired when both walking and standing, and that after a short time she had to rest, at which the pains lessened but by no means ceased. The pain was of an indefinite nature; one could gather that it was, roughly speaking, a painful fatigue. A fairly large, ill-defined area on the front of the right thigh was indicated as the focus of the pains; it was from here that they most often radiated and reached their greatest intensity. It was here too that the skin and musculature were particularly sensitive to pressing and pinching (pinpricks were given a somewhat indifferent reception). The same hyperalgesia of the skin and muscles could be detected not only in this one area, but around pretty much the entire circumference of both legs. The muscles were possibly even more painful than the skin; what was unmistakable was that both types of painfulness were most strongly developed on the thighs. The motor power of the legs could not be described as slight, the reflexes were of an average intensity, there were no other symptoms of any kind, so that there were no grounds for assuming a serious organic affection. The affliction had developed gradually over the last two years and varied greatly in intensity.

It was no easy matter for me to reach a diagnosis, but I resolved – for two reasons – to agree with that made by my colleague. First, it was striking that all the statements made by this highly intelligent patient about the nature of her pains were so indefinite. A patient who suffers from organic pains will, if he does not, say, also have a nervous condition, give a definite and calm description of them. They might, for example, be lancing pains, occur at certain intervals, extend from this place to that, and be caused, in his opinion, by this or that influence. The neurasthenic[1] who describes his pains gives as he does so the impression that he is engaged in a difficult intellectual task that far exceeds his powers. His features are tense and distorted as if under the control of a painful emotion, his voice becomes shriller, he struggles to express himself, rejects every definition that the doctor suggests for his pains, even when it later transpires that they were unquestionably appropriate; he is clearly of the opinion that language is too poor to supply words for his sensations, that these sensations are themselves something singular, something unprecedented that can in no way be described exhaustively, and this too is why he does not tire of adding more and more new details and, when he has to break off, he is certainly under the impression that he has not succeeded in making himself understood by the doctor. This is because his pains have utterly captured his attention. Fräulein v. R.'s behaviour was the opposite of this, and as such left one to conclude, since she did in fact attribute sufficient significance to the pains, that her attention was lingering over something else to which the pains were simply an accompanying phenomenon, probably some thoughts and feelings connected with the pains.

But what had to be of still greater consequence for my interpretation of the pains was the second factor. If you stimulate a painful area on someone who has an organic or a neurasthenic illness, their physiognomy displays a straightforward expression of discomfort or physical pain; the patient flinches more, draws back from the investigation, resists. But when, in Fräulein v. R.'s case, the hyperalgesic skin and musculature of the legs was pinched or pressed, her face took on a peculiar expression, more that of pleasure than pain, she cried aloud – I couldn't help thinking that it was as if she were being tickled voluptuously – her face became flushed, she threw back her head and closed her eyes, her trunk bent backwards. None of this was particularly gross, but it was clearly pronounced and could be reconciled only with the interpretation that she was suffering from hysteria and that the stimulation had touched on a hysterical zone.

The facial expression was not appropriate to the pain that was supposedly excited by the pinching of the muscles and skin, it was probably more in keeping with the content of the thoughts that lay behind this pain and that were awakened in the patient by stimulating areas of the body associated with them. I had repeatedly observed expressions of similar significance when stimulating hyperalgesic zones in definite cases of hysteria. The other gestures were clearly the vague signs of a hysterical attack.

For the time being, no explanation for the unusual location of the hysterogenic zone was forthcoming. The fact that the hyperalgesia affected principally the musculature was also food for thought. The illness that is most frequently to blame for muscular sensitivity to pressure, both diffuse and local, is the infiltration of the muscles by rheumatism, common chronic muscular rheumatism, whose liability to simulate nervous affections I have already discussed. The consistency of Fräulein v. R.'s painful muscles did not contradict this assumption, there were numerous hard strands in the muscular mass which in addition seemed to be particularly sensitive. This was then, in all probability, an organic alteration of the muscles of the kind indicated – the neurosis was supported by it and disproportionately magnified its significance.

Accordingly, the therapy proceeded on the assumption that this was a mixed illness. We recommended that a systematic kneading and faradization of the sensitive muscles be pursued regardless of the resulting pain, and in order to remain in contact with the patient I reserved for myself the treatment of the legs with a strong Franklinic spark discharge. In answer to her question whether she should force herself to walk, we gave a decisive 'Yes'.

In this way we achieved a slight improvement. She seemed, in particular, to warm to the painful shocks of the electrostatic machine, and the stronger these were, the more they seemed to repel the patient's own pains. Meanwhile my colleague was preparing the ground for a psychical treatment, and when, after four weeks of pseudo-treatment, I suggested this and gave the patient some information on the procedure and how it would work I met with swift comprehension and only slight resistance.

The work upon which I then embarked proved to be one of the hardest tasks that had ever fallen to me and the difficulty of giving a report on this work is equal to the difficulties that I overcame at the time. For a long time I could not understand the connection between the history of her suffering and what she was suffering from, although it must have been caused and determined by the sequence of events.

When undertaking a cathartic treatment such as this, one begins by putting the question to oneself: Is the patient familiar with the origin of her affliction and what caused it? If she is, then it is unlikely that any particular technique will be required to enable her to reproduce the history of her illness; the interest that you show her, the sympathetic understanding that you let her sense, and the hope of recovery that you give her will induce the patient to give up her secret. In the case of Fräulein Elisabeth it seemed likely to me from the very start that she was conscious of the reasons for her affliction, and that all that she had in her consciousness was a secret, not a foreign body. Looking at her one could not help thinking of the words of the poet, 'Das Mäskchen da weissagt verborgnen Sinn' ['That little mask reveals a hidden meaning'].[2]

For the time being, then, I could do without hypnosis – with the proviso, however, that I could use it later should connections result in the course of the confession which could not be sufficiently elucidated by her recollections. And so it was that during this, the first complete analysis of a hysteria that I had undertaken, I arrived at a procedure that I later elevated to the status of a method and would initiate deliberately. This procedure involved a level-by-level clearing out of the pathogenic psychical material, and we liked to compare it to the technique of excavating a buried city. I began by getting the patient to tell me what she knew and paid careful attention to those areas where a connection remained enigmatic, where a link in the chain of cause and event seemed to be missing. Later, I would penetrate further into deeper layers of memory, by operating on these areas using investigation under hypnosis or a similar such technique. The premise for all of this work was, of course, that a perfectly adequate set of determining factors would be demonstrated. The methods for deep investigation will be discussed shortly.

The history that Fräulein Elisabeth told of her affliction was a lengthy one, woven together from many different painful experiences. She was not under hypnosis when she recounted it, but I made her lie down and keep her eyes shut, though I did not prevent her from opening them from time to time, changing her position, sitting up, and so on. When she was more deeply moved by a part of her story, she seemed to me to shift spontaneously into a state similar to hypnosis. Then she would remain lying down, motionless, and keep her eyes tightly shut.

I will now repeat what proved to be the most superficial layer of her memories. She had spent her youth on an estate in Hungary and, as the youngest of three daughters, loved her parents tenderly. Her mother's health was frequently marred by an eye complaint as well as by nervous states. As a result she developed a particularly intimate attachment to her father, a vivacious man of the world, who used to say that his daughter took the place of a son and friend with whom he could share his thoughts. However much the girl gained in intellectual stimulus from this intercourse, it did not escape the father that she was at the same time departing from the mental constitution that ideally one likes to see realized in a girl. He jokingly called her 'cocky' and a 'know-all', warned her against being too sure of her judgement and against her tendency to merciless truth-telling, and often expressed the opinion that she would have difficulty finding a husband. Indeed, she was quite discontented with being a girl; she was full of ambitious plans, wanted to study or train as a musician, was outraged by the thought that a marriage would force her to sacrifice her inclinations and the freedom of her judgement. In the meantime she prided herself on her father, and the prestige and social standing of her family, and she kept jealous guard over everything connected with these possessions. But the selflessness with which she put her mother and elder sisters before herself, when the occasion arose, reconciled her parents completely with the gruffer side of her character.

In view of the girls' ages, the family decided to move to the capital where Elisabeth could for a time enjoy a fuller and brighter home life. But then the blow came that destroyed the happiness of this family. Their father had hidden, or perhaps overlooked, a chronic heart complaint. One day he was brought home unconscious after his first attack of pulmonary oedema. He was nursed for the next eighteen months, and throughout this time Elisabeth made sure that she had first place at his bedside. She slept in her father's room, woke at night when he called, watched over him by day, and even forced herself to appear bright and cheerful while he, for his part, bore his hopeless condition with good-natured resignation. This period of nursing had to be connected with the beginning of her illness, for she could remember that during the last six months of the nursing she had been confined to bed for a day and a half because her right leg was so painful. But she claimed that these pains soon passed and had aroused neither concern nor attention on her part. In fact it was not until two years after the death of her father that she felt ill and that her pains prevented her from walking.

The gap left by the death of the father in the life of this family of four women, their social isolation, the cessation of so many connections that had promised stimulation and pleasure, the now increased fragility of her mother's health – all this cast a shadow over our patient's mood, but at the same time it stirred in her the burning wish that her family would soon find a substitute for the happiness that they had lost and led her to concentrate all her affection and care on her surviving mother.

After the year of mourning had passed the eldest sister married a gifted and industrious man, who held a prestigious position and whose intellectual capacity seemed to mark out a great future for him. With his close acquaintances, however, he developed a morbid sensitivity and an egoistic insistence that his whims be met; he was the first of the family circle to dare to show a lack of consideration towards the old lady. This was more than Elisabeth could stand; she felt it was her mission to take up arms against her brother-in-law whenever he gave her cause to, whereas the other women did not take the outbursts of his excitable temperament to heart. It was a painful disappointment to her that the rebuilding of the old family happiness should be disrupted in this way, and she could not forgive her married sister's feminine compliance in forever attempting to avoid taking sides in any way. A whole series of scenes of this kind had been preserved in Elisabeth's memory and attached to them were grievances against her first brother-in-law that had in part remained unspoken. But the greatest reproach was still that, for the sake of a prospective promotion, he and his small family had moved to a remote town in Austria, thereby helping to increase her mother's isolation. On this occasion Elisabeth felt all too keenly her helplessness, her inability to afford her mother any substitute for the happiness she had lost, and the impossibility of implementing the resolution that she had made on the death of her father.

The marriage of the second sister seemed to promise a happier future for the family, for this second brother-in-law, although not as highly intellectual, was a man after the heart of these sensitive women, schooled in the cultivation of consideration for others, and his behaviour reconciled Elisabeth with the institution of marriage and with the thought of the sacrifices that were bound up with it. The second young couple continued to live close to their mother, and the child of this brother-in-law and second sister became Elisabeth's favourite. Unfortunately, the year in which this child was born was overshadowed by another event. The mother's eye complaint required her to spend several weeks in total darkness and Elisabeth accompanied her in this programme of treatment. An operation was then declared necessary and the upset leading up to it coincided with the first brother-in-law's preparations for moving house. When at last the operation was over (and had been expertly performed), the three families met up at a summer resort, and Elisabeth, exhausted by the worries of the last few months, should have made a full recovery in this first period free of suffering and fear that had been granted to the family since the death of the father.

But it was at precisely the time of this summer stay that Elisabeth first experienced pains and weakness when walking. She had been aware of the pains to an extent for a while before, but they first occurred violently after a hot bath that she took in the bathing house of the small spa. A long walk, really half a day's hike, of a few days previously, was then connected with the appearance of these pains, making it easy to take the view that Elisabeth must first have become 'over-tired' and then 'caught a chill'.

From now on Elisabeth was the invalid of the family. On doctor's advice she was to spend the rest of the summer following a course of hydropathic treatment at Gastein; she travelled there with her mother, but not without a new worry having surfaced. The second sister was again pregnant and her state of health was reported to be so very bad that Elisabeth had barely wanted to undertake the journey to Gastein. After barely two weeks' stay in Gastein, mother and sister were called back – the invalid, who was now confined to bed, was 'not at all well'.

An agonizing journey, during which, for Elisabeth, pains intermingled with terrible anticipations; then, at the station, certain signs which led them to expect the worst; and finally, when they entered the invalid's room, the certainty that they had come too late to take leave of a living person.

Elisabeth suffered not only from the loss of this sister, whom she had dearly loved, but also – and almost as much – from the thoughts that were prompted by this death, and from the changes that it brought with it. The sister had succumbed to a heart condition that had been aggravated by her pregnancy.

Now it occurred to them that heart disease was hereditary on the paternal side of the family. Then it was remembered that, as a young girl, the deceased had suffered from chorea accompanied by a slight heart disorder. They reproached themselves and the doctors for having permitted the marriage and could not help reproaching the unfortunate widower for endangering the health of his wife with two pregnancies in immediate succession. From that time on, Elisabeth could think of nothing but the unhappy impression that if ever the rare conditions for a happy marriage were met, this happiness should come to such an end. But what was more, this was the second time that she saw everything that she had longed for for her mother collapse. The widowed brother-in-law was inconsolable and withdrew from his wife's family. It seems that his own family, from whom he had become estranged during his short and happy marriage, found this the right moment to draw him back into their sphere. No means could be found to sustain the companionship they used to have: it was impracticable for him to live with her mother, as his sister-in-law was unmarried, and by refusing to entrust the two women with the child – the only inheritance left by the deceased – he gave them their first opportunity to accuse him of hard-heartedness. Finally, but no less distressingly, Elisabeth had received dark tidings of a dispute that had broken out between the two brothers-in-law. She could only guess at its cause, but it seemed that the widower had made financial demands which the other brother-in-law termed unjustified and which, in view of their mother's grief at this time, he could go so far as to describe as blackmail of the worst kind. Such was the story of how this ambitious girl who craved affection had suffered. Resenting her fate, embittered by the failure of all her little plans to restore her family's former glory – her loved ones either dead, or distant, or estranged – in no way inclined to seek refuge in the love of a man she did not know, she had been living in almost complete seclusion for eighteen months, with only her mother and her own pains to care for.

If we were to leave greater misfortune to one side and enter into this girl's feelings, it would be impossible to have anything but heartfelt human sympathy for her. But what of the medical interest of this tale of suffering, of its connections to her painful unsteadiness when walking, and of the prospects for an elucidation and cure for this case that might arise from our knowledge of these psychical traumas?

For the doctor, the patient's confession was at first a great disappointment. It was, after all, a case history made up of commonplace emotional upheavals, which explained neither why the person concerned should necessarily fall ill with hysteria, nor why the hysteria had assumed precisely this form of painful abasia. It clarified neither what caused nor what determined the hysteria in question. One could assume, for example, that the patient had produced an association between her painful psychical impressions and the physical pains which she had happened to feel at the same time, and that now, in the life of her memories, she was using the physical sensation as a symbol for the psychical one. What motive she might have had for this substitution, and at which point it was carried out, remained unclear. But these were, of course, questions which it had not been common practice for doctors to raise. One tended to rest content with the explanation that the patient simply was of a hysterical constitution and liable to develop hysterical symptoms under the pressure of intensive excitations *of whatever kind*.

If little of the case seemed to have been elucidated by this confession, still less had been achieved in terms of a cure. It was impossible to see what kind of beneficial influence Fräulein Elisabeth might draw from telling the story of her suffering of recent years to a stranger, who received it with a moderate degree of sympathy, when it was already well known to all the members of her family. Nor did the confession have any visibly curative effect. Not once during this first period of treatment did the patient miss the opportunity of saying to the doctor, 'But I still feel ill, I have the same pains as before', and when she accompanied this with a sly look of satisfaction at my failure, I could not help being put in mind of the judgement that old Herr v. R. had passed on his favourite daughter, that she was often 'cocky' and 'naughty'. Still, I had to admit that she was right.

Had I given up the psychical treatment of the patient at this stage, the case of Fräulein Elisabeth v. R. would undoubtedly have become quite irrelevant to the theory of hysteria. But I continued my analysis because I was convinced that the deeper layers of consciousness would yield an understanding of both the cause and the determining factors of the hysterical symptoms.

I therefore resolved to put a direct question to the patient's enlarged consciousness: what was the psychical impression with which the first emergence of the pains in her legs was connected?

To this end the patient needed to be put under deep hypnosis. But unfortunately I could not help observing that the procedures I used to this effect did not bring the patient into any state of consciousness other than that in which she had made her confession to me. Still, I could be genuinely glad that this time at least she refrained from triumphantly proclaiming to me, 'You see, I'm not asleep at all. I'm not to be hypnotized.' In this quandary it occurred to me to use the trick of applying pressure to her head (see the previous report on Miss Lucy for a comprehensive description of how this procedure was developed). This I implemented by demanding that the patient tell me, without fail, what appeared to her inner eye or drifted through her memory at the moment of pressure. She was silent for a long time, then, at my insistence, confessed that she had thought of an evening on which a young man had accompanied her home after a party, of the conversations that had occurred between the two of them, and of the feelings with which she then returned home to care for her father.

At this first mention of the young man a new shaft was opened, the contents of which I now gradually brought to the surface. This time a secret was actually involved, for, other than a girl who was a mutual friend, she had initiated no one into her relations with the young man and the hopes that were bound up with them. The person in question was the son of a family who were friends of long standing and who lived near to their former estate. The young man, who was himself an orphan, had formed the most devoted attachment to her father, followed his advice in choosing a career, and extended his admiration from the father to the ladies of the family. Numerous memories of reading together, of exchanging ideas, things he had said that had been repeated to her, all characterized the gradual growth of her conviction that he loved and understood her and that a marriage with him would not expose her to the sacrifice that she feared from marriage. He was unfortunately only a little older than she and at that time still very far from being independent, but she had been firmly resolved to wait for him.

The severe illness of her father and the demands made on her in her role as nurse meant that she had less and less contact with him. The evening that she had first remembered marked the culmination of her feelings, but even then they had not spoken openly to one another. On that occasion she had, at the insistence of her family and even of her father, allowed herself to be persuaded to leave the sick bed to go to a party where she might expect to find him. She then wanted to hurry back early, but was urged to stay, and gave in when he promised to accompany her home. Never had her feelings for him been as warm as when he walked her home that evening; but when in this state of bliss she arrived back late, she found her father's condition had worsened and reproached herself most bitterly for having sacrificed so much time to her own pleasure. It was the last time that she forsook her sick father for a whole evening; she only ever saw her friend again on rare occasions; after the death of her father he seemed to keep his distance out of respect for her pain and then life took him along a different path; she had had gradually to accustom herself to the thought that his interest in her had been repressed by other feelings and that she had lost him. But this disappointment in her first love was still painful to her whenever she thought of him.

It was therefore in this relationship and in the scene (described above) to which it led that I could search legitimately for what had caused the first hysterical pains. The contrast between the blissful happiness that she had allowed herself at that time and the distress of her father that she encountered at home produced a conflict, a case of incompatibility. The result of the conflict was that the erotic idea was repressed from association and the affect attached to it was used to heighten or revive a physical pain which was present simultaneously (or shortly beforehand). This was, then, the mechanism of *conversion for the purpose of defence*, which I have discussed in detail elsewhere.[3]

Various other observations could, of course, be made here. I must stress that I was not successful in proving from what she could remember that the conversion had been completed at the very moment of her return home. I therefore looked for similar experiences from the time of her nursing and summoned up a series of scenes among which her jumping out of bed barefoot in a cold room, in response to her father's call, stood out because it happened repeatedly. I was inclined to attribute a certain significance to these moments because, apart from the complaint of pain in her legs, she complained of an agonizing feeling of cold. Yet even here I was unable to make out any scene that could have been described with certainty as the scene of conversion. My subsequent inclination was to admit that there was a gap in the explanation, but then I remembered that the hysterical pains in the legs were entirely absent during the time that she had been nursing. Her memory cited one isolated attack of pain that lasted only a few days and attracted no attention at the time. My scrutiny now turned to this occasion on which the pains first emerged and I succeeded in reviving the memory of it with certainty: it was at precisely that time that a relative had come to visit, whom she was unable to see because she was in bed and who on a subsequent visit two years later again had the misfortune of finding her in bed. But in spite of repeated attempts, the search for a psychical cause for these first pains was unsuccessful. I thought it safe to assume that the first pains really had occurred as a slight attack of rheumatism *without* any psychical cause and was further able to discover that this organic illness, the model for the later hysterical imitation, was in any case to be dated prior to the scene in which she was accompanied home. At any rate, it was quite possible, given the nature of the thing, that these pains, which were organic in origin, had continued for a time in a milder form that attracted little attention. The lack of clarity is due to the fact that the analysis indicates a conversion of psychical excitation into physical pain at a time when this pain was certainly neither sensed nor remembered, and this is a problem that I hope to be able to solve on the basis of further considerations and examples.[4]

With the uncovering of the motive for the first conversion, a second, fruitful period of treatment began. At first the patient surprised me by announcing soon afterwards that she now knew why the pains only ever came from that particular area on her right thigh and were most intense there. She said that this was, in fact, the place where her father's leg rested every morning while she replaced the bandages which bound up his severely swollen leg. This must have happened a hundred times, and yet strangely enough she had not thought of this connection until today. Thus she provided me with the desired explanation for the genesis of an *atypical* hysterogenic zone. What is more, her painful legs started to 'join in the conversation' during our analyses. By this I mean to indicate the following curious state of affairs: the patient was, for the most part, free of pain when we set to work together; if I then wakened a memory, whether by asking a question or pressing on her head, the first response was a painful sensation, for the most part so vivid that the patient would start and put her hand on the painful area. The pain that had been woken remained for as long as the patient was controlled by the memory, reached its peak when she was on the point of talking through the most significant and decisive part of what she had to say and, with the last words, it had disappeared. Gradually, I learnt to use the pain that had been woken as a compass; when she fell silent but admitted that she still had pains, I knew that she had not yet said everything, and pressed her to continue the confession until the pain had been talked away. Only then did I waken a new memory.

In this period of 'abreaction', the patient's condition, both physical and psychical, was so markedly improved that I was only half joking when I used to maintain that on each occasion I was carrying away a certain quantum of her motives for pain, and that once I had cleared everything away she would be healthy. She soon reached a point at which she was free of pain for most of the time and allowed herself to be persuaded to walk a lot and to give up her previous isolation. Over the course of the analysis I followed now the spontaneous fluctuations in her condition, now – when I thought that a part of her story of suffering was not yet sufficiently exhausted – my own evaluation. In the course of this work I made some interesting observations and the conclusions I drew from them were later confirmed in other patients.

The first observation, as regards the spontaneous fluctuations, was that none in fact occurred that had not been provoked by association with something that had happened during the day. On one occasion she had heard of an acquaintance of hers falling ill and was reminded of a detail of her father's illness; on another, the child of her dead sister had been visiting and its resemblance to her sister awoke the pain of her loss; on yet another occasion it was a letter from the sister living far away from them which clearly proved the influence of her inconsiderate brother-in-law and awoke a pain that forced her to speak of a family scene that she had not yet recounted.

Since she never brought up the same cause of pain twice it seemed justifiable to suppose that we would exhaust the supply in this way, and I did not shy from getting her into situations that were apt to summon up new memories that had not yet surfaced, as, for example, sending her to her sister's grave or having her go to a party where she might see the friend from her youth, who was around again.

I then gained an insight into the genesis of what might be termed a *monosymptomatic* hysteria. I found that her right leg became painful during our hypnoses when they involved memories of nursing her father, of her relations with her childhood sweetheart, and of other things that fell within that first part of the pathogenic period; by contrast, the pain in the other, left leg responded as soon as I had woken a memory of the sister she had lost or of her two brothers-in-law; in short, an impression from the second half of the story of her illness. Alerted by the regularity of this behaviour, I continued my investigation and had the impression that the specification went further still, as if each new psychical cause of a painful sensation had formed a link with another point on the painful section of the leg. The original painful area on the right thigh had referred to her nursing her father; from that point on new traumas caused the region of pain to grow by apposition, so that, strictly speaking, there was not one *single* physical symptom linked with several psychical memory complexes, but rather a majority of similar symptoms, which, viewed superficially, seemed to be fused into one symptom. I did not, however, attempt to pursue the delimitation of the zones of pain corresponding to the individual psychical causes, as I discovered that the patient's attention was not drawn to these relationships.

I did, however, pay further interest to the way in which the whole complex of symptoms of abasia might have built up from this painful zone, and with this in mind asked various questions, such as: where do the pains come from when walking, standing, lying? – She answered these in part without being influenced, in part under the pressure of my hand. Two things resulted from this. On the one hand she gathered all the scenes bound up with painful impressions into groups for me, according to whether she had been sitting or standing during them and so on. – So, for example, she was *standing* by a door when her father was brought home with a heart attack and in her fright remained *standing* as if rooted to the ground. She then added further memories to this first 'fright when *standing*', up until the frightening scene in which she was once more *standing* as if spellbound at the bedside of her dead sister. The entire chain of reminiscences might be taken as demonstrating the justifiable connection between the pains and the standing up and could even count as proof of association, save that one had to bear in mind that another factor must be proved to be present on all these occasions, one that had specifically drawn her attention to the standing (walking, sitting, etc.), the further consequence of which was the conversion. The explanation for her attention having been thus directed could hardly be sought in any circumstances other than that walking, standing and lying are linked to the actions and states of those parts of the body where the painful zones were located, that is, the legs. So the connection between the astasia-abasia and the first case of conversion in this medical history was not difficult to understand.

Among the scenes that, according to this review, had made *walk-ing* painful, one in particular came to the fore, a walk that she had taken at the spa together with a large party of people and that had, supposedly, gone on for too long. The more precise circumstances surrounding this event were only hesitantly revealed and left much that was puzzling unsolved. She was in a particularly gentle and compliant mood and was glad to join the party of friends; it was a beautiful day, not too hot, her Mama stayed at home, her older sister had already left, the younger felt ill, but did not want to spoil her pleasure – this second sister's husband at first explained that he would stay with his wife, but then for her (Elisabeth's) sake went along too. This scene seemed to have a great deal to do with the first emergence of the pains, for she remembered that she had come back from the walk feeling very tired and suffering violent pains, but she said that she was unsure whether she had already been aware of having pains beforehand. I maintained that had she had any serious pains she would hardly have committed herself to this long walk. When asked where on this walk the pains might have come from, she gave the rather obscure answer that the contrast between her isolation and her sister's happy marriage (which was incessantly kept in view by her brother-in-law's behaviour) had been painful to her.

Another scene, which was very closely related in time to the previous one, played a role in linking the pains with *sitting*. It was a few days later – sister and brother-in-law had already departed; she was in an agitated mood, full of longing; she got up early in the morning, climbed a small hill to a place that they had very often visited together and that had a splendid view, and there sat down on a stone bench and gave herself up to her thoughts. Her thoughts again concerned her loneliness and the fate of her family, and this time she quite openly confessed her ardent wish to become as happy as her sister. Returning from this morning meditation she had violent pains and on the evening of that same day she took the bath after which the pains made their definitive and lasting appearance.

There was also no doubt that the pains when walking and standing were initially eased when lying down. The connection between lying down and her pains was not established until the time that she had received news of her sister's falling ill, departed from Gastein, and that night lay sleepless, stretched out in the railway carriage, tormented at once by her concern for her sister and by raging pains – for quite a time after this lying down was even more painful to her than walking and standing.

In this way the painful area had, first, grown by apposition, in that each new theme which had a pathogenic effect occupied a new region of the legs; secondly, each of the scenes that made a powerful impression left behind a trace by establishing a permanent and constantly increasing 'cathexis' of the various functions of the legs, a linking of these functions with the sensations of pain; but yet a third mechanism had unmistakably been collaborating in the formation of the astasia-abasia. When the patient concluded the account of a whole series of events with the complaint that she had throughout felt the pain of 'standing alone'; when, in another series which encompassed her abortive attempts to establish a new family life, she never tired of repeating that what had been painful about it was her feeling of *helplessness*, the sense that she 'could not make any headway', then I had to allow that her reflections had had some influence on the formation of the abasia, to accept that she had sought out a direct symbolic expression for her markedly painful thoughts and found it in the intensification of her suffering. The possibility of somatic symptoms of hysteria arising through a symbolization of this kind has already been advanced in our 'Preliminary Statement'; I will cite some conclusive examples of it in the critical analysis of the present case history. In the case of Fräulein Elisabeth v. R., the psychical mechanism of symbolization was not of primary importance; it had not created the abasia, yet everything seemed to indicate that the pre-existing abasia had been considerably intensified by it. The stage of development at which I encountered this abasia was, accordingly, to be equated not only with a functional paralysis based on psychical associations, but also with one based on symbolization.

Before I continue with the history of my patient, I want to add a few words about her behaviour during this second period of treatment. Throughout this analysis I used the method of pressing on her head to call up images and thoughts, a method, then, that is impracticable without the full co-operation and willing attentiveness of the patient. Sometimes she did in fact behave just as I would have wished and in periods such as this it really was surprising how promptly and with what faultless chronology the individual scenes pertaining to a theme presented themselves. It was as if she were reading from a long picture book, the pages of which were being turned before her eyes. At other times there seemed to be impediments of a kind that at the time I did not yet suspect. I would exert my pressure and she would claim that nothing had come to mind; I would repeat the pressure, tell her to wait, but still nothing would come. The first few times that this recalcitrance manifested itself, I allowed myself to be led into breaking off the work – it wasn't a good day for it, I'd try another time. But two observations led me to change my attitude. First, that the method only ever failed in this way when I had found Elisabeth to be in good spirits and without pain, never when I came on a bad day; second, that she frequently made this claim that nothing appeared to her when she had allowed a long interval to elapse, an interval during which her tense and preoccupied expression nevertheless betrayed that something was happening internally. I therefore resolved to assume that the method never failed, that Elisabeth did have an idea in mind or an image before her inner eye every time that I applied the pressure of my hand, but that she was not prepared to communicate it to me every time and tried instead to suppress what had been evoked. I could imagine two motives for remaining silent in this way, either Elisabeth was subjecting her idea to criticism (which she had no right to do) and found that it was not sufficiently valuable, not suitable as an answer to the question posed, or perhaps she was nervous of stating it because – she found it too disagreeable to communicate. I proceeded, therefore, as if I were completely convinced of the reliability of my technique. I no longer accepted her claim that nothing had occurred to her, assured her that something must have done, that she had perhaps not been sufficiently attentive, in which case I would willingly repeat the pressure, or that she perhaps thought that what had occurred to her was not the right thing. But that wasn't her business; it was her duty to remain wholly objective and to say what had come to mind, whether it was suitable or not; finally, I said that I knew for certain that something had occurred to her and that she was keeping it secret from me, but that she would never get rid of her pains as long as she kept anything secret. By pressing her in this way I managed to reach a point at which no subsequent pressure was unsuccessful. I had to assume that I had correctly identified the state of affairs and through this analysis I gained what was indeed an unconditional trust in my technique. It often happened that she would not communicate something to me until I had pressed for the third time, but would then herself add, 'I could have told you that straightaway the first time.' – 'Oh yes, then why didn't you say it straightaway?' – 'I thought that it wasn't the right thing', or, 'I thought I could get round it, but it came back every time'. During this difficult work, I began to attach a deeper significance to the resistance that the patient showed when reproducing her memories and carefully made a collection of those occasions on which it was betrayed in a particularly striking way.

I now come to the description of the third period of treatment. The patient felt better, the strain on her psyche had been relieved and her general capacity restored, but the pains had obviously not been removed – they continued to appear from time to time, and, indeed, to appear with their former violence. The incompleteness of the cure corresponded to the incompleteness of the analysis: I still did not know precisely at which moment and by what mechanism the pains had arisen. During the reproduction of the many different scenes in the second period, when I had observed the patient's resistance to recounting them, a particular suspicion had taken shape in me, but I did not yet venture to make it the basis of my actions. A chance perception was the decisive factor. Once, when working with the patient, I heard a man's footsteps in the room next door, a pleasant-sounding voice, which seemed to be asking a question, and at this my patient got up and asked if we could break off for today – she had heard her brother-in-law coming in and asking after her.

Until then she had been free of pain; after this disruption her face and gait betrayed the sudden emergence of violent pains. My suspicion was confirmed and I decided to induce the decisive explanation.

I therefore questioned her about the circumstances and causes of the first appearance of the pains. In answer, her thoughts were drawn to the summer stay at the spa before the journey to Gastein, and a few scenes reappeared that had already been treated before, but in less detail: her state of mind at that time, her exhaustion after having been so anxious about her mother's eyesight and having nursed her at the time of the eye operation, her final despair of ever, as a girl on her own, being able to enjoy anything of life or achieve anything in life. Until then she had thought herself strong enough to do without the support of a man, now she was overpowered by a feeling of her weakness as a woman, a longing for love, in which, to quote her own words, her frozen nature began to melt. In this mood her younger sister's happy marriage made a deep impression on her, how touchingly he cared for her, how they understood each other at a glance, how sure they seemed to be of one another. Of course it was regrettable that the second pregnancy had followed so soon after the first, and her sister knew that this was the cause of her illness – but how willingly she bore this suffering because he was the cause of it. On the occasion of the walk that was so intimately bound up with Elisabeth's pains, her brother-in-law had at first not wanted to join in, he preferred to stay with his sick wife. But with a glance she persuaded him to go too, because she thought that it would bring Elisabeth pleasure. Elisabeth stayed in his company throughout; they talked to one another about all sorts of things, even the most intimate ones; she found that she was so very much in accord with everything that he said, and her wish to have a husband like him became overpowering. There then followed the scene of a few days later when, the morning after their departure, she made her way to the place with the view that had been a favourite walk of the absent couple. She sat down on a rock there and dreamt once more of finding such happiness in life as had fallen to her sister, and of a husband who would know how to capture her heart as this brother-in-law did. She stood up in pain, but the sensation disappeared again, and not until the afternoon, after the hot bath that she took at the resort, did the pains break over her – they had not left her since. I tried to find out what kinds of thoughts had occupied her when she was taking the bath, but all that came of this was that the bathing-house reminded her of her sisters who had gone away because that was the building in which they had stayed.

I must long since have become aware of what this was about; the patient, immersed in her bitter-sweet memories, seemed not to notice the disclosure towards which she was steering and continued to recite her reminiscences. There followed the time at Gastein; the anxiety with which she awaited each letter; finally the news that her sister was in a bad way; the long wait until the evening that was her first opportunity to leave Gastein. The journey, passed in a torment of uncertainty, a night without sleep – all of these factors accompanied by a violent increase in her pains. I asked whether during the journey she had imagined the sad possibility that did then come about. She answered that she had carefully avoided the thought, but that, in her opinion, her mother had expected the worst from the very beginning. – There now followed her memory of the arrival in Vienna, the impressions made on them by the relatives who were expecting them, the short journey from Vienna to the nearby summer resort where her sister was staying, the arrival there in the evening, the path hurriedly crossed through the garden up to the door of the small garden pavilion – the stillness inside, the stifling darkness; that her brother-in-law did not come to greet them; then they stood in front of the bed, saw the dead woman, and in that moment of dreadful certainty that her beloved sister had died without having taken leave of them, without her last days having been brightened by their care – at that same moment another thought flashed through Elisabeth's mind, a thought that had now presented itself again unavoidably and came like a bolt in the dark: now he is free again, and I can become his wife.

Now everything was indeed clear. The analyst's efforts had been amply rewarded: the concepts of the 'fending off' of an intolerable idea and of the genesis of hysterical symptoms through the conversion of psychical excitation into something physical, the formation of a separate psychical group through the act of will that leads to the fending off – at that moment all of this moved palpably into view. This is what had happened here, there was no alternative. This girl had developed an affection for her brother-in-law and her whole moral being was struggling to prevent its admission into consciousness. She had succeeded in sparing herself the painful certainty that she loved her sister's husband by creating physical pains in its place and at moments when this certainty threatened to force itself on her (on the walk with him, the daydreams during that morning bath, in front of her sister's bed) a successful conversion into the somatic had given rise to those pains. At the time that I took on her treatment the group of ideas relating to this love had already been separated from her knowledge, otherwise I think that she would never have agreed to a treatment of this kind; the resistance with which she had repeatedly countered the reproduction of scenes of a traumatic effect really corresponded to the energy with which the intolerable idea was being forced out of association.

For the therapist, however, the period that followed was a bad one. The re-admission of that repressed idea had a shattering effect on the poor child. She screamed aloud when, summarizing the matter drily, I said: 'You had been in love with your brother-in-law for a long time, then.' She complained of the most dreadful pains at this moment and made one more desperate effort to reject the explanation – it wasn't true, I had talked her into it, it was impossible, she wasn't capable of such wickedness. Nor would she ever forgive herself such a thing. It was easy to prove to her that what she herself had said admitted no other interpretation, but as for my two reasons for consolation – I told her that one was not responsible for one's feelings and that her behaviour, falling ill on those occasions, was proof enough of her moral nature – it was a long time before either made any impression on her.

At this point I had to adopt more than one way of alleviating the patient's suffering. At first I wanted to give her the opportunity to use 'abreaction' to discharge the store of excitation that had been accumulating for a long time. We investigated the first impressions of her relations with her brother-in-law, of the beginning of the affection that she had unconsciously held. Here were to be found all the small signs and intimations of which, in retrospect, a fully developed passion can make so much. On his first visit to the house he had taken *her* for the bride who was meant for him and greeted her before the older but plainer sister. One evening they were having such an animated conversation and seemed to be getting on so well together that his fiancée interrupted them with an observation, made half in earnest, 'Actually, you two would have suited each other very well.' On another occasion, at a party where no one yet knew anything about the engagement, the young man was the subject of conversation and one lady was critical of a defect in his figure which suggested that in his youth he had suffered from bone disease. His fiancée herself remained quiet at this, but Elisabeth flared up and intervened to defend the upright build of her future brother-in-law with a zeal that she herself subsequently found incomprehensible. As we worked our way through these reminiscences it became clear to Elisabeth that her tender feelings for her brother-in-law had lain dormant in her for a long time, perhaps since the beginning of their relations, and that they had long been hidden by the mask of mere familial affection, which she could understand in the light of her highly developed sense of family.

This abreaction unquestionably did her much good, but I was able to give even more relief by taking a friendly interest in her present circumstances. With this in mind I sought an audience with Frau v. R. and found her to be a lady of understanding and sensitivity, though her spirit had been adversely affected by her recent misfortunes. I learnt from her that the charge of unfeeling blackmail that the elder brother-in-law had brought against the widower and that had been so painful for Elisabeth had had, on closer inquiry, to be retracted. The young man's character could remain unsullied: there had, quite understandably, been a difference between the value attached to the money by the businessman, for whom money was a tool of the trade, and the value attached to it by the civil servant – and this misunderstanding was all that remained of what had seemed so nasty an incident. I asked Elisabeth's mother to give her all the explanations that she needed from then on and to continue to offer her the opportunity of voicing her innermost thoughts to which I had accustomed her.

I was, of course, also concerned to discover what prospect the girl's wish had of coming true, now that it had become conscious. Here things were less favourable! The mother said that she had long suspected Elisabeth's affection for her brother-in-law; what she had not known was that it had come into effect while the sister was still alive. Whoever saw them in each other's company – even though this had become infrequent – could not have doubted the girl's intention to please him. Yet neither she, the girl's mother, nor the senior members of the family were particularly inclined to the couple being joined in marriage. The young man's health was, she said, not sound and it had suffered another blow with the death of his wife; it was also not at all certain that he had made a sufficient emotional recovery to enter into a new marriage. It was, she thought, probably for that reason that he was behaving with such reserve, perhaps too because, unsure of whether he would be accepted, he wanted to avoid the gossip that would be likely. Given this reserve on both sides the happy resolution for which Elisabeth longed was unlikely to be successful.

I informed the girl of everything that I had learnt from her mother, had the satisfaction of doing her some good by clearing up the matter of the money, and, on the other hand, appealed to her to bear calmly a future whose uncertainty could not be dispelled. But so much of the summer was now past that concluding the treatment had become a pressing matter. She was feeling better again and there had been no more talk of her pains since we had dealt with the cause to which they had been traced. We both had the sense of having finished, although I thought to myself that the abreacting of the tender feelings that she had held back had not been carried out in a particularly exhaustive manner. I regarded her as cured and pointed out to her that things would resolve themselves of their own accord now that a path had been opened up – she did not contradict me. She left with her mother to join her eldest sister and her family for the summer vacation together.

It remains for me to give a brief report on the further course of Fräulein Elisabeth v. R.'s illness. A few weeks after we parted I received a despairing letter from her mother that informed me that on the first attempt to speak to Elisabeth about her affairs of the heart her daughter had rebelled in utter indignation and subsequently experienced violent pains again; she was furious with me for having betrayed her secret and now appeared to be quite unapproachable – the cure had been a thorough failure. What was to be done now? Elisabeth didn't want anything more to do with me. I did not reply; it was to be expected that once she had been freed from my tight rein she would make one more attempt to reject her mother's interference and shut herself off again. But I had a kind of certainty that everything would turn out all right and that my efforts had not been spent in vain. Two months later they had come back to Vienna and the colleague to whom I owed the introduction to my patient brought me the news that Elisabeth felt perfectly well and was behaving as if she were healthy, although she did still have some pain from time to time. Since then she has repeatedly sent me similar messages, always promising to call on me, but it is characteristic of the personal relationship that develops in treatments such as this that she has never done so. According to my colleague's assurances she is to be regarded as cured; her brother-in-law's relationship with the family has not changed.

In spring 1894 I heard that she would be attending a private ball, to which I could also obtain an invitation, and I did not let the opportunity escape me of seeing my erstwhile patient fly past in a lively dance. Since that time she has, by her own inclination, married a man unknown to me.

CRITICAL ANALYSIS

I have not always been a psychotherapist but was trained, like other neuropathologists, to use local diagnosis and electro-prognosis, and I myself still find it strange that the case histories that I write read like novellas and lack, so to speak, the serious stamp of science. I have to console myself with the thought that the nature of the object rather than my own personal preference is clearly responsible for this; local diagnosis and electrical reactions are simply not effective in the study of hysteria, whereas an in-depth portrayal of the workings of the inner life, such as one expects to be given by novelists and poets, together with the application of a few psychological formulas, does allow me to gain a kind of insight into the course of a hysteria. Case histories such as these demand to be judged as psychiatric, but they have one advantage over the latter, namely the intimate relationship between the story of the patient's suffering and the symptoms of their illness, a relationship that we still seek in vain in the biographies of other psychoses.

I have endeavoured to weave the explanations that I can give regarding the case of Fräulein Elisabeth v. R. into my description of the history of her cure, but the essential points do perhaps bear recapitulating in context at this stage. I have portrayed the patient's character – the traits that recur in a great many hysterics and really cannot be put down to degeneracy: her gifted nature; her ambition; her moral sensitivity; her excessive need for love, which was, to begin with, satisfied by her family; the independence of her nature that went beyond the feminine ideal and was expressed in a good deal of stubbornness, pugnacity and reserve. According to my colleague's reports there was no evidence of any significant hereditary illness in either family; it is true that her mother suffered for many years from a neurotic depression that did not receive close examination, but her mother's brothers and sisters, her own father and his family could be counted as well-balanced people, free of any nervous complaint. There had been no severe case of neuropsychosis in the near family.

This, the patient's nature, was then affected by painful emotions, the first of which was the debilitating influence of a long period of nursing her beloved father.

There are good reasons why nursing should play such a significant role in the prehistory of hysterias. Indeed, there is clear evidence of a series of factors that are operative in this: disturbance of one's physical state by interrupted sleep, neglect of one's physical well-being, and the repercussions of continually gnawing anxiety on the vegetative functions. But in my estimation what is most important lies elsewhere. Anyone whose mind is occupied by the hundred and one tasks of nursing that follow each other interminably over weeks and months will, on the one hand, become accustomed to suppressing every sign of his own emotional involvement and, on the other, find that he is soon distracted from paying any attention to his own impressions because he lacks the time as well as the strength to give them their due. The nurse, then, stores up within himself a wealth of impressions that could be intensely emotional; these impressions have hardly been perceived with sufficient clarity and in any case have not been weakened by abreaction. He is providing himself with the material for a retention hysteria. Should the patient recover, all of these impressions will lose their value; but if he dies and the period of mourning sets in – a time when the only things of value seem to be those connected with the departed – then those impressions that are waiting to be dealt with will take their turn as well and after a short period of exhaustion the hysteria, the seeds of which were sown during the nursing, breaks out.

Occasionally one comes across this same instance of traumas that have accumulated during nursing being dealt with retrospectively when the overall impression is not one of ill-health, but the mechanism of hysteria is nevertheless preserved. Such is the case of a highly gifted woman of my acquaintance who suffers from slight nervous conditions and whose entire being testifies to hysteria, although she has never burdened doctors with it, nor had to interrupt her duties. This woman has already nursed three or four of her loved ones up until their death, on each occasion to the point of complete physical exhaustion, and even these unhappy exertions did not cause her to fall ill. But a short time after the death of the invalid, the work of reproduction begins in her, making the scenes of illness and dying appear to her once more. Every day she experiences each impression anew, cries about it, consoles herself – at her leisure, one is tempted to say. This manner of dealing with things goes on throughout her daily business, without the two activities becoming confused. The whole thing runs past her in chronological order. Whether or not the memory-work of one day corresponds exactly to a day in the past, I do not know. I suspect that this depends on the leisure that her regular household duties allow her.

Apart from these 'deferred tears' that follow closely after the bereavement, this woman periodically holds annual commemorations at the time of the individual catastrophes and here her vivid visual reproduction and expressions of emotion keep faithfully to the date. I might, for example, come across her crying and ask sympathetically what happened today. Half-annoyed, she will brush off the query. 'Oh no, it's just that the consultant, Dr N., was here again today, and he gave us to understand that there is no hope. I didn't have any time back then to cry about it.' She is referring to the last illness of her husband, who died three years ago. It would be very interesting to know if she constantly repeats the same scenes during these annually recurring commemorations, or whether, as I surmise in the interests of my theory, she is presented with different details for abreaction on each occasion. But I cannot discover anything about it with any certainty; this woman, who is as clever as she is strong, is ashamed of the violence with which these reminiscences affect her.[5]

I want to emphasize once more: this woman is not ill, the deferred abreaction is, despite all similarity, not a hysterical process. One might well ask why hysteria should result after one period of nursing and not after another. It cannot be due to the individual disposition, as a disposition of this kind was amply present in the woman whom I have in mind here.

I will return now to Fräulein Elisabeth v. R. It was, then, while she was looking after her father that she first developed a hysterical symptom, namely a pain in a particular area of her right thigh. The mechanism of this symptom can be adequately elucidated as a result of the analysis. It was a moment at which the sphere of ideas relating to her duties towards her sick father entered into conflict with what was at the time the content of her erotic longing. Reproaching herself keenly she made a decision in favour of the former, and in so doing created her hysterical pain. According to the view advanced by the conversion theory of hysteria, the process could be depicted as follows. She repressed the erotic idea from her consciousness and transformed its quantity of affect into a somatic sensation of pain. Whether this first conflict presented itself to her just the once or repeatedly did not become clear; the latter is more likely. A very similar conflict – but of higher moral significance and even more clearly borne out by the analysis – was repeated years later and led to the same pains increasing and spreading beyond the borders that they occupied at the outset. Once again it was a sphere of erotic ideas that entered into conflict with all her moral ideas, for the inclination related to her brother-in-law, and both in her sister's lifetime and after her death the thought that of all men he should be the one for whom she longed was unacceptable to her. Detailed information about this conflict, which represents the mid-point of the case history, is given by the analysis. The germ of the patient's inclination for her brother-in-law may have been present long ago, but its development was favoured by the physical exhaustion of further nursing and the moral exhaustion of disappointments over many years; her inner coldness did then begin to give and she admitted to herself that she needed a man's love. During their contact, which went on for some weeks (at the spa), this erotic inclination and her pains simultaneously reached a point at which both were fully formed; the analysis gave evidence too that during this same period the patient had been in a particular psychical state – the connection of this state with her inclination and pains seems to enable an understanding of the process in terms of the conversion theory.

I have, therefore, to venture the assertion that at this time, however intense her inclination for her brother-in-law, the patient did not become clearly conscious of it other than in a few isolated instances and even then only momentarily. Had it been otherwise she would also have had to become conscious of the contradiction between this inclination and her moral ideas, and to overcome a spiritual torment such as I saw her suffer after our analysis. Her memory could report nothing about any suffering of this kind – she had spared herself this and as a consequence the inclination itself had not become clear to her; then, as at the time of the analysis, the love for her brother-in-law was present as a kind of foreign body in her consciousness, which had not entered into any relation with the rest of her ideational life. What presented itself, as regards this inclination, was the peculiar state of at once knowing and not knowing, that is, the state of the detached psychical group. This is all that is meant when we assert that this inclination was not 'clearly conscious' to her; it is not meant to indicate an inferior quality or a lesser degree of consciousness, but rather a detachment from any free associative traffic of thought with the remaining ideational content.

But how did it happen that a group of ideas of such intense emphasis was kept so isolated? In general the affective quantity of an idea will grow in proportion to its role in association.

This question can be answered by taking into account two facts that can be taken as firmly established: 1. that the formation of those separate psychical groups was simultaneous with the development of the hysterical pains; 2. that the patient put up a strong opposition to the attempt to produce an association between the separate psychical group and the remaining content of her consciousness, and when in spite of this they were brought together, she experienced great psychical pain. Our conception of hysteria makes a connection between these two factors and the splitting of consciousness by asserting that 2. gives an indication of the *motive* for the splitting of consciousness and 1. of its *mechanism*. The motive was that of defence, the reluctance on the part of the whole self to tolerate this group of ideas; the mechanism was that of conversion, i.e. physical pains emerged in the place of the emotional pains that she had spared herself, thus initiating a transformation, in which the *advantage* proved to be that the patient had extracted herself from an unbearable psychical state, albeit at the expense of a psychical anomaly – the splitting of consciousness that was allowed – and of physical suffering, the pains, on which an astasia-abasia was built up.

I am not, it should be said, able to give instructions for producing a conversion of this kind. Clearly one doesn't do it in the same way that one would intentionally carry out a voluntary action. It is a process that is accomplished under the impetus of the individual's motive of defence, if the organization of that individual – or the current modification of it – is thus suited.

One might quite justifiably press the theory more closely and ask: what is it that is being converted into physical pain here? The cautious answer would be: something that could and should have become psychical pain. If one wanted to venture further and attempt a kind of algebraic representation of the ideational mechanism, one might ascribe a certain amount of affect to the ideational complex of the inclination that has remained unconscious and say that this quantity is what has been converted. A direct consequence of this conception would be that the 'unconscious love' would forfeit so much of its intensity through such a conversion that it would be reduced to a weak idea; this weakening alone would then enable it to exist as a detached psychical group. The present case is, however, not suited to giving a clear picture of such a tricky matter – it probably corresponds only to an incomplete conversion; other cases allow one to show the probability that complete conversions occur too, and that in such cases the incompatible idea has indeed been *'repressed'*, as only an idea of very slight intensity can be. Once the bringing together by association is complete, the patients affirm that since the emergence of the hysterical symptom their thoughts have ceased to be occupied with the intolerable idea.

I maintained above that on certain occasions, even if only fleetingly, the patient also consciously recognized her love for her brother-in-law. One such moment was, for example, at her sister's bedside, when the thought went through her mind, 'Now he is free and you can become his wife'. I need to discuss in some detail the significance of these moments for our conception of the neurosis in its entirety. It seems to me that our acceptance of the notion of a 'defence hysteria' demands that at least *one* such moment has occurred. Consciousness does not, of course, have advance knowledge of when an incompatible idea will present itself; the incompatible idea, which, together with its attachments, will later be excluded to form a separate psychical group, must initially have been part of the general traffic of thought, otherwise the conflict leading to its exclusion would not have arisen.[6] Precisely these moments are, then, to be termed *'traumatic'*; during them the conversion occurred that resulted in the splitting of consciousness and the hysterical symptom. In Fräulein Elisabeth v. R.'s case everything indicates that there were many such moments (the scenes during the walk, the morning meditation, in the bath, at her sister's bedside); it may even be that new moments of this kind occurred during the treatment. For what makes it possible for there to be so many traumatic moments of this kind is that an experience similar to that which first introduced the incompatible idea supplies the detached psychical group with new excitation and thus temporarily undoes the success of the conversion. The self has to deal with this idea that has suddenly flared up and to reproduce the previous state through a further conversion. Fräulein Elisabeth, who was constantly in the company of her brother-in-law, must have been particularly vulnerable to the emergence of new traumas. It would have been preferable for my account to have a case whose traumatic history had been concluded in the past.

Now I must attend to a point that I have described as problematic for our understanding of the above case history. On the basis of the analysis, I assumed that an initial conversion occurred in the patient while she was nursing her father, at the time when her duties as a nurse entered into conflict with her erotic longing, and that this process was the model for the later one that led to the outbreak of her illness at the spa in the Alps. But the information given by the patient shows that at the time when she was nursing and in the interval following this, which I have termed the 'first period', she *did not in the least suffer from pains or weakness when walking*. During her father's sickness she had in fact once been confined to bed for a few days, on account of pains in her feet – but whether one would have to attribute the attack to hysteria at this stage remains debatable. No causal connection between these first pains and any kind of psychical impression could be proven in the analysis; it is possible, probable even, that at this time it was a matter of common, rheumatic muscular pains. Even if one wanted to assume that this first attack of pain was the result of a hysterical conversion owing to the rejection of her erotic thoughts at this time, the fact still remains that the pains disappeared after a few days, so that the patient's behaviour was in reality different from that which she seemed to indicate during the analysis. During the reproduction of the so-called first period she accompanied all the stories about the sickness and death of her father, the impressions of her contact with her first brother-in-law and so on, with expressions of pain; whereas she felt no pains at the time that she was experiencing these impressions. Doesn't this pose a contradiction fit to lessen one's confidence in the elucidatory value of an analysis such as this quite considerably?

I believe that I can resolve the contradiction by assuming that the pains – the product of the conversion – may not have arisen while the patient was experiencing the impressions of the first period, but belatedly, that is in the second period, when the patient reproduced these impressions in her thoughts. The conversion would not then have ensued from the fresh impressions but from the memories of these same impressions. Actually, I think that a process such as this may be nothing out of the ordinary in hysteria, and may make a regular contribution to the genesis of hysterical symptoms. But since such an assertion is in no way self-evident, I will try to make it more credible by drawing on other experiences.

It once happened that during an analytic treatment of this kind a new hysterical symptom developed in the patient, so that I could tackle the matter of clearing it away the very day after it had arisen.

I will insert the main traits of this patient's story here; it is fairly simple, but not without interest.

Fräulein Rosalia H., twenty-three years old, who has for some years endeavoured to train as a singer, complains that in certain registers she loses control over her beautiful voice. A feeling of choking occurs, of her throat being constricted, so that her voice sounds strained; because of this, her teacher has not yet been able to allow her to make a public appearance as a singer; although this imperfection affects only the middle register, it cannot be attributed to a fault in the organ; at times the disturbance fails to appear at all, so that the teacher declares himself quite satisfied; on other occasions, at the slightest excitement, and even without any apparent reason, the sensation of constriction starts again and the voice is impeded from unfolding freely. It was not difficult to recognize hysterical conversion in this bothersome sensation; I did not take steps to ascertain whether there was in fact a contraction of certain muscles of the vocal chords.[7] In the hypnotic analysis which I undertook with the girl, I learnt the following about her fate and thus about the cause of her troubles; she was orphaned at a young age, taken into the home of an aunt who already had many children of her own, and so became the participant in a deeply unhappy family life. The husband of this aunt, who was clearly a pathological personality, ill-treated his wife and children in the roughest fashion; he hurt them in particular by showing an undisguised sexual prefer-ence for the maids and nannies in the house and this became all the more offensive as the children grew up. When her aunt died, Rosalia became the protector of this swarm of orphaned children, who were threatened by their father. She took her duties seriously, fighting through all the conflicts into which her position led her, but it demanded the greatest effort on her part to suppress the expression of her hatred and contempt for her uncle.[8] It was at that time that the sensation of constriction in her throat arose: whenever she had to check her answer, whenever she had forced herself to keep quiet in the face of an outrageous accusation, she felt the scratching in her throat, the knotting up, the failure of her voice, in short, all the localized sensations in the larynx and pharynx that now disrupted her singing. It was understandable that she sought the opportunity to become independent as a way of escaping the upsets and painful impressions that every day in her uncle's house brought. She was taken up by a very competent singing teacher, who, setting aside his own interests, assured her that her voice justified her in her choice of career as a singer. She then began to take lessons with him in secret, but since she often hurried off to her singing lessons with the constriction in her throat left over from violent scenes at home, a connection between the singing and the hysterical paraesthesia was consolidated – a connection that had already been brought under way by the sensation in the organ when singing. The apparatus that should have been perfectly at her command when singing proved to be cathected with the remains of innervations from those numerous scenes of suppressed excitement. Since then she had left her uncle's house and moved to another town in order to keep her distance from the family, but the obstacle had not been overcome.

There was no sign of any other hysterical symptoms in this beautiful and unusually intelligent girl.

I attempted to resolve this 'retention hysteria' by reproducing and belatedly abreacting all of the impressions that were the cause of excitement. I made her grouse and grumble, harangue, tell her uncle the truth to his face, and so on. This treatment did her a great deal of good; but in the meantime she had unfortunately been living here in extremely unfavourable circumstances. She did not have much luck with her relatives. She was staying as a guest with another uncle, who did in fact take her in in a friendly way; but it was in precisely this that she excited the displeasure of her aunt. This woman suspected that her husband had a deeper interest in his niece and made every effort to spoil the girl's stay in Vienna thoroughly. She herself had had to give up her artistic leanings in her youth and now envied her niece for being able to cultivate her talent, although it was not a leaning but the urge to become independent that had brought about this decision. Rosalie[9] felt so constrained in the house that she did not, for example, dare to sing or play the piano if her aunt was in hearing distance and she scrupulously avoided playing or singing anything to her uncle – who was incidentally of an advanced age, the brother of her mother – if there were any possibility of her aunt coming in. While I attempted to erase the traces of old excitations, new ones were developing from this relationship with her hosts, which eventually interfered with the success of my treatment and broke off the cure prematurely.

One day the patient turned up with a new symptom that was barely twenty-four hours old. She complained of an unpleasant prickling in her fingertips, which had occurred every few hours since the day before and compelled her to make a particular kind of flicking movement with her fingers. I was not able to see the attack, otherwise I would probably have guessed what had caused it by observing the finger movements; but I tried straight away to trace the grounds for the symptom (which was in fact a small hysterical attack) using hypnotic analysis. Since the whole thing had existed for only a very short period of time, I hoped to be able to elucidate and resolve it swiftly. To my astonishment, the patient gave me – without hesitation and in chronological order – a whole series of scenes, beginning in early childhood, which had more or less in common that she had tolerated an injustice without defending herself, so that as it was happening she could feel her fingers twitching; scenes like, for example, at school having to hold out her hand, which the teacher then hit with a ruler. But these were banal reasons and I would willingly have disputed the legitimacy of their entering into the aetiology of a hysterical symptom. But a scene from early in her girlhood that then followed was a different matter. The bad uncle, who suffered from rheumatism, had asked her to massage his back. She did not dare refuse him. He had been lying in bed; suddenly he threw off the covers, got up, and tried to grab hold of her and throw her down. Evidently she broke off the massage and a moment later had fled and locked herself in her room. She was clearly loath to remember this event, nor did she want to say whether she had seen anything when this man had suddenly bared himself. The sensation in her fingers might then be explained by the suppressed impulse to beat him, or it might simply have come from the massaging action. Only after this scene did she come to speak about the one she had experienced the day before, after which the sensation and twitching in her fingers had recurred as a memory-symbol. The uncle with whom she was now living had asked her to play something to him; she sat down at the piano and accompanied her playing with a song, thinking that her aunt had gone out. Suddenly her aunt was at the door; Rosalie jumped up, slammed down the piano lid, and threw the sheet of music away. One can guess at the memory that surfaced in her and the thought process that she was fending off at this moment – it was her rage at an unjust suspicion which really should induce her to leave the house, and yet because of her medical treatment she was compelled to stay in Vienna and had no other accommodation. The twitching movement of the fingers that I saw when she reproduced this scene was a flicking away, in such a way as – both literally and figuratively – to reject something, to brush away a sheet of music or dismiss an unreasonable demand.

She was quite definite in her assurance that she had not sensed this symptom before, that is, that it had not been occasioned by the scenes that she had first recounted. The only other assumption was that the experience of the day before had at first wakened the memory of earlier experiences of a similar content and that the formation of a memory-symbol had then applied to the whole group of memories. The conversion had on the one hand been provided with affect that was newly experienced and on the other with affect that was remembered.

On closer consideration of the situation, it has to be admitted that this kind of process should be termed the rule rather than the exception in the genesis of hysterical symptoms. On almost every occasion that I was investigating the determining factors of conditions such as these, not one but a group of similar traumatic causes was uncovered (some fine examples of this are given in the second case history, Frau Emmy). For some of these cases it was possible to establish that the symptom in question had already appeared for a short time after the first trauma, only then to retreat until it was brought on once more and stabilized by a subsequent trauma. Yet there is, in principle, no distinguishable difference between this temporary appearance and the general state of latency that may follow the first occasions; indeed, in the great majority of instances it transpired that the first traumas had not left any symptoms behind, whereas a later trauma of the same kind brought on a symptom whose genesis could not in fact have done without the involvement of the earlier occasions, and the resolution of this symptom really demanded that all occasions be taken into account. Translated into the terms of the conversion theory, the incontrovertible fact of the summation of traumas and of the initial latency of symptoms means that the conversion can proceed equally well from fresh and remembered affect, and if we make this assumption it fully explains the apparent contradiction between the case history and the analysis of Fräulein Elisabeth v. R.

Unquestionably, those who are healthy can, to a great degree, bear the continuing presence of ideas with unresolved affect in their consciousness. The assertion that I have just defended simply brings the behaviour of the hysteric closer to that of the healthy person. The decisive factor is a quantitative one, namely *how much* affective tension of this kind an organization can tolerate. Even the hysteric will be able to retain a certain amount that is unresolved; should similar occasions cause this amount to grow by summation beyond the individual's capacity, then the impetus to conversion is given. To say that the formation of hysterical symptoms might also proceed at the expense of remembered affect is not an unfamiliar proposition, but almost a postulate.

I have thus far been concerned with the *motive* and *mechanism* of this case of hysteria. What remain to be discussed are the *determining factors* of the hysterical symptom. Why did those particular pains in the legs take on the representation of the psychical pain? The circumstances of the case indicate that this somatic pain was not created by the neurosis, but simply used, heightened and maintained by it. I want to add straight away that something similar happened in the great majority of cases of hysterical pains into which I was able to gain an insight; there was always a real, organically founded pain present at the beginning. It is mankind's most common, most widespread pains that seem to be called upon most frequently to play a role in hysteria – above all the periosteal and neuralgic pains of dental illness; headaches that may come from any number of different sources; and, no less, rheumatic muscular pains that so often go unrecognized. Similarly, I consider the foundation of the first attack of pains that Fräulein Elizabeth v. R. had while still nursing her father to be organic. For I gained no information when I searched for a psychical cause, and I am, I admit, inclined to attribute differential-diagnostic significance to my method of calling forth hidden memories, if it is carefully handled. This pain, which was rheumatic[10] in origin, then became a memory-symbol for the patient's painful psychical excitations, and this happened, as far as I can see, for more than one reason. First, and most probably also foremost, because it was present at roughly the same time as were the excitations in her consciousness; second, because it was connected or could be connected with the ideational content of that time in several ways. It may actually have been only a remote consequence of the nursing, that is, of the restricted movement and poor diet that her duties as nurse entailed. But the patient did not really become aware of this. Of greater consideration is likely to be that she must have felt the pain at significant moments during the nursing, such as, for example, having to jump out of bed in the cold of winter to answer her father's call. But what was really decisive in determining the direction taken by the conversion was undoubtedly the other type of associative connection, the fact that over a period of many days one of her painful legs would come into contact with her father's swollen leg as she was changing the bandages. From then on the area of her right leg marked out by this contact remained the focus and starting point of her pains, an artificial hysterogenic zone, whose genesis was, in this case, clearly visible.

Should surprise be expressed that this associative connection between physical pain and psychical affect is too diverse and artificial, I would reply that there is as little justification for this as for being surprised 'that of all people it should be the wealthiest in the world who have the most money'. When such numerous connections present, a hysterical symptom will not be formed, the conversion does not find a path; and I can say for sure that the example of Fräulein Elisabeth v. R. is among the simpler cases as regards determining factors. I have had the most knotted threads of this kind to disentangle, in particular with Frau Cäcilie M.

I have already discussed in the case history how the patient's astasia-abasia was built up on these pains once a certain path was opened for the conversion. But I also advanced the claim there that the patient had created or heightened the functional disturbance by symbolization, that she found in the abasia-astasia a somatic expression for her lack of independence, her inability to change her circumstances, and that the turns of phrase, 'not being able to make any headway', 'having no support', and so on, formed the bridge for this new act of conversion. I will attempt to back up this conception with other examples.

Conversion on the basis of simultaneity, when an associative connection is already present, seems to make the least claims on the hysterical disposition; conversion by symbolization, on the other hand, seems to require a higher degree of hysterical modification, as can be demonstrated by the case of Fräulein Elisabeth, although not until the later stage of her hysteria. I observed the finest examples of symbolization in the case of Frau Cäcilie M., which I may say was my most difficult and most instructive case of hysteria. I have already indicated that, unfortunately, it is not possible to give a detailed reproduction of this case history.

Frau Cäcilie was suffering, among other things, from an extremely violent facial neuralgia, which would appear suddenly two to three times a year, last for five to ten days, defy every kind of therapy, and then stop as if it had been cut off. It was limited to the second and third branch of one trigeminal, and since there was undoubtedly uratosis and because a not altogether clear case of 'rheumatismus acutus' played a certain role in the patient's history, taking it to be gouty neuralgia seemed plausible enough. This view was shared by the consultant doctors who were able to see every attack; the neuralgia was to be treated with the customary methods – electric brushing, alkaline water, laxatives – but remained unaffected throughout, until it chose to make room for a new symptom. In previous years – the neuralgia was fifteen years old – her teeth had been blamed for sustaining this neuralgia; they were condemned to extraction and one fine day saw the execution of seven of the culprits under anaesthetic. Not that this was so easily done. The teeth were so firmly embedded that the roots of most of them had to be left behind. This cruel operation was completely unsuccessful, both in the short and long term. The neuralgia then raged on for months. The dentist was summoned at each attack of neuralgia, even when I was treating her; on every occasion he would declare that he had found diseased roots and set to work, but would usually be interrupted after a short while, for the neuralgia would suddenly stop and with it the demand for the dentist. In the intervals the teeth didn't hurt at all. One day, just as an attack was raging yet again, I was summoned by the patient to give a hypnotic treatment: I set a very forceful ban on the pains and from that moment on they stopped. It was then that I began to harbour doubts as to whether this neuralgia was genuine.

About a year after this successful cure by hypnosis, the state of Frau Cäcilie's illness took a new and surprising turn. Conditions suddenly appeared that were different from those that had been characteristic of the last few years, but after some reflection the patient explained that she had had all of these conditions once before, and indeed that they had been scattered throughout the period of her long illness (thirty years). What then unfolded really was a surprising wealth of hysterical attacks, which the patient was able to locate correctly in her past, and soon even the trains of thought that determined the sequence of these attacks and were often very entangled could be made out. It was like a series of pictures with explanatory texts. Pitres must have had something like this in mind when he put forward his *Délire ecmnésique*. The way in which this kind of hysterical condition belonging to the past was reproduced was extremely curious. There first emerged, when the patient was feeling perfectly well, a pathological mood of a particular tone, which the patient would regularly fail to recognize and which would be attributed to a trivial event of the last few hours. Then, as her consciousness dulled, the hysterical symptoms ensued – hallucinations, pains, cramps, long declamations; following which, in conclusion, an experience from the past emerged as a hallucination, which made it possible to explain her initial mood and to determine the current symptoms. With this last piece of the attack, lucidity was restored, her troubles disappeared as if by magic, and she felt well again – until the next attack, half a day later. I was usually sent for at the height of the condition, would induce the hypnosis, call forth the reproduction of the traumatic experience, and hasten the end of the attack by artificial means. In going through several hundred of these cycles with the patient I acquired the most instructive information about how hysterical symptoms are determined. Moreover, it was this curious case that I observed jointly with Breuer that was the immediate reason for the publication of our 'Preliminary Statement'.

In this connection we finally came to the reproduction of the facial neuralgia, which I had treated myself when it occurred as an attack. I was curious whether a psychical cause would be forthcoming here. When I tried to call forth the traumatic scene, the patient saw herself transported to a time of great emotional sensitivity towards her husband, reported a conversation that she had had with him and an observation on his part that she had taken to be deeply offensive, then suddenly she grabbed her cheek, cried aloud in pain, and said, 'That was like a slap in the face.' – At this, both the pain and the attack were over.

There was no doubt that this was an instance of symbolization; she had felt that she really had received the slap in the face. Now this raises the question, how might the sensation of a 'slap in the face' have been externalized as a neuralgia of the trigeminal nerve, restricted to the second and third branches, and heightened when opening the mouth and chewing (not talking!).

The following day the neuralgia was there again, save that this time it could be solved by the reproduction of another scene, whose content was likewise a supposed insult. So it went on for nine days; what seemed to transpire was that the offences of many years, particularly those that were verbal, had brought on new attacks of this facial neuralgia by means of symbolization.

But at last we managed to penetrate as far as the very first attack of neuralgia (of more than fifteen years previously). Here I did not find any instance of symbolization, but rather a conversion by means of simultaneity: at the sight of something painful a reproach arose within her, causing her to force back another set of thoughts. It was, then, a case of conflict and defence; the genesis of the neuralgia at this moment could not be explained any further unless one assumed that she had been suffering from slight toothache or facial pains, and this was not improbable as she was in the first months of her first pregnancy at precisely this time.

So the explanation turned out to be that this neuralgia had become the marker of a specific psychical excitation by the usual means of conversion, but that it could, thereafter, be roused by associative echoes from her mental life and by conversion through symbolization – the same behaviour, in fact, that we found in Fräulein Elisabeth v. R.

I will introduce a second example to illustrate the efficacy of symbolization in other circumstances. At a certain time, Frau Cäcilie was plagued by a severe pain in her right heel, with shooting pains at every step making it impossible for her to walk. The analysis led us to a time when the patient was at a sanatorium abroad. She had stayed in her room in bed for a week and should then have been taken by the doctor to her first communal meal. The pain had arisen at that moment when the patient took his arm to leave the room; it disappeared during the reproduction of this scene, when the patient uttered the following phrase: she said that at the time she had been gripped by the fear that she might not be able to *'find herself on a right footing'* in this unfamiliar company.

Now, this appears to be a conclusive, almost comic example of the genesis of hysterical symptoms through symbolization by means of verbal expression. Yet closer inspection of the circumstances suggests that a different view might be favourable. The patient was, at that time, suffering above all from pains in her feet; she had remained in bed for so long because of her foot pains; and all that can be claimed is that the fear that had seized her as she took her first steps sought out from among the various pains present at this same time the one that was suitable as a symbol, in the right heel, so as to develop it into a psychical pain and help it to acquire a particular persistence.

While the mechanism of symbolization appears to be demoted to second place in these examples – this is certainly the rule – I have other examples at my disposal that seem to prove the genesis of hysterical symptoms through symbolization alone. One of the finest of them, again referring to Frau Cäcilie, is as follows. She was lying in bed – she was fifteen at the time – watched over by her strict grandmother. Suddenly the child let out a cry; she had a piercing pain in her forehead between her eyes, which then lasted for weeks. In the analysis of this pain, which was reproduced after almost thirty years, she reported that her grandmother had looked at her so 'penetratingly' that her gaze had pushed deep into her brain. She was, in fact, frightened of being regarded suspiciously by the old woman. On telling me this thought she broke out laughing and the pain was over again. In this instance I can find nothing save the mechanism of symbolization, which is in a sense placed midway between the mechanism of *autosuggestion* and that of *conversion*.

My observation of Frau Cäcilie M. gave me nothing less than the opportunity to draw up a collection of symbolizations of this kind. A whole set of physical sensations, which are normally regarded as being transmitted organically, had, in her case, a psychical origin or, at least, came with a psychical interpretation. A certain series of her experiences were accompanied by a stabbing pain in the area of the heart. ('It made my heart bleed.') The pain that occurs in hysteria as of nails being driven into the head could in her case be unambiguously resolved as a pain related to thinking ('Something is stuck in my mind'), and was in fact cleared up whenever the problem in question had been cleared up. The feeling of the hysterical aura in the throat was paralleled by the thought, 'I have to swallow that', whenever she had been offended and this feeling arose. There was a whole series of sensations and ideas running in parallel, in which sometimes the sensation would awaken the idea as an interpretation of it, sometimes the idea would create the sensation by symbolization, and not infrequently did the question of which of the two elements had been the primary one remain unresolved.

I have not been able to discover such an extensive application of symbolization in any other patient. True, Frau Cäcilie M. was an unusually gifted person, in particular artistically, whose highly developed sense of form was expressed in some perfectly beautiful poems. Still, I maintain that it is not as singular and arbitrary as one would think for the hysteric to use symbolization to create a somatic expression for the affectively marked idea. In taking the verbal expression literally – feeling the 'heart bleeding' and the 'slap in the face' when spoken to in a wounding way as a real event – she is not practising some kind of witty verbal misuse, but simply reviving the sensations to which the expression owes its justification. How else would we come to say of someone who has been offended 'it made his heart bleed' if the offence were not in fact accompanied by a precordial sensation that could be interpreted in this way and were not recognizable by this sensation? Is it so unlikely that the expression 'to swallow something', applied to an insult that has gone unanswered, really comes from the sensations of innervation that appear in the throat if one stops oneself from speaking and prevents oneself from reacting to the insult? All of these sensations and innervations belong to the 'expression of emotions', which, as Darwin has taught us, is made up of actions that were in origin meaningful and served a purpose. They may now for the most part have been so much weakened that their verbal expression seems to be a figurative translation, yet it is likely that all this was at one time literally meant, and hysteria is right to express its stronger innervations by restoring the original meaning of the words. Indeed, it is perhaps wrong to say that it creates these kinds of sensation by symbolization; it may be that it has not taken linguistic usage as its model at all, but that both hysteria and linguistic usage draw from a common source.[11]

(1895)

Notes

1. (A hypochondriac, someone afflicted with anxiety neurosis.)
2. It will transpire that I was mistaken in this.
3. 'Die Abwehrneuropsychosen' [The Neuro-Psychoses of Defence'], *Neurologisches Zentralblatt*, 1 June 1894 [*Standard Edition*, vol. III].
4. I cannot exclude the possibility, but nor can I prove for a fact, that these pains, which principally affected the thigh, were *neurasthenic* in nature.
5. I was once astonished to learn that a 'deferred abreaction' – following on from impressions other than those of nursing – can form the content of an otherwise puzzling neurosis. Such was the case of Fräulein Mathilde H., a pretty nineteen-year-old girl, who had a partial paralysis of the legs when I first saw her, but who came for treatment months later because of a change in her character: she had grown so depressed that she had lost her appetite for life and become inconsiderate towards her mother, irritable and unapproachable. Taken in its entirety, the picture of this patient did not allow me to assume this to be an ordinary case of melancholy. She could very easily be put into a state of deep somnambulism, and I made use of this peculiar characteristic of hers to impart commands and suggestions to her on every occasion. She would listen to these in her deep sleep and

accompany them with copious tears, but otherwise very little in her condition
was changed. Under hypnosis one day she became talkative and informed
me that the cause of her depression was the breaking off, several months
previously, of her engagement. Closer acquaintance with her fiancé had
brought more and more things to light that her mother and she found
undesirable; on the other hand, the material advantages of the union had
been too palpable for it to be easy to decide to break it off: so both of them
had wavered for a long time, she herself had ended up in a state of listless
indecision, allowing everything to wash over her, and in the end her mother
spoke the decisive 'no' for her. A little while later it was as if she had woken
from a dream and in her mind she began assiduously to attend to the
decision that had already been passed and to weigh up the pros and cons,
and this process was still going on in her. She was living in that time of
doubt; each day she experienced the mood and thoughts that would have
suited that day in the past – so too, the only grounds for her irritability with
her mother lay in the circumstances pertaining at that time – and alongside
this mental activity her present life seemed to her nothing but an illusory
existence, as if it were something she had dreamt. – I did not manage to
get the girl to speak again. I continued to give my words of advice and
encouragement during her deep somnambulism, saw her burst into tears
each time without ever giving me an answer; then one day, roughly on the
anniversary of her engagement, the whole state of depression was over, and
this was credited to me as a highly successful cure by hypnosis.

6. Unlike hypnoid hysteria where the content of the separate psychical
group would never have been present in the consciousness of the self.

7. I have witnessed another case in which a contraction of the masseters
made it impossible for a singer to practise her art. Unfortunate family
circumstances had obliged the young woman to take to the stage. She was
in Rome singing for an audition in a state of great excitement, when suddenly
she had the sensation that she could not close her opened mouth; she fell
to the ground in a faint. The doctor who was fetched pressed her jaws
together with all his might; but from then on the patient was incapable of
moving her jaws any more than a finger-width apart from each other and
had to give up her newly chosen profession. Years later, when she came to
be treated by me, the causes of that excitement were evidently long since
finished with, for a massage under light hypnosis was sufficient to open her
mouth wide. Since then the lady has sung in public.

8. [*Addition 1924*:] Here, too, it was in reality her father, not her uncle.

9. [Freud's text gives these two variants on the patient's name.]

10. Though perhaps spinal-neurasthenic?

11. In conditions of more profound psychical modification there is clearly also a symbolic version in sensory images and sensations of more artificial turns of speech. Frau Cäcilie M. went through a period in which her every thought was transposed into a hallucination which frequently demanded a great deal of ingenuity to solve. During this time, she complained to me that she was being troubled by a hallucination that her two doctors – Breuer and I – were hanging from *two* trees that were close to one another in the garden. The hallucination disappeared after the analysis had uncovered the following course of events: the evening before, Breuer had refused her request for a specific medicament and he had turned her away; she then set her hopes on me, but found me just as hard-hearted. She was furious at both of us for this and in her anger thought: There is nothing to choose between these two, one is the *pendant* of the other.

III

Theoretical Issues

(Breuer)

In the 'Preliminary Statement' that forms the introduction to this study we set out the views to which our observations led us, and I believe that we can, in the main, stand by them. But the 'Preliminary Statement' is so short and concise that for the most part we could give only an intimation of our thoughts. Now that the case histories have provided evidence for our views, it may be permissible to set them out in greater detail. Even here, of course, we should not and indeed cannot deal with 'hysteria in its entirety', but we may give a somewhat closer, clearer and indeed more restricted discussion of those points that were not sufficiently substantiated or were given too little emphasis in the 'Preliminary Statement'.

In the course of these inquiries little will be said about the brain and nothing at all about molecules. Psychical processes should be treated in the language of psychology; indeed, it really is not possible to do otherwise. If we chose to say 'excitation of the cortex' instead of 'idea', then the former would be meaningful to us only in as much as we see the old friend through the disguise and tacitly reinstate the 'idea'. For while ideas are constantly the objects of our experience and familiar to us in their every nuance, 'excitation of the cortex' is more of a postulate, an object that we hope to understand in the future. This substituting of terms seems to be a pointless masquerade.

I hope, then, that the reader will forgive the almost exclusive use of psychological terms. I have one more demand that I want to make in advance on the reader's patience. If a science is progressing swiftly, thoughts that were at first spoken by individuals quickly become common property. No one, then, who tries to put forward his views on hysteria and its psychical foundation today, can avoid repeating much of what others have thought and that has, precisely, passed from being individual to common property. It is almost impossible always to be able to acknowledge who first voiced these ideas and there is also the real danger that one considers as a product of one's own what has already been said by others. And so I hope it will be excused if few quotations are used here and if no strict differentiation is made between what is our own and what is the work of others. Originality is the least claim in what is to be put forward over the following pages.

1 *Are All Hysterical Phenomena Ideogenic?*

In the 'Preliminary Statement' we spoke about the psychical mechanism of 'hysterical phenomena' and not that of 'hysteria' because we did not want to claim that this mechanism or the psychical theory of hysterical symptoms has unlimited validity. We do not believe that all manifestations of hysteria come into being in the way that we have detailed, nor do we believe that all are *ideogenic*, that is, determined by ideas. In this we differ from Möbius,[1] who in 1888 proposed the definition: 'All pathological manifestations caused by ideas are hysterical.' This proposition was subsequently refined to the effect that only some of the manifestations of the illness correspond in content to the ideas causing them, namely those engendered by the suggestion of a second party or by auto-suggestion, as, for example, when the idea of not being able to move one's arm causes it to be paralysed. Another group of hysterical phenomena, while caused by ideas, do not correspond to them in terms of content, as, for example, when in one of our observations the paralysis of the arm is engendered by the sight of snake-like objects.

In giving this definition, Möbius is not merely endorsing a change in nomenclature, so that henceforth only those manifestations of the illness caused by ideas, the ideogenic phenomena, would be termed hysterical; rather, it is his opinion that all hysterical symptoms are ideogenic. 'Because ideas are very frequently the cause of the mani-festations of hysteria, we believe that this is always the case.' He calls this an inference by analogy; I would prefer to call it a generaliz-ation, the justification for which must first be investigated.

Clearly, before any discussion can take place we need to establish what is understood by hysteria. I take hysteria to be a clinical picture that has been discovered empirically and stems from observation, in just the same way as tubercular pulmonary phthisis. Clinical pictures like this that have been empirically established are made clearer, deeper and more comprehensible as our knowledge progresses; but they should not and indeed cannot be abolished by it. Aetiological research has shown that the various constituent processes of pulmon-ary phthisis are determined by various causes – tuberculosis by *bacillus Kochii*; the disintegration of tissue, the formation of cavities, and septic fever, all by other microbes. Nevertheless, tubercular phthisis remains a clinical unity and it would be incorrect to abolish it by attributing only the 'specifically tubercular' changes – that is, the changes in the tissue determined by Koch's bacillus – to it and separating these from the other changes. In the same way, the clinical unity of hysteria must be maintained even if it emerges that its phenomena are determined by various causes, some coming into being by way of a psychical mechanism, others without a mechanism of this kind.

It is my conviction that this really is the case. Only a number of hysterical phenomena are ideogenic and accepting Möbius's defi-nition means tearing apart the clinical unity of hysteria and indeed the unity of one and the same symptom in one and the same patient.

An inference that is completely analogous to Möbius's inference by analogy might proceed as follows: 'Because ideas and perceptions very frequently give rise to erections, we assume that they alone do so and that even peripheral stimuli trigger this vasomotor process only by a detour through the psyche.' We know that this would be wrong and yet this conclusion would be founded on at least as many facts as is Möbius's proposition regarding hysteria. To take the analogy with a great number of physiological processes, such as the secretion of saliva or tears, variations in the action of the heart, and so on, it is possible and plausible to assume that the same process can equally well be triggered by ideas as by peripheral or other non-psychical stimuli. The opposite needs to be proved and we are still very far short of that. Indeed, it seems certain that many phenomena termed hysterical are not caused by ideas alone.

Let us consider a quite everyday case. A woman may, whenever she undergoes an intense emotion, produce a patchy, then confluent erythema on her neck, breast and face. This is determined by ideas and so, according to Möbius, it is a hysterical phenomenon. Yet the same erythema may appear, albeit to a lesser extent, when the skin is irritated, touched and so on. This would not be hysterical. So what is without doubt a perfectly unified phenomenon is on one occasion hysterical and on another not. It is questionable whether this, the erythema of the vasomotors, should in any case be counted as a specifically hysterical manifestation, or if it would not be better classified as a simple 'nervosism'. But according to Möbius, this disintegration of a unified process would in any case necessarily occur and only the affectively determined erythema would be termed hysterical.

The hysterical pains that are of such great practical importance behave in exactly the same way. There is no doubt that these are often determined directly by ideas; they are 'pain-hallucinations'. On somewhat closer examination, it appears that for the hallucinations to develop it is not enough that the idea be very vivid; rather, a particular, abnormal state of the apparatuses that conduct and feel pain is necessary, as is the abnormal excitability of the vasomotors in the development of an affective erythema. The word 'pain-hallucination' undoubtedly gives the most succinct description of the nature of this neuralgia, but it also compels us to transfer onto it the views that we have formed on hallucinations in general. This is not the place to enter into a more detailed discussion of these views. I declare myself to be of the opinion that the 'idea', the memory-image alone, without any excitation of the apparatus of perception, never, even at its most vivid and intense, achieves the character of objective existence that distinguishes hallucinations.[2]

This is true of sensory hallucinations and still more so of pain-hallucinations. For it does not seem to be possible for a healthy person to endow the memory of a physical pain with even the degree of vividness, the distant approximation to the real sensation, which can, after all, be attained by optical and acoustic memory-images. Even in the normal hallucinatory state of someone who is healthy – that is, in sleep – pains are, I believe, never dreamt unless a real sensation of pain is present. The 'regressive' excitation that emanates from the organ of memory and acts on the perceptual apparatus by means of ideas is then in the normal course of things more difficult in the case of pain than in that of visual or aural sensations. The great ease with which pain-hallucinations arise in hysteria must be posited as an abnormal excitability of the apparatus that senses pain.

This excitability, then, does not only appear when aroused by ideas but also when aroused by peripheral stimuli, in just the same way as the erythema of the vasomotors considered above.

It is a matter of everyday observation that in people with normal nerves pathological processes that are not in themselves painful cause peripheral pains in other organs; as, for example, headaches caused by relatively insignificant changes in the nose and sinuses, neuralgias of the intercostal and brachial nerves by changes in the heart and so on. If the abnormal excitability that we had to assume as the precondition of pain-hallucinations is present in a patient, then it is, so to speak, at the disposal of the aforementioned irradiations. The irradiations that occur, too, in those not of a nervous disposition become more intense and are formed in a way only to be found in those with nervous illnesses but based in fact on the same mechanism. Thus I believe ovarian neuralgia to be dependent on states of the genital apparatus. That it is transmitted psychically would have to be proven and the fact that this pain, like any other, can be engendered in hypnosis as a hallucination, or that ovarian neuralgia may have a psychical origin, does not supply this proof. It arises, just like the erythema or any of the normal secretions, from psychical as well as purely somatic causes. Should we then term only the first kind hysterical – those pains that we know to have a psychical origin? In that case we would have to exclude ovarian neuralgia as

Studies in Hysteria

it is commonly observed from the complex of hysterical symptoms and this is hardly appropriate.

If a joint experiences a slight trauma, following which a severe neurosis of that joint develops, there is bound to be a psychical element to this process – the concentration of attention on the injured part that increases the excitability of the affected nerve-tracks; but this can hardly be expressed by saying that the hyperalgia is determined by ideas.

The same is true of the pathological diminution of sensation. It is thoroughly unproven and improbable that general analgesia or analgesia of individual parts of the body without anaesthesia is caused by ideas. And even were Binet and Janet's discovery that hemi-anaesthesia is determined by a peculiar psychical state – the splitting of the psyche – to be fully confirmed, this would be a psychogenic phenomenon, not an ideogenic one, and therefore, according to Möbius, should not be termed hysterical.

If, therefore, a large number of characteristic hysterical phenomena cannot be taken as ideogenic, then it seems right to limit Möbius's proposition. We do not say 'Pathological manifestations that are caused by ideas are hysterical', but simply that *very many hysterical phenomena, probably more than we know of today, are ideogenic*. But the common and fundamental pathogenic change, which enables ideas as well as non-psychological stimuli to have a pathogenic effect, is an abnormal excitability of the nervous system.[3] The degree to which this itself is psychical in origin is another question.

Only a certain number of hysterical phenomena may, then, be ideogenic, yet it is precisely these that might specifically be termed hysterical, and the investigation of these phenomena, the uncovering of their psychical origin, constitutes the most significant recent progress in the theory of the disorder. The further question then arises: How do these phenomena come into being – what is their 'psychical mechanism'?

In terms of this question the two groups of ideogenic symptoms differentiated by Möbius behave very differently. Those symptoms in which the content of the pathological phenomenon corresponds to the idea that is the cause of excitation are relatively comprehensible and transparent. If the idea of hearing a voice does not just, as in a healthy person, make it quietly discernible in the 'inner ear', but rather, through hallucination, makes it perceptible as a real objective auditory sensation, this corresponds to familiar phenomena of healthy life (dreams) and is quite comprehensible under the assumption of abnormal excitability. We know that in the case of every voluntary movement it is the idea of the result to be obtained that triggers the corresponding contraction of the muscle; it is not inconceivable that the idea that this is impossible should hinder the movement. (Suggestive paralysis.)

It is a different matter in the case of those phenomena that have no logical connection with the precipitating idea. (For these, too, analogies can be found in normal life, as, for example, blushing with shame and so on.) How do these come into being? Why does an idea in someone who is sick trigger one particular quite irrational movement or hallucination that does not correspond to it in the slightest?

In the 'Preliminary Statement' we felt that we were able to say something about this causal connection on the basis of our observations. In our exposition we introduced and used the concept *'of excitation which drains away or has to be abreacted'* without further discussion. But this concept, which is of fundamental importance for our topic and for the theory of neuroses in general, seems to demand and deserve a more thoroughgoing investigation. Before I proceed to this I must apologize for revisiting the fundamental problems of the nervous system. There is always something oppressive about this kind of 'descent to the mothers', but the attempt to dig up the roots of a phenomenon is always bound to lead irresistibly to fundamental problems that cannot be avoided. With this in mind, I hope that the abstruse nature of the following observations will not be judged too harshly.

2 *Intracerebral Tonic Excitation – Affects*

A

We know two extreme states of the nervous system – dreamless sleep and wide-awakeness. States of diminishing clarity of every degree form the passage from one to the other. What interests us here is not the question of the purpose and physical basis of sleep (chemical or vasomotor conditions), but that of the fundamental difference between the two states.

We can say nothing directly about the deepest, dreamless sleep, precisely because all observations and experiences are excluded from this state of complete unconsciousness. But we do know that in the neighbouring state of dream-sleep we intend to make voluntary movements, to speak, to walk, and so on, but that this does not voluntarily trigger the relevant muscular contractions as it does when we are awake. We know too that sensory stimuli may be perceived (as they often enter dreams), but not apperceived, that is, they do not become conscious perceptions. Again, emergent ideas do not, as when we are awake, actualize all the ideas that are connected with them and present in our potential consciousness; indeed, large numbers of them are not excited (as, for example, if we talk to someone who has died, without remembering their death). Even incompatible ideas can exist simultaneously without inhibiting each other, as they would when we are awake. The association that ensues is therefore inadequate and incomplete. We may assume, then, that in deepest sleep this removal of connections between the psychical elements is even more extensive and, indeed, complete.

By contrast, when we are wide awake every act of will triggers the corresponding movement, sensory impressions become perceptions, ideas are associated with everything held in potential consciousness. The brain then functions as a unity with complete internal connections.

We are perhaps simply paraphrasing these facts when we say that in sleep excitation of the psychical elements (cortical cells?) cannot pass along the paths of connection and conduction in the brain, but that when we are awake they are completely passable.

The existence of these paths of conduction in two different states can only be understood by assuming that when we are awake they are in a state of tonic excitation (Exner's 'intercellular tetanus'), that this tonic *intracerebral excitation* determines their conductive capacity, and that it is precisely the diminution and disappearance of the excitation that produces the state of sleep.

We should not picture a cerebral path of conduction as a telephone wire that is excited electrically only when operating (which, in this case, means transmitting a signal), but rather as if it were one of those telephone lines along which there is a constant flow of galvanic current and which cannot be excited if this current dwindles. Alternatively, we might do better to think about an electrical system with many different branches for supplying light and transmitting motor power, a system that is required to make each lamp and machine operate simply by establishing a contact. For this to be possible, that is, for everything to be ready for work, a certain degree of tension must be present throughout the entire network of conductors, even when the system is at rest, and to this end the dynamo has to expend a certain amount of energy. Similarly, a degree of excitation is present in the conducting paths of the brain when it is resting, but awake and ready for work.[4]

What favours this picture is that simply being awake, even without productive activity, is tiring and engenders the need to sleep; it necessitates the consumption of energy in itself.

Let us imagine a person in a state of tense expectation that does not, however, relate to any one sensory field. In this instance the brain is at rest, but ready for activity. We may rightly suppose that the conducting paths of this brain are all set at the maximum of their conductive capacity, i.e. in a state of tonic excitation. It is significant that when talking about this state we in fact call it 'tension'. We know from experience what a strain this state is and how tiring, although no actual motor or psychical work is done in it.

This is an exceptional state which, precisely because of the great consumption of energy, cannot be tolerated for long. But even the normal state of being wide awake demands a measure of intracerebral excitation that varies between limits that are not too far apart; all the gradations of wakefulness down to the point of sleepiness and real sleep are accompanied by correspondingly lower degrees of excitation.

When actually performing work the brain does, of course, demand a greater consumption of energy than when it is simply ready for work (in the same way that the electrical system cited for the purposes of comparison above has to allow a greater quantity of electrical energy to flow into the conductors when many lamps or appliances are switched on). When functioning normally no more energy is made available than will immediately be consumed by the activity. The brain, however, behaves like an electrical system of limited capacity and cannot, for example, produce great quantities of light and mechanical work at the same time. If power is being transmitted little energy will be available for lighting, and vice versa. So we see that intense muscular effort makes it impossible for us to engage in sustained reflection, or that concentrating one's attention on one sensory field reduces the capacity of other cerebral organs, that, in sum, the brain works with a varying but limited quantity of energy.

The non-uniform distribution of energy is probably determined by 'attentional breaching' (Exner) in that the conductive capacity of the paths in use is heightened and that of others is reduced, so that in the working brain the 'intracerebral tonic excitation' too is not uniformly distributed.[5]

We wake up someone who is asleep, that is, we suddenly raise the quantum of their tonic intracerebral excitation, by bringing a vivid sensory stimulus to bear on them. Whether changes in the circulation of the blood to the brain are significant links in the causal chain here, whether the vessels are enlarged primarily by the stimulus, or whether this is the consequence of excitation of the cerebral elements, has yet to be established. But what is certain is that the state of excitation that penetrates through the gateway of one of the senses spreads from that point throughout the brain, is diffused, and raises the breaching capacity of all the paths of conduction.

It is still not in the least clear, of course, how spontaneous awakening occurs, whether one and the same part of the brain is always first to enter the state of waking excitation that then spreads from this point, or whether sometimes one and sometimes another group of elements assumes the role of waking the others.

Yet waking up spontaneously, which occurs even in complete dark and quiet without external stimuli, proves that the generation of energy is based on the vital processes of the cerebral elements themselves.

If it is not stimulated a muscle will remain still, even if it has rested for a long time and accumulated the maximum tensile force. This is not the case with the cerebral elements. We are no doubt right in assuming that they regain their previous state during sleep and accumulate tensile force. When this happens to a certain degree and, so to speak, reaches a certain level, the surplus will flow off along the paths of conduction, breaching them and producing the intracerebral excitation of the waking state.

It is instructive to observe the same process in waking life. When the brain is awake but has remained inactive for a lengthy period, having not exercised any function that would transform tensile force into living energy, then the need and impulse for activity set in. Long motor rest creates both the need for movement (as with the aimless running around of animals in cages) and a feeling of distress if this need cannot be satisfied. Lack of sensory stimuli, darkness, complete silence, all become agonizing; mental repose, a lack of perceptions, ideas and associative activity all engender the torment of boredom. These unpleasurable feelings correspond to an 'excitement', an increase in normal intracerebral excitation.

Even when at rest, then, the fully restored cerebral elements also free up a certain degree of energy which, if not put to functional use, increases the intracerebral excitation. This engenders a feeling of 'unpleasure'. Feelings such as this always arise when the organism has a need that cannot be satisfied. Since those discussed here diminish whenever the surplus quantum of excitation that has been freed up is put to functional use, we can conclude that this removal of surplus excitation is a need of the organism, and this is where we first encounter the fact that there exists in the organism a *'tendency to maintain intracerebral excitation at a constant'* (Freud).

A surplus of excitation is a nuisance and a burden and so the drive to expend it arises. If expenditure is not possible by means of sensory or ideational activity, then the surplus flows off into aimless motor action, pacing up and down and so on. We will come across this later too as the most common means of discharging excessive tensions.

It is well known that there is a great variation between individuals in this respect: the great differences between lively people and those who are lethargic and torpid; those who 'cannot sit still' and those who have an 'innate talent for lounging around'; the intellectually agile and those who are dull and can bear unlimited periods of intellectual rest. These variations, which make up a person's 'intellectual temperament', are certainly based on profound differences in the nervous system – on the extent to which the cerebral elements that are functionally dormant free up energy.

We spoke of the organism's tendency to maintain cerebral excitation at a constant; but such a tendency is comprehensible only if we can appreciate the need that is fulfilled by it. We can understand the tendency in warm-blooded animals to maintain the mean temperature at a constant, because we know by experience that this is optimal for the functioning of the organs. And we make a similar assumption about the constancy of the water content of the blood, and so on. I believe that one can assume similarly that there is an *optimum* degree of intracerebral excitation. At this level of tonic excitation the brain is accessible to all exterior stimuli, the reflexes are breached, but only to the extent of normal reflex activity, the fund of ideas is capable of being aroused and is open to association in that mutual relationship between individual ideas that corresponds to a clear and composed state of mind: this is the state of optimum readiness for work. The relations are already altered by the uniform heightening of tonic excitation that constitutes 'expectation'. This makes the organism hyperaesthetic towards sensory stimuli, which quickly become distressing, and it heightens the reflex excitability beyond what is useful (liability to fright). This state is, of course, useful for many purposes and situations; but when it occurs spontaneously, without preconditions such as these, it does not improve our efficiency, but rather impairs it. In everyday life we call this 'being nervous'. But in by far the greater number of forms in which excitation is heightened we are dealing with non-uniform over-excitation, which is directly detrimental to efficiency. We describe this as 'excitement'. Far from being inconceivable, it is in fact in line with other of the organism's regulative procedures that it should strive to retain optimum excitation and to regain it once it has been exceeded.

I should like, at this point, to return to the comparison with an electrical lighting system. Even the tension in the conducting network of a system such as this has an optimum level; if this is exceeded, then the functioning can easily be impaired in that, for example, the filaments quickly burn through. The damage done to the system itself by a fault in the insulation or a 'short circuit' will be the subject of later discussion.

B

Our language, the result of many generations' experience, distinguishes with admirable subtlety those forms and degrees of heightened excitation that are still useful to mental activity because they raise the free energy of all cerebral functions uniformly, from those which influence them in a non-uniform way by in part raising, in part inhibiting the psychical functions.

Linguistically, then, the first are termed stimulation or 'incitement', the second 'excitement'. An interesting conversation, tea or coffee, incites; an argument or a considerable dose of alcohol, excites. Whereas incitement wakens only the drive to put increased excitation to functional use, excitement seeks to discharge itself in more or less violent processes that either border on or really are pathological. Excitement constitutes the psychical-physical basis of the affects, and these will be discussed below. But I must first touch briefly on the physiological and endogenous causes of increases in excitation.

These are, in the first instance, the great physiological needs and drives of the organism, the hunger for oxygen, food and water. Since the excitement that they set off is bound up with specific sensations and objectives, it cannot be observed in as pure a form as can that increase of excitation described above that arises solely when the cerebral elements are dormant. It always has its own particular tone. But it is unmistakable in the anxious excitement of dyspnoea, as it is in the restlessness of the starving.

The increase in excitation that issues from these sources is determined by the chemical alteration of the cerebral elements themselves, which are lacking either in oxygen, tensile force or water; it is discharged along preformed motor paths that lead to the satisfaction of the need that triggered it. Dyspnoea leads to breathing with effort, hunger and thirst to the seeking and securing of food and water. The principle of the constancy of excitation in reality hardly comes into effect as regards this kind of excitement; for the interests served by the increase in excitation are of far greater importance for the organism than the restoration of normal conditions of functioning in the brain. It is true that animals at the zoo are seen to run excitedly to and fro before feeding time; but this may well be the remains of the preformed motor activity of looking for food, which has now become redundant in their captivity, rather than a means of freeing the nervous system of excitement.

If the chemical structure of the nervous system has been permanently altered by a continuous supply of foreign substances, then a lack of these substances will cause states of excitement as does a lack of normal nutrients in a healthy person; such is the excitement of *abstinence* from narcotics.

The transition from these endogenous increases in excitation to the psychical affects in the narrower sense is provided by sexual excitation and sexual affect. Sexuality appears at puberty in the first of these forms as a vague, indefinite, aimless increase in excitation. In later development (in the normal course of things) this endogenous increase in excitation caused by the functioning of the sex glands becomes firmly connected with the perception or idea of the opposite sex and, of course, with the idea of a particular individual, when the wonderful phenomenon of falling in love occurs. This takes over the entire quantity of excitation that has been freed up by the sexual drive, so becoming an 'affective idea'. In other words, when the idea is actualized in consciousness it releases an increase in excitation that really originates from another source, the sex glands.

The sexual drive is certainly the most powerful source of long-persisting increases in excitation (and consequently of neuroses); the distribution of such heightened excitation throughout the nervous system is unequal in the extreme. At higher degrees of intensity the course of ideas is disturbed and the relative value of ideas altered; during sexual orgasm thought is almost totally extinguished.

Perception – the psychical working out of sense-impressions – also suffers; an animal that is otherwise timid and cautious becomes deaf and blind to danger. On the other hand, the strength of the aggressive instinct (at least in males) is intensified; peaceful animals will become dangerous until their excitation has been discharged in the motor activities of the sexual act.

C

A similar disturbance of the dynamic equilibrium of the nervous system – a non-uniform distribution of increased excitation – is what constitutes the psychical side of affects.

This is not the place to attempt to formulate either a psychology or a physiology of affects. Only one point, which is important for pathology, should come under discussion, and moreover only for ideogenic affects, for those that are called up by perceptions and ideas. (Lange[6] rightly points out that affects are almost as likely to be caused by toxic substances and, as psychiatry proves, primarily by pathological changes, as they are by ideas.)

It may, then, be taken as self-evident that all these disturbances of the psychical equilibrium that we call acute affects are accompanied by an increase in excitation. (In the case of chronic affects, such as worry and grief, i.e. protracted anxiety, there is the complication of a severe state of fatigue, in which the non-uniform distribution of excitation – and hence the disrupted equilibrium – is maintained, but its level is reduced.) But this increased excitation cannot be used in psychical activity. All strong affects impair association, the course of ideas. One becomes 'senseless' with anger or fright. Only the group of ideas that has excited the affect persists in consciousness, and it does so with the greatest intensity, thereby preventing excitement from being evened out by associative activity.

Affects that are 'active' or 'sthenic', however, even out the increased excitation by motor removal. Shouting and jumping for joy, the increased muscular tone of anger, angry words and acts of retaliation allow excitation to flow away through movement. Psychical pain discharges it in heavy breathing and acts of secretion, sobbing and crying. The fact that these reactions diminish and calm excitement is part of everyday experience. As has been noted above, we express this linguistically through phrases such as 'to cry one's eyes out' and 'to let off steam', and what is being given out is precisely the increased cerebral excitation.

Only some of these reactions – as, for example, the angry words or deeds – serve their purpose, in that they can change something about the situation. The others serve no purpose at all, or rather they have no purpose other than evening out the increased excitation and establishing a psychical equilibrium. In accomplishing this, they serve the 'tendency to maintain cerebral excitation at a constant'.

The 'asthenic' affects of fright and anxiety do not have this reactive discharge. Fright directly paralyses motility as well as association, and such is also the case with anxiety when the one reaction that would serve a purpose – running away – is prevented by the cause of the feeling of anxiety or by circumstances. The excitation of fright disappears only by being gradually evened out.

Anger has reactions appropriate to its cause. If these are impossible or inhibited, surrogates appear in their place. Angry words are themselves surrogates of this kind. But even other, quite aimless acts can function as substitutes. Whenever Bismarck had to suppress angry excitement in front of the king, he would seek relief afterwards by smashing a valuable vase to the ground. This voluntary substitution of one motor action by another corresponds exactly to the substitution of natural pain reflexes by other kinds of muscular contraction. The preformed reflex when a tooth is being removed is to push the dentist away and give a shout. But if instead we contract our arm muscles and press against the sides of the chair, we are displacing the quantum of excitation released by the pain from one muscle group to another. In the case of violent toothache that happens spontaneously and has no preformed reflex other than groaning, the excitation flows away in aimless running to and fro. Similarly, we transpose the excitation of anger from the appropriate reaction onto others and feel relieved only if it is used up by some strong motor innervation.

But if the affect is denied any of these ways of removing excitation, then the situation is the same in anger as in fright and anxiety: the intracerebral excitation undergoes an immense increase, but it is not used up in either associative or motor activity. In a normal person the disturbance will gradually even out; but in some, abnormal reactions occur and an *'abnormal expression of the emotions'* (Oppenheim) is formed.

3 *Hysterical Conversion*

I shall hardly be suspected of identifying nervous excitation with electricity if I return once more to the comparison with an electrical system. If the tension in a system of this kind becomes too high, there is the danger of breaks occurring at weak points in the insulation. Electrical phenomena then appear at abnormal points. Or, if two wires are lying next to each other, a 'short circuit' is produced. Since a permanent change is established at these points, there is always the possibility of the disturbance that is caused by it reappearing whenever the tension is sufficiently increased. An abnormal 'breaching' has taken place.

The assertion that the conditions in the nervous system are to a degree similar is quite plausible. It forms a thoroughly coherent unity, but at various points great, although not insurmountable, resistances are inserted that prevent the general and even spreading of excitation. Thus for the normal person who is awake the excitation of the ideational organs does not pass on to the organs of perception; we do not hallucinate. In the interests of the safety and efficiency of the organism, strong resistances separate the nervous apparatuses of those vital complexes of organs, such as the circulation and digestion, from the organs of ideation; their independence is preserved, they are not directly influenced by ideas. But only resistances of varying individual strength can prevent the passage of intercerebral excitation into the circulatory and digestive apparatuses: there is every degree of emotional excitability separating what is nowadays a rare ideal – the person who is quite free from 'nerves', the action of whose heart remains constant in every situation and is influenced only by the work it has to do, and who maintains a good appetite and digestion whatever danger he is in – from the 'nervous' person for whom the slightest occurrence is cause for palpitations and diarrhoea.

But in any case there are resistances in the normal person to the passage of cerebral excitation on to the vegetative organs. These correspond to the insulation of electrical cables. Under high tension, cerebral excitation breaks occur at those points that are abnormally weak and this, the excitation of the affect, passes over to the peripheral organ. There develops an 'abnormal expression of emotion'.

One of the two conditions that we have mentioned above as responsible for this has already been discussed in detail. There is a high degree of intracerebral excitation which cannot be evened out, whether by a process of ideation or by removal through motor activity, or which is too great to be dealt with in this way.

The other determining condition is an abnormal weakness of the resistances in particular paths of conduction. This may lie in the individual's original constitution (innate disposition); it can also be determined by protracted states of excitation which, as it were, loosen the structure of the nervous system and lower all resistances (disposition in puberty); or by debilitating influences, illness, undernourishment etc. (disposition due to states of exhaustion). The resistance of individual paths of conduction can be lowered by a prior illness of the organ in question, which breaches the paths to and from the brain. A diseased heart is more susceptible to the influence of an affect than a healthy one. 'I have a sounding-board in my abdomen,' I was told by a woman suffering from chronic parametritis, 'if anything happens it wakens my old pain' (disposition due to local illness).

The motor acts through which the excitation of affects is normally discharged are organized and co-ordinated, even if frequently without purpose. But excessive excitation can circumvent or break through the centres of co-ordination and flow off in elementary movements. In infants, with the exception of the respiratory act of screaming, affects produce and are expressed only through unco-ordinated muscular contractions such as arching the body and flailing about. As development continues, the musculature falls increasingly under the control of will-power and co-ordination. But opisthotonus, which represents the maximum motor effort of the body's entire musculature, and the clonic movements of flailing and thrashing about, remain the forms of reaction for the maximal excitation of the brain throughout life, whether it be for the purely physical excitation of epileptic attacks or for the discharge of maximal affects as more or less epileptoid convulsions (that is to say, the purely motor component of hysterical attacks).

Abnormal affective reactions such as these are of course part of hysteria, but they also occur outside this illness: they indicate a more or less high degree of nervousness rather than hysteria itself. One can only describe such phenomena as hysterical if they appear not as the consequences of an affect which, although of high intensity, is objectively founded, but as seemingly spontaneous manifestations of an illness. Many observations, including our own, have proved that these phenomena are based on recollections that revive the original affect. Or rather, *they would revive the affect if these very reactions had not already arisen*.

There is no doubt that a stream of ideas and recollections flows through the consciousness of anyone of a lively mind when they are psychically at rest, and these ideas are for the most part so little vivid that they leave no trace in the memory and one cannot say how association occurred. But should an idea emerge that was in origin bound up with a strong affect, then the affect will be revived to a greater or lesser degree of intensity. The 'affectively marked' idea will then enter consciousness clearly and vividly. The strength of the affect that a recollection can release varies greatly according to the extent to which it was exposed to 'erosion' by various influences. And this depends above all on the extent to which the original affect had been 'abreacted'. In the 'Preliminary Statement' we indicated the varying degrees in which, for example, the feeling of anger at being insulted can be awakened by a recollection, according to whether the insult was repaid or suffered in silence. If the psychical reflex really occurred on the original occasion, then the recollection will release a far smaller quantum of excitation.[7] If not, then the recollection will repeatedly bring to the tip of one's tongue the words of abuse that were suppressed at the time and that would have been the psychical reflex to that stimulus.

If the original affect has been discharged in an 'abnormal' rather than a normal reflex, then it too will be released again by the recollection; the excitation emitted by the affective idea is '*converted*' into a physical phenomenon (Freud).

If the breaching of this abnormal reflex is completed by frequent repetition, then it would appear so completely to exhaust the effectiveness of the releasing ideas that the affect itself either develops to only minimal strength or does not develop at all; at this point the '*hysterical conversion*' is complete. But the idea that no longer exercises any psychical effects can be overlooked by the individual or forgotten as quickly as it surfaces, as is the case with other ideas lacking in affect.

It may be easier to accept that cerebral excitation which should bring about an idea is replaced by an excitation of peripheral paths, if we remember the inverse behaviour when a preformed reflex does not take place. I shall choose an extremely trivial example, the reflex of sneezing. If a stimulus to the mucous membrane of the nose for some reason fails to release this preformed reflex, then, as is known, a feeling of excitation and tension arises. It is this excitation that cannot flow off along motor paths and that now spreads throughout the brain, inhibiting all other activities. This most banal of examples provides the schema for what happens when even the most complicated psychical reflexes fail to materialize. The excitement of the revenge drive discussed above is in essence the same; and we can even trace the process to the highest spheres of human achievement. Goethe could not get over an experience until he had resolved it in poetic activity. This, for him, was the preformed reflex of an affect, and a distressing increase in excitation persisted until it was accomplished.

The intracerebral excitation and the excitatory process in the peripheral paths are of reciprocal strengths: the former increases if and as long as a reflex is not released; it diminishes and disappears when it has been converted into peripheral nervous excitation. Similarly, then, it is quite comprehensible that no noticeable affect arises if the idea that should have given rise to it instead directly releases an abnormal reflex, into which the excitation flows off as soon as it arises. The 'hysterical conversion' is then complete; the original intracerebral excitation of the affect has been converted into the excitatory process in the peripheral paths; what was originally an affective idea no longer gives rise to the affect but only the abnormal reflex.[8]

This has allowed us to take a step further, beyond the 'abnormal expression of the emotions'. Hysterical phenomena (abnormal reflexes) do not appear to be ideogenic – even to intelligent and observant patients – because the ideas that gave rise to them are no longer affectively marked, nor are they distinguished from other ideas and recollections; they appear to be purely somatic phenomena, seemingly without any psychological roots.

What, then, determines the discharge of affective excitation, so that an abnormal reflex rather than any other kind of reflex is created? Our observations provide an answer to this question in many cases by showing that the discharge again follows the 'principle of least resistance' and occurs along those paths where the resistance has already been lowered by competing circumstances. Such is the case discussed earlier in which a specific reflex has already been breached by somatic illness: if, for example, someone often suffers from cardiac pains, these will also be brought on by strong emotions. – Or a reflex will be breached by the particular muscular innervation having been deliberately intended at the moment when the affect originally occurred: thus, with an intense feeling of fright, Anna O. (Case 1) tries to stretch her right arm to fend off the snake, but it has been paralysed by the pressure applied to it. Henceforth, tetanus of the right arm is brought on by the sight of all snake-like objects. Or she is affected and forces her eyes together in order to make out the hands of the clock – *strabismus convergens* becomes one of the reflexes of this affect, and so on.

This, then, is the effect of simultaneity, which of course also controls our normal association; every sense perception calls back into consciousness another sense perception that had originally appeared at the same time (as in the textbook example of the visual image and bleating of a sheep).

If a vivid sense impression was present at the same time as the original affect, this impression will be called up again by the revived affect and, indeed, since this is a matter of the discharge of excessive excitation, it is called up not as a memory but as a hallucination. Almost all our observations provide examples of this. Another such example is given by the case of a woman who experienced a painful emotion while she had severe toothache due to periostitis – whenever this emotion was revived, or even simply recollected, it brought on an infra-orbital neuralgia.

Such is the breaching of abnormal reflexes according to the general laws of association. Sometimes, however, and admittedly only at higher levels of hysteria, there are genuine sequences of associated ideas lying between the affect and its reflex: this is *determination through symbolism*. The connection between the affect and its reflex is often a ridiculous play on words or a sound association, but this happens only in dreamlike states in which the critical capacity is reduced and does not fall into the group of phenomena that we are considering here.

In a great number of cases the determination cannot be understood because our insight into the psychical state and our knowledge of the ideas that were current when the hysterical phenomenon arose are often severely lacking. But we can make the assumption that the process will not be entirely dissimilar from what can clearly be seen in more favourable cases.

We termed those experiences that released the original affect, and whose excitation was then converted into a somatic phenomenon, '*psychical traumas*', and the symptoms which arose in this way '*hysterical symptoms of traumatic origin*'. (The term 'traumatic hysteria' has already been allocated to phenomena that, as the consequence of physical injuries – traumas in the narrowest sense of the word – are part of the category of 'traumatic neuroses'.)

There is a perfect analogy between the genesis of hysterical phenomena that are caused by trauma and the hysterical conversion of psychical excitation that arises neither from external stimuli nor from the inhibiting of normal psychical reflexes, but from the inhibition of the course of association.

The most elementary example and paradigm for this is provided by the excitation that arises when a name does not occur to us, when we cannot solve a riddle and so on. If we are told the name or the answer to the riddle, the excitation disappears as the chain of association closes, just as it does when a chain of reflexes is closed. The strength of excitation that comes from the interruption to a series of associations is in direct proportion to the interest that this series has for us, i.e. the extent to which our will is moved by it. But since the search for a solution to the problem or such like will always involve a great deal of work, regardless of whether it is successful or not, even strong excitation will find an application and will not press to be discharged, thus never becoming pathogenic.

This does, however, occur when the course of association is inhibited because ideas of equal value are *irreconcilable*; when, for example, new thoughts come into conflict with deep-rooted complexes of ideas. Such is the torment of religious doubt to which so many succumb and to which many more succumbed in the past. Even here, however, there is a significant increase in excitation and so in psychical pain – the feeling of aversion – only when a volitional interest of the individual comes into play, if the doubter feels that his happiness or the salvation of his soul is threatened.

But this is always the case when there is a conflict between the firm complex of moral ideas that has been instilled into one and the memory of one's own actions or even simply of thoughts that are incompatible with it: such are the *pangs of conscience*. The volitional interest in taking pleasure in one's own personality and being content with it steps into action here and raises the excitation due to the inhibition of associations to the highest level. That a conflict such as this between irreconcilable ideas should have a pathogenic effect is the stuff of everyday experience. For the most part it involves ideas and processes relating to sexual life: masturbation in morally sensitive adolescents or, in a married woman who is extremely moral, the consciousness of an attraction to a stranger. Indeed, it is very often the case that the first emergence of sexual feelings and ideas is itself enough for the conflict with the deep-rooted idea of moral purity to create an extreme state of excitation.[9]

This excitation usually has psychical consequences, such as pathological depression or states of anxiety (Freud). Sometimes, however, competing circumstances will establish an abnormal somatic phenomenon into which the excitation is discharged: vomiting, for example, when the feeling of being morally sullied engenders a physical feeling of disgust, or a nervous cough (*tussis nervosa*) as in the case of Anna O. (Case 1), when moral anxiety provokes spasms of the glottis and so on.[10]

There is a normal and appropriate reaction to the excitation engendered by very vivid and irreconcilable ideas – to communicate them by speaking. We find a comically exaggerated version of the urge to do this in the story of Midas's barber, who spoke his secret aloud to the reeds; we find it, too, as one of the fundamental principles of a great historical institution – the Catholic confessional. Communication affords relief, it discharges tension even when it is not made to a priest or followed by absolution. If excitation finds that this way out is blocked, it will sometimes be converted, as is the excitation of traumatic affects, into a somatic phenomenon, and we can, as does Freud, describe the entire group of hysterical phenomena which originate in this way as *hysterical retention phenomena*.

Thus far, this exposition of the psychical mechanism by which hysterical phenomena arise is open to the criticism of schematizing the process and portraying it as simpler than it is in reality. For a healthy person who was not originally neuropathic to form a truly hysterical symptom, that is, a symptom that appears to be independent from the psyche and has a somatic existence of its own, there must *almost always be a number of competing circumstances*.

The following case may serve as an example of how complicated this process is: a twelve-year-old lad, who used to suffer from *pavor nocturnus* [night terror] and whose father suffered greatly from nerves, came home from school one day feeling unwell. He complained of difficulty swallowing and headaches. The family doctor took a sore throat to be the cause. But after several days the condition had still not improved. The boy refused to eat, vomited when he was forced to do so, dragged himself around in a tired and listless fashion, wanted to stay in bed all the time, and physically became very run down. When I saw him five weeks later he gave the impression of being a shy child who kept himself to himself, and I became convinced that the condition had a psychical foundation. When pressed he gave a trivial reason – that his father had given him a stern rebuke – which was obviously not the real grounds for his falling ill. Nor could anything be discovered from the school. I promised that I would extract the information from him later under hypnosis. But this was, in the end, unnecessary. When at one point his mother, a clever and energetic woman, upbraided him severely, he began, in floods of tears, to tell his story. On his way home from school he had gone into a urinal where a man had held out his penis to him and asked him to take it in his mouth. He had run away in utter fright, and nothing else had happened to him. But from that moment on he was ill. As soon as he had made this confession his condition improved and full health was restored. – In order to produce the phenomenon of anorexia, the difficulty in swallowing and the vomiting, several factors were necessary: his innate nervous constitution, his fright, the irruption of sexuality in its most brutal form into his childish temperament and, the determining factor, the idea of disgust. The illness persisted because of his silence, which prevented the excitation from being discharged normally.

As in this case, then, several factors must always take effect at the same time before someone who has previously been well can develop a hysterical symptom; this symptom is always, to use Freud's expression, '*overdetermined*'.

Overdetermination such as this can also be taken to include those instances when the same affect is brought on by a number of repeated causes. The patient and those around him will relate the symptom only to the last cause, but this cause will on the whole have brought to light only what had already been almost completely accomplished by other traumas.

A young girl[11] had her first hysterical attack when a cat jumped onto her shoulder in the dark and this was then followed by a series of further attacks. This seemed simply to be the effect of fright. But closer investigation revealed that this seventeen-year-old girl, who was strikingly beautiful and poorly looked after, had recently on a number of occasions been pursued – with varying degrees of brutality – and had herself been sexually excited by this. (Disposition.) A few days earlier, on this same dark stairway, she had been assaulted by a young man and had had difficulty escaping from his grasp. This was the real psychical trauma and its effect only became manifest through the cat. But in how many cases is the cat taken as a perfectly sufficient *causa efficiens*?

For a conversion such as this to be effected by repetition of the affect does not always require a number of external causes; the renewal of the affect in memory is often sufficient if this ensues immediately after the trauma, before the affect has been weakened and in rapid and frequent succession. This is sufficient if the affect is very powerful. Such is the case in traumatic hysteria, in the narrower sense of the word.

In the days following a railway accident, for example, the terrifying scene will be relived when asleep and awake, and always with the renewed feeling of fright until finally, once this time of 'psychical working out' (Charcot) or *incubation* is past, the conversion into a somatic phenomenon has taken place. (An additional factor that is at work here will be discussed later.)

In normal circumstances, however, the affective idea is immediately eroded by all of those influences touched on in the 'Preliminary Statement', influences that gradually rob it of its affective value. As it re-emerges, it causes an ever-dwindling degree of excitation, and thus the recollection loses its capacity to contribute to the production of a somatic phenomenon. The breaching of the abnormal reflex is lost and at this the *status quo ante* is restored.

The 'eroding' influences are, however, all achieved by association, thought and correction by other ideas. This correction becomes impossible when the affective idea is withdrawn from 'the circulation of association', and in these cases the idea retains its affective value in its entirety. Because the idea repeatedly releases the original affect's entire sum of excitation whenever it is renewed, the breaching of an abnormal reflex that had been initiated at the time is finally completed or, if the breaching had already been achieved, it is preserved and stabilized. The phenomenon of hysterical conversion is then fully and permanently established.

Our observations have shown us that there are two ways in which affective ideas can be excluded from association.

The first is *'defence'*, the voluntary suppression of painful ideas which a person feels are a threat to their enjoyment of life or their self-esteem. Freud has spoken about this process, which is undoubtedly of great pathological significance, in his paper 'The Neuro-Psychoses of Defence' (*Neurol. Zentralblatt*, no. 10, 1894) ['Die Abwehr-Neuropsychosen', *Standard Edition*, vol. III] and in the above case histories.

While it is true that we are not able to comprehend how an idea can be repressed from consciousness at will, we are perfectly familiar with the corresponding positive process – namely, concentrating one's attention on an idea – and are just as incapable of saying how we accomplish this.

Ideas, then, from which consciousness is diverted and which are not thought about, also escape being eroded and retain their quantity of affect undiminished.

We have, in addition, found that another kind of idea escapes being eroded by thought, not because one does not *want* to remember it, but because one is *not able* to, because the thought originally emerged and was invested with affect in states for which in waking consciousness there is amnesia, that is, in those states that are hypnotic or similar to hypnosis. These states seem to be of the utmost significance for the theory of hysteria and so to deserve a discussion of greater depth.[12]

4 *Hypnoid States*

When, in the 'Preliminary Statement', we put forward the proposition that 'the foundation and condition of hysteria is the existence of hypnoid states', we overlooked the fact that in 1890 Möbius had made exactly the same statement. 'The precondition for the (pathogenic) operation of ideas is an innate, that is, hysterical disposition on the one hand and, on the other, a particular state of mind. One can gain only a very vague idea of this state of mind. It must be similar to the hypnotic state, it has to correspond to a certain emptiness of consciousness in which no emergent idea encounters opposition from another, in which, so to speak, the throne is free to the first-comer. We know that a state such as this can be induced not only by hypnosis, but by emotional shock (fright, rage, etc.) and exhausting influences (sleeplessness, hunger, etc.).'[13]

The question that Möbius moves towards solving in this passage is that of the genesis of somatic phenomena by means of ideas. He reminds us here of the ease with which this takes place in hypnosis and maintains that affects operate in a similar manner. A detailed exposition of our somewhat different view of this operation of the affects has been given above. Hence I do not need to go any further into the difficulty that lies in Möbius's assumption that in anger there is a 'vacancy of consciousness'[14] (a state which does, of course, exist during fright and protracted anxiety), or into the more general

difficulty of drawing any kind of analogy between the state of excitation in an affect and the peaceful state of hypnosis. But later we
will return to Möbius's propositions which, in my opinion, contain
an important truth.

For us the importance of these states that resemble hypnosis –
'hypnoid' states – lies additionally and primarily in the amnesia and
in their capacity to cause the splitting of the psyche, which will be
discussed later and is of fundamental significance to 'major hysteria'.
Even today we still attribute this importance to these states. But I
must set a substantial qualification to our proposition. Conversion,
the ideogenic genesis of somatic phenomena, can also occur outside
hypnoid states, and Freud has found in the voluntary amnesia of
defence a second source, independent of hypnoid states, for the
formation of ideational complexes that are excluded from associative
circulation. Even with this qualification, however, I maintain that
hypnoid states are the cause and condition of many, indeed most, of
the major and complex hysterias.

Genuine auto-hypnoses are of course the predominant type of
hypnoid state and they differ from artificial hypnoses only by virtue
of their spontaneous genesis. We find them in many fully developed
hysterias where they are of varying frequency and duration, and
often occur in very swift alternation with the normal waking state.[15]
Because of the dream-like ideas that they contain they often deserve
the name *'delirium hystericum'*. The inner processes of auto-
hypnosis are subject to more or less complete amnesia during waking
life, whereas in artificial hypnosis they are recalled completely. It is
precisely this amnesia that allows the psychical results of these states,
i.e. the associations formed within them, to escape any correction
during waking thought. And since in auto-hypnosis the critique and
surveillance exercised by other ideas are diminished, and for the
most part almost entirely fade away, the wildest delusions can stem
from it and be preserved intact for a long time. Hence it is almost only
ever in states such as this that there arises a somewhat complicated,
irrational 'symbolic relation between the precipitating cause and the
pathological phenomenon', which is often based on the most absurd
word associations and similarities in sound. The absence of critical

powers in these states is what causes auto-suggestions to arise so frequently in them, as, for example, when a paralysis remains after a hysterical attack. But in our analyses – perhaps by chance – we hardly ever came across an instance of hysterical phenomena originating in this manner. Whether under auto-hypnosis or not, we always found the genesis to be determined by the same process, the converting of an affective excitation.

This 'hysterical conversion' is in any case more easily achieved in auto-hypnosis than in a waking state, as indeed it is far easier for suggested ideas to take on the physical form of hallucinations and movements in artificial hypnosis. But the process of the conversion of excitation is in essence the same as that explicated above. Once this process has taken place, the somatic phenomenon is repeated whenever the affect and auto-hypnosis coincide again. And it appears that the hypnotic state can then be brought on by the affect itself. So initially, and for as long as the hypnosis is in pure alternation with a complete waking state, the hysterical symptom remains limited to the hypnotic state and is strengthened there by repetition. But the precipitating idea is still protected from correction by waking thought and its critical powers, precisely because it never surfaces in clear waking life.

Thus in the case of Anna O. (Case 1) the contracture of the right arm, which had been associated in her auto-hypnosis with the intense feeling of anxiety and the idea of the snake, was restricted for four months to the moments during which she was in a hypnotic state (or, if 'hypnotic' is held to be an unsuitable term to designate absences of very short duration, 'hypnoid' state), but recurred frequently. The same thing happened with other conversions completed in the hypnoid state, and so that great complex of hysterical phenomena formed and remained perfectly latent, becoming manifest only when the hypnoid state became continuous.

Phenomena that have arisen in this way do not appear in waking life until the splitting of the psyche (which will be discussed later) is complete and the alternation of waking and hypnoid states has been replaced by the co-existence of normal and hypnoid complexes of ideas.

Do hypnoid states such as this pre-date the illness and how do they come into being? I can say little on this subject since, with the exception of the case of Anna O., we have no observations at our disposal that could elucidate the matter. It seems certain that for this patient the auto-hypnosis was prepared by habitual reverie and then fully produced by an affect of protracted anxiety, which itself provided the basis for a hypnoid state. It is not improbable that this process holds true more generally.

A great variety of states can cause 'absent-mindedness', but only a few of them predispose to auto-hypnosis or pass directly into this. The researcher who is immersed in a problem is probably also anaesthetic to a degree and fails to form any conscious perceptions of large groups of sense impressions; the same is true of anyone using their imagination in a lively and creative way (the 'private theatre' of Anna O.). But in these states psychical work is energetically pursued; the excitation liberated from the nervous system is used up in this way. – In states of distraction or stupor, on the other hand, the intracerebral excitation drops below the level it maintains when the subject is wide awake; these states border on sleepiness and can turn into sleep. But if, in such states of 'immersedness' and when the course of ideas is inhibited, a group of affectively marked ideas is active, it will create a high level of intracerebral excitation that is not used up by psychical work but is at the disposal of abnormal functions, such as conversion.

Neither 'absent-mindedness' during energetic work nor twilight states devoid of emotion are, then, pathogenic, but it is likely that reverie filled with emotion and the state of fatigue brought about by protracted affects are. The brooding of someone who is care-laden, the anxiety of the person watching over the sick bed of someone who is dear to them, the lover's reverie, are all states of this kind. The concentration on the affective group of ideas is what first causes the 'absence'. Gradually the flow of ideas slows down, so that ultimately it almost stagnates; but the affective idea and its affect remain in place, as does the large quantity of excitation that has not been used up by any function. The similarity between these circumstances and the conditions of hypnosis seems unmistakable.

The person being hypnotized must not, of course, fall into a real sleep, i.e. his intracerebral excitation may not drop to the level of sleep; but the flow of ideas must be inhibited. The entire mass of excitation is then at the disposal of the suggested idea.

The origin of pathogenic auto-hypnosis in a number of people may then be that the affect enters into their habitual reverie. This is perhaps one of the reasons why in the anamnesis of hysteria we so often encounter the two great pathogenic factors: being in love and nursing. In the first, thoughts full of longing for the absent loved one create a state of 'rapture', causing external reality to fade and thought to be brought to a standstill laden with affect; nursing, with its calm environment, the concentration on the one object, the listening out for the patient's breathing, produces exactly the same conditions as many methods of hypnosis and fills the twilight state that has arisen in this way with the affect of anxiety. It may be that these states differ only quantitively from real auto-hypnoses, and that they turn into them.

Once this has happened, the hypnosis-like state will repeat itself again and again in these same circumstances, and in place of the two normal psychical states the individual has three: waking, sleeping and hypnoid, as we have often observed in cases where deep artificial hypnosis has been frequently repeated.

I am not in a position to say whether or not spontaneous hypnotic states can develop if the affect does not intervene in this way, that is, as the result of an innate disposition, but I believe it to be very probable. When we observe how much both sick and healthy people vary in their susceptibility to artificial hypnosis, with what facility it appears in some, then we have reason to suspect that in such people it can also occur spontaneously. And it may be that the disposition to this is necessary for reverie to be converted into auto-hypnosis. I am then far from presupposing that hysteria develops according to the mechanism which Anna O. taught us in all cases.

I am talking about hypnoid states rather than hypnosis itself, because the boundaries separating these states that are so important in the development of hysteria are very ill-defined. We do not know whether the reverie that was described above as a preliminary stage of auto-hypnosis is not itself able to produce the same pathogenic effect as auto-hypnosis and whether the same might not also be true of the protracted affect of anxiety. This is certainly the case with fright. Since fright inhibits the flow of ideas when an affective idea (danger) is simultaneously very active, it provides a perfect parallel to affect-filled reverie; and as the recollection that is constantly renewed repeatedly produces this psychical state, 'hypnoid fright' develops, in which the conversion is either accomplished or stabilized. This is the incubation stage of 'traumatic hysteria' in the strict sense of the term.

Since states that are extremely different but concur in what is most important can be classed with auto-hypnosis it seems preferable to adopt the expression 'hypnoid', since it stresses these inner similarities. It sums up the view represented by Möbius in the propositions cited above.

Most importantly, however, this term designates auto-hypnosis itself, which is important in the genesis of hysterical phenomena because it facilitates the conversion, protects (by amnesia) the converted ideas from being eroded, and ultimately leads to the splitting of the psyche.

If a physical symptom is caused by an idea and repeatedly released by it, one would expect that intelligent patients, capable of self-observation, would be conscious of this connection, that they would know from experience that the somatic phenomenon occurs at the same time as the memory of a specific process. It is true that they are not cognizant of the inner causal nexus, and yet we are all constantly aware of which ideas make us cry or laugh or blush, even if the nervous mechanism of these ideogenic phenomena is not in the least clear to us. – Sometimes patients really observe the connection and are conscious of it. A woman may say, for example, that her mild hysterical attack (shaking and palpitations, say) stems from some great emotional upset and recurs only when an event reminds her of it. But for very many hysterical symptoms, probably the majority of them in fact, this is not the case. Even intelligent patients do not know that their symptoms come on as the consequence of an idea and take them to be independent physical phenomena. If this were not so, the psychical theory of hysteria would already have reached a venerable old age.

Now it seems reasonable to believe that the symptoms in question did, in origin, arise ideogenically, but that repetition has, to use Romberg's expression, 'imprinted' them onto the body, so that rather than being based on a psychical process they would be based on the modifications in the nervous system that had arisen subsequently. They would have become independent, genuinely somatic symptoms.

This view is, from the outset, neither impossible nor improbable. But I believe that the way in which our observations advance the theory of hysteria is precisely in having proved that this view is, at least in a great many cases, inaccurate. We saw that all kinds of hysterical symptoms that had existed for years 'disappeared immediately and did not recur, if we succeeded in wakening the memory of the precipitating event with complete clarity, arousing with it the accompanying affect, and if the patient then depicted the event in the greatest possible detail and put words to the affect'. The case histories related here give some evidence in support of this assertion. 'By reversing the proposition *"cessante causa cessat effectus"* [when the cause ceases the effect ceases] we may conclude from these observations that the precipitating event in some way still continues to exercise an effect years later, not indirectly through a chain of intermediary causal links, but as a directly releasing cause, in something like the same way that a psychical pain remembered in waking consciousness will still produce the secretion of tears later on: *hysterics suffer for the most part from reminiscences*.'

But if this is the case, if the recollection of the psychical trauma is to be regarded as an agent that, like a foreign body, exercises an effect in the present long after it has forced its way in and yet the patient has no consciousness of these recollections and their emergence, then we have to admit that *unconscious ideas* exist and are operative.

In the analysis of hysterical phenomena we do not, however, simply find isolated instances of such ideas, rather we are forced to recognize that in reality, as the admirable work of French researchers has shown, large complexes of ideas as well as intricate psychical processes of great consequence remain completely unconscious in many patients and co-exist with the conscious life of the psyche; we have further to recognize that a splitting of psychical activity occurs and that this is of fundamental importance for our understanding of complicated hysterias.

I may perhaps be permitted to go into this difficult and obscure area somewhat further; the need to establish the meaning of the terms used may to an extent excuse the theoretical nature of the discussion.

5 *Ideas that are Unconscious or Inadmissible to Consciousness, Splitting of the Psyche*

We call those ideas of which we are aware 'conscious'. Man's self-consciousness is a miraculous phenomenon: we can see and observe ideas that emerge in us and follow on from each other as if they were objects. This does not always happen since there is seldom cause for self-observation. But it is an ability that everyone shares, since we all say: I have thought such and such. Ideas that we observe or would observe as active in ourselves if we paid attention to them, we call conscious. There are only very few of these at any moment in time and if others apart from them should be current, we would have to call them *unconscious* ideas.

To speak in support of the existence of current, but unconscious or subconscious ideas hardly seems necessary anymore. These are the facts of life at its most everyday. If I have forgotten to pay a medical visit, I feel a keen sense of disquiet. Experience has taught me that this feeling means forgetting. I check my memories in vain, and can find no reason until, often hours later, it suddenly enters my consciousness. I have, however, been uneasy throughout this time. The idea of this visit is then still operative, that is, continuously present, but not in consciousness. – A busy man is frustrated by something one morning. He is entirely preoccupied by his work, and, during this activity, his conscious thought is fully occupied and he does not think about what has irritated him. But his decisions will be influenced by it, and he will probably say no where he would otherwise say yes. In spite of everything the recollection is operative, that is, present. A large part of what we call mood comes from this source, namely from ideas that exist and are operative below the threshold of consciousness. – Indeed, our entire way of life is continuously influenced by subconscious ideas. It is a matter of daily observation that in mental decline, at the onset of paralysis for example, inhibitions that would otherwise prevent many actions become weaker and disappear. But the man who is paralysed and now tells dirty jokes in front of women was not, when healthy, restrained from this by conscious recollection and consideration. He avoided it 'instinctively' and 'automatically', i.e. he was held back from it by ideas that were roused by his impulse to act in this way, but which remained below the threshold of consciousness and at the same time inhibited the impulse. – All intuitive activity is directed by ideas that are for the most part subconscious. Only the clearest, most intense ideas are perceived by consciousness, while the great mass of current, but weaker ideas remains unconscious.

The objections to the existence and effectiveness of 'unconscious ideas' seem for the most part to be mere word-play. 'Idea' is, of course, a word belonging to the terminology of conscious thought and so 'unconscious idea' is a contradiction in terms. But the physical process that underlies the idea is the same as regards content and form (if not quantity), regardless of whether the idea steps above the threshold of consciousness or remains beneath it. Creating some kind of term like 'ideational substratum' would suffice to avoid the contradiction and escape that objection.

In principle, then, there does not seem to be any major obstacle to acknowledging unconscious ideas as causes of pathological phenomena. But closer investigation of the matter reveals other difficulties. In most cases, if the intensity of unconscious ideas increases, they enter consciousness *ipso facto*. They remain unconscious only at lesser intensity. But it seems difficult to see how an idea might be at once intense enough to produce a lively motor action, for example, and yet not enough to become conscious.

I have already mentioned a view that should not, perhaps, be dismissed out of hand. The clarity of our ideas and hence their capacity to be observed by our self-consciousness, to be conscious, then, is also conditioned by the feelings of pleasure or aversion that they awaken, that is, by their affective value. If an idea has direct and lively somatic consequences, the excitation flows off along the path in question, instead, as would normally happen, of being emitted and diffused throughout the brain. Precisely *because* the idea has physical consequences, because there has been a *conversion* of the sum of psychical stimulus into somatic stimulus, it loses the clarity that would otherwise distinguish it from the current of ideas and becomes lost among the others.

Suppose that a person has undergone a violent emotion during a meal but not 'abreacted' it. Subsequent attempts to eat are accompanied by choking and vomiting, which to the patient seem to be purely physical symptoms. Hysterical vomiting persists for some time, and does not disappear until the emotion has been renewed, recounted and reacted to under hypnosis. There is no question but that this recollection was roused by every attempt to eat and that it triggered the act of vomiting. But it does not enter consciousness clearly because it is now free of affect, whereas the vomiting absorbs the person's attention completely.

It is conceivable that for this reason some ideas that release hysterical phenomena are not recognized as having caused them. But the fact that ideas that have lost their affect through conversion are overlooked cannot explain why in other cases complexes of ideas that are anything but devoid of affect do not enter consciousness. Our case histories provide many examples of this.

As a rule, in this kind of patient, changes in mood such as anxiousness, angry irritability or grief will either precede the appearance of the somatic symptom or immediately follow on from it; they will then increase until speaking out brings resolution, or until the affect and somatic phenomena gradually disappear again. When the former occurred, it was still possible to comprehend the quality of the affect, even if its intensity necessarily appeared quite disproportionate to the healthy person and even, once it had been resolved, to the patient. These, then, are ideas that are of sufficient intensity not only to cause strong physical phenomena but also to bring on the accompanying affect, to influence the association by privileging ideas that are related to it – and yet they themselves still remain outside of consciousness. Hypnosis was required to bring these ideas into consciousness, as in Cases 1 and 2, or a laborious search had to be carried out with the strenuous help of a doctor (Cases 4, 5).

Ideas such as these that are (current but) unconscious not because of their relatively low degree of activity but in spite of their extreme intensity, may be described as *inadmissible to consciousness*.[16]

The existence of ideas such as these that are inadmissible to consciousness is pathological. In a healthy person every idea that is at all capable of becoming current will, if sufficiently intense, enter consciousness. In our patients we find that a large complex of ideas that are admissible to consciousness co-exists with a smaller complex of ideas that are inadmissible to consciousness. Their field of ideational psychical activity, then, does not coincide with potential consciousness, rather the latter is more restricted than the former. Here, ideational psychical activity disintegrates into conscious and unconscious activity; ideas likewise disintegrate into those that are admissible and those that are inadmissible to consciousness. We cannot, then, speak of a splitting of consciousness, but rather of a *splitting of the psyche*.

Conversely, these subconscious ideas can be neither influenced nor corrected by conscious thought. They frequently involve experiences that have subsequently lost their meaning – a fear of events that have not come about, fright that turned to laughter or joy at a rescue. These consequences remove all affectivity from the recollection in conscious thought; but the subconscious idea that arouses somatic phenomena remains perfectly untouched.

Permit me to present one more example of this. A young married woman was for a while intensely worried about what would become of her younger sister. During this time her periods, which had previously been regular, became longer, lasting for two weeks, her left hypogastrium became painful, and on two occasions the patient woke from a 'faint' to find herself lying rigid on the ground. This was followed by an ovarian neuralgia of the left side, with signs of a severe peritonitis. The absence of any fever, together with a contracture of the left leg (and back), indicated that the illness was a pseudo-peritonitis, and when, a few years later, the patient died and a post-mortem was carried out, all that was found was 'microcystic degeneration' of *both* ovaries without any trace of the peritonitis that had occurred. The severe symptoms gradually disappeared, leaving behind ovarian neuralgia, a contracture of the back muscles that made her trunk as stiff as a board, and a contracture of the left leg. This last symptom was removed by direct suggestion under hypnosis. The contracture of the back could not be altered. Her sister's situation had in the meantime righted itself completely and all her fears had faded away. But the hysterical phenomena that must have derived from them persisted in the same form. It seemed reasonable to suppose that these were changes in innervation that had become independent and were no longer bound to the idea that had caused them. But when the patient was compelled to recount under hypnosis the whole story up to her falling ill with 'peritonitis' (which she did most unwillingly), she straight away sat up in bed unaided, and her contracture of the back disappeared for good. (The ovarian neuralgia, which was undoubtedly much older in origin, remained unaffected.) – For months, then, the pathogenic anxious idea had continued to be active and operative; it had also been completely inaccessible to any correction by external events.

If, therefore, we have to acknowledge the existence of complexes of ideas that never enter waking consciousness and are not influenced by conscious thought, then we have also admitted that, even in such simple hysterias as the one just described, there is a splitting of the psyche into two relatively independent parts. I am not claiming that everything that is referred to as hysterical has a splitting of this kind as its basis and precondition, but rather that 'the splitting of psychical activity that is so strikingly present in the well-known cases as *double conscience*, exists in a rudimentary form in every "major" hysteria, and that this capacity and tendency to dissociation is the fundamental phenomenon of this neurosis'.

But before entering into a discussion of these phenomena, I want to add a remark relating to the unconscious ideas that give rise to somatic phenomena. As in the case of the contracture narrated above, many of the manifestations of hysteria continue uninterrupted for a long time. Should and can we assume that throughout this period the precipitating idea is always active and current? I think so. In healthy people, of course, we see that psychical activity takes place accompanied by rapid changes in ideas. But we see those who suffer from severe melancholy remain continuously immersed in the same distressing idea over a long period of time and this idea remains active and current throughout. Indeed, we may well believe that even when healthy people have a serious concern it is constantly present, since it controls their facial expression even when their consciousness is filled with other thoughts. But that part of psychical activity which is separated off in hysterics, and which we think of as being filled with unconscious ideas, is, on the whole, so poorly supplied with them and so inaccessible to any exchange with external impressions that it is quite conceivable that an idea could remain permanently active there.

If we take the view shared by Binet and Janet that the splitting off of one part of psychical activity is central to hysteria, then we are obliged to seek the greatest possible clarity regarding this phenomenon. It is all too easy to slip into the habit of assuming that there is a substance behind every substantive, of gradually coming to understand 'consciousness', or, in the French, *'conscience'*, as a thing; and if one has become accustomed to making metaphorical use of spatial relations like 'subconscious', then over time an idea really has formed in which the metaphor is forgotten and which can easily be manipulable as if it were real. At this point the mythology is complete.

All of our thinking is irresistibly accompanied and aided by spatial ideas, and we speak in spatial metaphors. Thus images of the trunk of a tree standing in the light with its roots in the dark, or of a building with its dark basement, come almost inevitably to mind when we talk about ideas found in the area of clear consciousness and unconscious ideas that never enter the bright light of self-consciousness. But if we always keep in mind that everything that is spatial here is a metaphor and do not allow ourselves to be misled into situating it in the brain, then we can speak of a consciousness and a subconsciousness. But only on this condition.

We are not in danger of being duped by our own turns of speech if we remain mindful that both conscious and unconscious thoughts have their origin in the same brain and in all probability in the same cerebral cortex. We are unable to explain how this is possible. But then we know so little about the psychical activity of the cerebral cortex that the addition of one more puzzling complication can hardly do anything to extend our boundless lack of knowledge. The fact that we have to acknowledge is that in hysterics one part of psychical activity cannot be accessed by the self-conscious perception of the waking person, and hence that the psyche is split.

A well-known instance of this division of psychical activity is given by hysterical attacks in a number of their forms and stages. At the beginning of the attack conscious thinking is often completely extinguished but then gradually wakens. Many intelligent patients are heard to confess that their conscious self was quite lucid during the attack and was intrigued and astonished to observe all the mad things that they did and said. Patients such as this are then also likely to believe (mistakenly) that, had they put their mind to it, they would have been able to inhibit the attack and are inclined to consider themselves guilty of it. 'They needn't have done it.' (When they accuse themselves of simulation it is also for the most part based on this feeling.) Then, when the next attack occurs, the conscious self is just as little able to take control of events as during the previous one. – Here, then, the thinking and ideation of the conscious waking self exist alongside ideas which, normally confined to the darkness of the unconscious, have gained control of the musculature, of speech, and even of a large part of ideational activity itself, and the splitting of the psyche is manifest.

The findings of Binet and Janet, in fact, deserve to be described as a splitting not only of psychical activity but also of consciousness. It is generally known that these observers succeeded in establishing contact with their patients' 'subconsciousness', with that part of psychical activity that is unknown to the conscious waking self; and in a number of cases they proved that all psychical functions are present within it, including that of self-consciousness, since it contains the memory of earlier psychical events. This half psyche is then quite complete and conscious in itself. In our cases the split-off part of the psyche is 'brought into darkness', in the same way that the Titans, imprisoned in the crater of Etna, can shake the earth but never appear in the light of day. In Janet's cases, a complete division of the realm has taken place. There is still a hierarchical difference, but even this disappears when, as in those well-known cases of *double conscience*, the two halves of consciousness alternate and there is no difference in their capacity to function.

But let us return to those ideas that we have proved to be the cause of hysterical phenomena in our patients. We are far from able simply to say that they are all 'unconscious' and 'inaccessible to consciousness'. From the fully conscious idea that releases an unusual reflex through to that which never enters consciousness when the subject is awake but only under hypnosis, there is an almost unbroken scale passing through every degree of vagueness and obscurity. In spite of this we believe it to be proven that at higher levels of hysteria there is a splitting of psychical activity and this alone seems to enable a psychical theory of the illness.

What, then, can be asserted or suspected as likely as regards the cause and genesis of this phenomenon?

The theory of hysteria owes an immense debt to P. Janet, and on most points we agree with him, but he has developed one view on this matter which we cannot ourselves adopt:

Janet holds that the 'splitting of personality' is based on an innate mental weakness (*'insuffisance psychologique'*). All normal mental activity presupposes a certain capacity for 'synthesis', the possibility of joining several ideas together into one complex. Fusing various sense perceptions to create an image of one's surroundings is already a synthetic activity of this kind; but in hysterics this psychical capacity lies well below the norm. If the attention of a normal person is focused to the maximum possible on one point, as, for example, on perception involving only one of the senses, he will temporarily lose the capacity to apperceive impressions from the other senses, i.e. to admit them to conscious thought. In hysterics this is the case without there being any particular concentration of attention. When they perceive something they are unreceptive to other sense impressions. Indeed, they are not even capable of taking in the impressions of any one sense completely. They can, for example, apperceive sensations of touch on only one half of the body; those on the other side reach the centre and are used to co-ordinate movement, but they are not apperceived. A person who experiences this is hemi-anaesthetic.

In a normal person, an idea will call a great many others to consciousness by association; these will form either a supportive or an inhibiting relation with the initial idea, and only those ideas at maximum intensity are so excessively strong that their associations remain beneath the threshold of consciousness. In hysterics this is always the case. Every idea monopolizes their limited mental activity in its entirety; it is this that determines their excessive affectivity.

Janet terms this peculiarity of the hysterical psyche the 'restricted field of consciousness', in analogy with the 'restricted field of vision'. On the whole, sense impressions that are not apperceived and ideas that have been aroused but have not entered consciousness expire without further consequence; sometimes, however, they aggregate and form complexes – this is the psychical level that is withdrawn from consciousness, the subconsciousness.

Hysteria, which is fundamentally based on this splitting of the psyche, is, according to Janet, *'une maladie de faiblesse'* ['an illness due to weakness']; and hence it is most likely to develop if a psyche that is innately weak suffers additional debilitating influences or has great demands made on it that appear further to diminish its mental strength.

In the above exposition of his views, we see that Janet has already answered the important question of the disposition to hysteria, of the *typus hystericus* (a term used in the sense in which one speaks of a *typus phthisicus*, meaning the long, narrow thorax, the small heart, etc.). For Janet, the disposition to hysteria is a certain form of congenital mental weakness. Counter to this, we would like to give the following brief formulation of our view: splitting of consciousness does not occur because patients are weak-minded; rather, patients appear weak-minded because their psychical activity is divided and only one part of its capacity is available to conscious thought. We cannot regard mental weakness as the *typus hystericus*, or essence of the disposition to hysteria.

What is meant by the previous sentence may be clarified by an example. On many occasions we were able to observe the following course of events in one of our patients (Frau Cäcilie M.): while she was in relatively good health, a hysterical symptom would appear – a tormenting, obsessive hallucination, a neuralgia or something similar, whose intensity would for a period of time increase. Simultaneously, her capacity to perform mentally would continually decrease, and after a few days any uninitiated observer would have to say that the patient was weak-minded. Then she would be delivered of the unconscious idea (the memory of a psychical trauma that had often happened long ago), either by the doctor during hypnosis, or by suddenly recounting the thing when in a state of excitement and intensely affected. After this she would not simply become peaceful and cheerful, freed from the symptom that had been tormenting her; rather one was always surprised by the richness and clarity of her intellect, the acuity of her understanding and judgement. She took special pleasure in chess, which she played excellently, preferably two games at once – hardly a sign that her powers of mental synthesis were lacking. It was impossible to avoid the impression that during a course of events such as this the unconscious idea seized an increasingly large share of the psychical activity for itself and that the more this happened the smaller the share of conscious thought became, until it dropped to the level of complete imbecility; but that when the patient was, to use the curiously apt Viennese expression, 'with it' [*beisammen*], she possessed a remarkable mental capacity.

To draw a comparison with the mental states of a normal person we would like to refer not to a concentration of attention, but to the state of *preoccupation*. If someone is 'preoccupied' by a vivid idea, a worry, for example, their mental capacity will be diminished accordingly.

Every observer is overwhelmingly under the influence of the object of his observation and we would like to believe that Janet's conception took shape predominantly in his penetrating study of those weak-minded hysterics, who are in hospital or a home because their illness and resultant mental weakness prevent them from being able to support themselves in life. Our observation of educated hysterics compels us to form a significantly different opinion of their psyche. We believe 'that people of the clearest intellect, strongest will, greatest character, and highest discrimination are to be found among hysterics'. Genuine and effective psychical gifts are not to any degree excluded by hysteria, even if real achievement becomes impossible *because* of the illness. The patron saint of hysteria was, after all, St Theresa, a woman of genius and of the greatest practical competence.

It is, however, equally true that no degree of silliness, uselessness and weak will is a protection from hysteria. Even if one disregards everything that is simply a consequence of the illness, one has to recognize that the weak-minded hysteric is a common type. But even here it is not a case of torpid, phlegmatic stupidity, but rather of an excessive degree of mental mobility that makes them incompetent. I will discuss the question of innate disposition later. Here I want simply to establish that Janet's opinion – that mental weakness as such is the basis of hysteria and psychical splitting – is untenable.

Quite contrary to Janet's view, I believe that in very many cases an excess of psychical efficiency – the habitual co-existence of two heterogenous series of ideas – is at the basis of the disaggregation. It has often been pointed out that we are frequently not only 'mechanically' active while series of ideas pass by that have nothing in common with our activity, but that we are also capable of unquestionable psychical performance while our thoughts are 'busy elsewhere' – as, for example, when we read aloud in an appropriate tone of voice and without making any mistakes yet afterwards know absolutely nothing about what we have read.

There is no doubt a whole range of activities – from those that are mechanical, like knitting, or playing scales, to those that demand some degree of psychical performance – which many people manage when only half their mind is turned to them. Particularly those who, while very lively, are tormented by monotonous, simple, unappealing activity, and who at first deliberately entertain themselves by thinking of other things. ('Private theatre' in Anna O., Case 1.) Another similar case comes about when an interesting series of ideas, which may come from reading or the theatre or such like, comes forcibly and intrusively to mind. This intrusion is all the more energetic when the foreign series of ideas is strongly 'marked with affect', in the form of worry, or the longing of the lover. This produces the state of preoccupation touched on above, which does not, however, prevent many people from performing moderately complex activities. Social circumstances often demand this kind of doubling even of intense thought, as, for example, when a woman tormented by worry or excited by passion fulfils her social duties and the functions of the kind hostess. We all accomplish minor achievements of this kind in the course of our work, but self-observation also seems generally to reveal that the group of affective ideas is not just occasionally aroused by association but is continually current in the psyche and moves into consciousness unless it is taken up with any lively external impression or act of will.

Even in people who do not habitually allow daydreams to flow alongside their daily activity, a number of situations cause the changing impressions and reactions from external life to co-exist in this way over substantial periods of time with an affectively marked group of ideas. *Post equitem sedet atra cura* [Black care sits behind the horseman]. Nursing loved ones and being in love are the most common situations of this kind. Experience shows that nursing and strong sexual feelings also play the main role in most of the more closely analysed case histories of hysterics.

I suspect that the habitual doubling of psychical capability or the doubling determined by affect-laden situations significantly predisposes to a genuine pathological splitting of the psyche. It turns into this when the two co-existing series of ideas cease to have the same kind of content, when one of them contains ideas that are inadmissible to consciousness, ideas that have been fended off or those that come from hypnoid states. The confluence of the two chronologically separated streams that occurs regularly in healthy people is then impossible and a split-off area of unconscious psychic activity is permanently established. This hysterical splitting of the psyche has the same relation to the healthy person's 'double self' as do hypnoid states to normal daydreaming. The pathological quality in the latter is determined by amnesia, and in the former by the inadmissibility of the ideas to consciousness.

Case 1 (Anna O.), to which I am constantly obliged to return, offers a clear insight into what happens. When in complete health, the girl was accustomed to letting series of imaginative ideas flow alongside her everyday occupations. In a situation suited to auto-hypnosis, the intense feeling of anxiety enters her reverie and creates a hypnoid state for which she has amnesia. This is repeated on various occasions and the ideas contained within this state gradually become more abundant, but it continues to alternate with the state of perfectly normal waking thought.

After four months the hypnoid state has taken complete control of the patient: as the single attacks run into one another, an *état de mal* takes shape, an acute hysteria of the most severe kind. It lasts for several months in various forms (somnambulistic period) and is then violently interrupted and alternates once again with normal psychical behaviour. But even here there is a persistence of somatic and psychical phenomena (contracture, hemi-anaesthesia, changes in speech) which in this case we *know* to be based on ideas from the hypnoid state. It is thereby proven that even during normal behaviour the ideational complex of the hypnoid state, the 'subconsciousness', is present and that the splitting of the psyche continues to exist.

I am unable to supply a second example of this kind of development, but I do believe that this one throws some light on the formation of traumatic neuroses. In traumatic neuroses, during the days immediately after the accident, both the memory of it and the hypnoid state of fright are repeated. As this happens with increasing frequency, the intensity of the hypnoid state diminishes to such a degree that it ceases to alternate with waking thought and simply exists alongside it. Now it becomes continual and the somatic symptoms that previously occurred only in attacks of fright acquire a permanent existence. I can, however, only suppose that this is what happens since I have not analysed a case of this kind.

Freud's observations and analyses prove that the splitting of the psyche can also be caused by 'defence', that is, by the deliberate diverting of consciousness from distressing ideas. But this happens only in some people to whom we must therefore attribute a psychical peculiarity. Normal people either succeed in suppressing ideas of this kind, in which case the ideas disappear completely, or they do not succeed, in which case the ideas surface repeatedly in consciousness. I do not know what the nature of this peculiarity is. I can only venture the supposition that the assistance of the hypnoid state is necessary if defence is to result not just in making single converted ideas unconscious, but in a real splitting of the psyche. The auto-hypnosis has created what might be called the space or area of unconscious psychical activity into which the ideas that have been fended off are forced. Yet however this may be, the fact of the pathogenic significance of 'defence' has to be acknowledged.

I do not believe, though, that the genesis of the psychical splitting would be anything like exhausted by the half-understood processes discussed above. Thus, in their initial stages higher degree hysterias usually reveal for a time a syndrome that can be described as acute hysteria. (In the anamnesis of male hysterics one often encounters this form of illness described as 'inflammation of the brain'; in female hysterias ovarian neuralgia is usually the reason for diagnosing 'peritonitis'.)

During this acute stage of the hysteria psychotic traits are very clear: manic and angry states of excitement, a swift changing of hysterical phenomena, hallucinations, and so on. In a state like this, the splitting of the psyche may perhaps ensue in a different way from that which we have sought to explain above.

Perhaps this stage in its entirety should be regarded as a long hypnoid state, the residues of which provide the nucleus of the unconscious ideational complex, while waking thought is amnesic to it. Since the conditions for the genesis of an acute hysteria of this kind are for the most part unknown (I would not venture to take the process in Anna O.'s case to be generally valid), this would be a further type of psychical splitting, which, in contrast to that described above, would be termed 'irrational'.[17] And so there will certainly be yet more varieties of this process, which have eluded our young psychological science. For we have undoubtedly taken only the first steps in this area and further discoveries will significantly alter the views we hold today.

Now let us ask what the knowledge gained in recent years about the splitting of the psyche has achieved for our understanding of hysteria. A great deal, it seems, and much that is significant.

These discoveries make it possible to trace what seem to be purely somatic symptoms back to ideas that cannot, however, be found in the patient's consciousness. It is unnecessary to go into this again here.

They have taught us to understand attacks, at least in part, as products of the unconscious ideational complex (Charcot).

They also explain some of the psychical characteristics of hysteria and this point perhaps deserves more detailed discussion.

'Unconscious ideas' never, or only seldom and with difficulty, enter waking thought, but they do influence it. They do so first through their effects, as, for example, when a patient is tormented by a hallucination that is completely incomprehensible and sense-less, the significance and motivation of which becomes clear under hypnosis.

In addition, they influence association, by allowing individual ideas to become more vivid than they would be without this reinforcement from the unconscious. Particular groups of ideas are constantly forced on patients with a certain compulsion and they are obliged to think about them. (Something similar happens when Janet's hemi-anaesthetics do not feel that their insensitive hand is being touched repeatedly, but, when asked to pick any number, always choose the one that corresponds to the number of times it has been touched.) Unconscious ideas also govern temper of mind or emotional state. When Anna O. unwound her recollections and approached an event that was originally bound up with vivid affect, the corresponding emotion had already manifested itself days before, prior to the recollection even appearing clearly in her hypnotic consciousness.

Thus the patient's 'moods', those inexplicable, unfounded depressions that have no motive in waking thought, become comprehensible. Hysterics are impressionable for the most part simply because of their innate excitability; but the vivid affects in which they are caught up for relatively minor reasons can more readily be understood if we consider that the 'split-off psyche' acts like a sounding-board to the note of a tuning-fork. Every event that excites 'unconscious' recollections frees up the entire affective power of these ideas that have not been subject to erosion, and the affect that is brought on is then quite without relation to the one that would have arisen in the conscious psyche alone.

An account was given above (p. 232) of a patient whose psychical performance is always in inverse proportion to the vividness of her unconscious ideas. Her conscious thought is diminished in part, but only in part, because of a peculiar kind of distractedness; after each momentary 'absence' (these appearing constantly) she does not know what she thought while it was happening. She oscillates between the '*condition prime*' and '*seconde*', between the conscious and unconscious ideational complex. But her psychical performance is not diminished by this alone, nor simply by the affect that controls her from the unconscious. In this state her waking thought is devoid of energy, her judgement childish; she seems, as has been said, virtually imbecile. In my opinion, the reason for this is that less energy is available to waking thought when a large amount of psychical excitation is being used by the unconscious.

If this is not just temporarily the case, if the split-off psyche is constantly in a state of excitation – as in Janet's hemi-anaesthetic patients, in whom all perceptions on one side of the body are perceived only by the unconscious psyche – so little mental capacity is left for waking thought that the psychical weakness portrayed by Janet and held to be innate is fully accounted for. There are very few people of whom one might say, as of Uhland's Bertrand de Born, 'that they never need more than half their mind'. The majority of people whose psychical energy is reduced in this way do become weak-minded.

The mental weakness caused by psychical splitting does, however, also provide the basis for a characteristic with positive consequences in *some* hysterics – their suggestibility. (I say 'some hysterics' because it is certain that people of the surest judgement and most critical intelligence also suffer from hysteria.)

By suggestibility we mean, in the first instance, simply the inability to criticize ideas and ideational complexes (judgements) that surface in one's own consciousness or are introduced to it from the external world by listening to others' talking or by reading. Any criticism of ideas like these that are newly entering consciousness is based on their ability to waken other ideas by association, among which are some that are irreconcilable with them. The resistance to them depends on the fund of these kinds of conflicting ideas in potential consciousness, and the strength of this resistance corresponds to the ratio between the vividness of the new ideas and that of those wakened from memory. Even in those of normal intellect this ratio varies greatly. What we call intellectual temperament is to a great extent dependent on it. Those who are sanguine, always delighted by new people and things, are probably like this because the intensity of their memory-images in comparison with that of new impressions is less than in quieter, 'phlegmatic' people. In pathological states the predominance of new ideas and the lack of resistance towards them increases in proportion to the low number of memory-images wakened, which is to say in proportion to the weakness and poverty of association; this already occurs in sleep and dreams, under hypnosis, whenever mental energy is decreased, as long as it does not also damage the vividness of the new ideas.

The unconscious, split psyche of hysteria is eminently suggestible because of the poverty and incompleteness of its ideational content.

But the suggestibility of the conscious psyche of some hysterics also seems to be based on this. They have an innate tendency to excitability and experience new ideas as extremely vivid. On the other hand, real intellectual activity, that is, association, is reduced because the splitting-off of an 'unconscious' means that only a part of their psychical energy is at their disposal.

As a consequence, their capacity to resist auto-suggestion as well as the suggestion of others is lessened and sometimes destroyed. Even the suggestibility of their will seems to result from this alone. Hallucinatory suggestibility, on the other hand, which immediately changes every idea of a sense-perception into the perception itself, demands, as do all hallucinations, an abnormal degree of excitability of the perceptual organ and cannot be derived from psychical splitting alone.

6 *Innate Disposition; The Development of Hysteria*

At almost every stage in these expositions I have had to acknowledge that most of the manifestations we are trying to understand can also be based on a congenital idiosyncrasy. This idiosyncrasy escapes any explanation that seeks to go beyond a statement of the facts. But even the *ability to acquire hysteria* is undoubtedly connected with an idiosyncrasy of the individual and the attempt to define this somewhat more precisely may not be entirely unprofitable.

I have explained above why Janet's view – that the disposition to hysteria is based on congenital psychical weakness – is unacceptable. The medical practitioner, who as family doctor observes the members of hysterical families at all ages, will undoubtedly be more inclined to look for this disposition in an excess than in a defect. Adolescents who later become hysterical are for the most part lively, talented and full of intellectual interests until they fall ill; they often have a remarkably energetic will. This category includes girls who get up during the night to pursue in secret some kind of study that their parents have forbidden them for fear of over-exertion. They are certainly no more plentifully endowed than others in their capacity for considered judgement. But one seldom finds simple, dull sluggishness of mind or stupidity in them. The overflowing productivity of their psyche led one of my friends to claim that hysterics are the flower of humanity, as sterile, admittedly, but also as beautiful as forced blooms.

Their liveliness and restlessness, their need for sensations and mental activity, their inability to tolerate monotony and boredom, can be formulated as follows: they belong to that group of people whose nervous system at rest liberates an excess of excitation which demands to be expended (p. 199). During and as a result of development in puberty, the innate surplus is supplemented by that massive increase in excitation that comes from awakening sexuality, from the sex glands. Now, an excessive quantum of free nervous energy is available for pathological phenomena: but, clearly, for this to take the form of hysterical symptoms requires a further specific idiosyncrasy on the part of the individual, for the great majority of those who are lively and excited do not become hysterical.

I could find only the vague and insubstantial words 'abnormal excitability of the nervous system' to describe this idiosyncrasy above. Yet one can perhaps go further and say that this abnormality lies in the fact that in this kind of person excitation from the central organ can flow into the sensory nervous apparatuses, which are normally accessible only to peripheral stimuli, and into the nervous apparatuses of the vegetative organs, which are isolated from the central nervous system by strong resistances. It is possible that this idea of an ever-present surplus of energy, which has access to the sensory, vasomotor and visceral apparatuses, in itself accounts for some pathological phenomena.

In people of this disposition, as soon as attention is forcibly concentrated on one part of the body, the 'attentional breaching' (Exner) of the sensory conductor in question exceeds the normal level; the free, floating excitation as it were places itself onto this path and local hyperalgesia results, which means that any pains, whatever their cause, reach maximum intensity and that any afflictions are 'terrible' and 'unbearable'. However, once the quantity of excitation has cathected a sensory path, it does not always leave it again, as it does in normal people, nor does it simply remain behind, but rather is increased by the constant influx of new excitations. So if a joint suffers a slight trauma a *neurosis of the joint* develops; the painful sensations of a swelling of the ovaries become permanent *ovarian neuralgia*.

The circulatory nervous apparatuses are more accessible to cerebral influence than in normal people: hence nervous palpitations, a tendency to syncope, excessive blushing and blanching, etc.

However, the peripheral nervous apparatuses are not just more readily excitable as regards central influences: they also react to appropriate, functional stimuli in an excessive and perverse way. Palpitations follow moderate exertion and emotional excitement alike, and the vasomotors cause arteries to contract ('dead fingers') without any psychical influence. And just as a slight trauma is followed by neurosis of the joint, so a short bronchitis leaves behind nervous asthma, and indigestion, frequently, cardiac pains. We have, then, to recognize that accessibility to sums of excitation originating centrally is simply a special case of general, abnormal excitability,[18] even though it is the most important one for our topic.

For this reason too I do not believe that we should entirely dismiss the old 'reflex theory' of these symptoms, which one might do better simply to call 'nervous', but which belong to the empirical clinical picture of hysteria. The vomiting that accompanies the dilation of the uterus in pregnancy can, when there is abnormal excitability, easily be set off as a reflex action by minor uterine stimuli and possibly even by the variable swelling of the ovaries. We know of so many distant effects caused by changes in the organs, so many strange instances of 'points of conjugation', that the possibility cannot be dismissed that very many nervous symptoms, which are caused psychically on one occasion, might in other cases be the distant effects of reflex action. Indeed, I would even venture the highly old-fashioned heresy that the motor weakness of a leg might sometimes be caused by a genital disorder, not psychically, but as the direct result of reflex action. In my opinion we would do well not to make overly exclusive claims for our new insights, nor try to apply them in all cases.

Other forms of abnormal sensory excitability still escape our understanding completely: general analgesia, for example, anaesthetic patches, real restriction of the field of vision, and so on. It is possible, and perhaps probable, that further observations will prove the psychical origin of one or other of these stigmata and thus explain the symptom – but to date this has not occurred (I do not dare to generalize the evidence of Case 1) and I do not believe it justifiable to assume the origin before it has been traced back successfully.

On the other hand, the idiosyncrasy of the nervous system and the psyche as we have described it does seem to explain some well-known characteristics of many hysterics. The surplus excitation liberated by their nervous system when it is at rest makes them incapable of bearing a monotonous life or boredom and causes their need for sensation, which, following the outbreak of the illness, drives them to interrupt the monotony of their invalidism with all sorts of 'events', which, according to the nature of the thing, tend above all to take the form of pathological phenomena. They are often supported in this by auto-suggestion. They are led still further in it by their need for illness, that curious trait that is so pathognomonic for hysteria, as the fear of illness is for hypochondria. I know one hysteric who often inflicted very significant injuries on herself simply for her own use, without her friends and family or her doctor finding out about it. If nothing else she would do all sorts of mischief when alone in her room just to prove to herself that she was not normal. She simply has a clear feeling of being unwell, performs her duties inadequately, and through acts such as these justifies herself in her own eyes. Another patient, a severely ill woman, who was pathologically conscientious and full of mistrust against herself, felt guilt at every hysterical phenomenon, because according to her she need not have had it, had she put her mind to it. When the paresis of her legs was mistakenly declared to be a disease of the spine, she felt relief, whereas the explanation that it was 'only due to nerves' and would pass was enough to give her severe pangs of conscience.

The need for illness arises from the patient's longing to convince herself and others of the reality of her illness. If this is subsequently accompanied by the distress caused by the monotony of the sickroom, then the inclination to have more and more new symptoms develops most powerfully.

But if this becomes deceitfulness and leads to actual simulation – and I believe that we now err just as far on the side of denying simulation as we used to do in accepting it – it is not based on the hysterical disposition, but rather, as Möbius so finely expresses it, on the complication of this disposition with other types of degeneration, of innate moral inferiority. The 'malicious hysteric' develops in exactly the same way, when an innately excitable but emotionally impoverished person also falls prey to the egoistic stunting of character that is so easily engendered by chronic infirmity. The 'malicious hysteric' is, in any case, hardly any more common than the malicious patient in the later stages of tabes.

In the motor sphere, too, the surplus of excitation engenders pathological phenomena. Children who are so disposed very easily develop tic-like movements which at first stimulated by a sensation in the eyes or face, or an uncomfortable item of clothing, straightaway become permanent unless they are opposed immediately. The reflex paths are very easily and swiftly 'worn in'.

Nor can we dismiss the possibility that there are purely motor convulsive attacks, independent of any psychical factor, in which the mass of excitation that has accumulated by summation is discharged, just as the mass of stimulus caused by anatomical changes is discharged in epileptic attacks. This, then, would be non-ideogenic hysterical convulsion.

We so often see excitable but healthy adolescents fall ill with hysteria during puberty, that we have to ask if this process might not create the disposition where it is not present innately. And indeed we are obliged to attribute more to it than the mere increase of the quantum of excitation: sexual maturation affects the entire nervous system, increasing excitability everywhere and lowering resistances. We know this from the observation of adolescents who are not hysterical, and are therefore justified in thinking that it might also give rise to the hysterical disposition, in so far as it consists of this idiosyncrasy of the nervous system. By saying this we are already acknowledging sexuality as one of the major components of hysteria. We will see that its part here is much greater still and that it contributes in very many different ways to the construction of the illness.

If stigmata arise directly from the innate breeding ground of hysteria and are not of ideogenic origin, then it follows that it is impossible to place ideogenesis at the centre of hysteria as is sometimes done nowadays. What could be more genuinely hysterical than the stigmata, the pathognomonic findings that determine the diagnosis – and yet precisely they seem not to be ideogenic. But if the basis of hysteria is an idiosyncrasy of the entire nervous system, the complex of ideogenic, psychically determined symptoms is raised up from it, like a building from its foundations. And it is a *multi-storey building*. In the same way that the structure of a building like this can be understood only if one differentiates the floor plans of the various storeys, so, I believe, the understanding of hysteria depends on taking into account the various kinds of complication in the ways that symptoms are caused. If one disregards this and attempts to undertake an explanation of hysteria using one single causal nexus, a very large number of unexplained phenomena will always be left over; it is just as if one wanted to enter the various rooms of a multi-storey house into the plan of a single storey.

As with the stigmata, a number of other nervous symptoms – some pains, vasomotor phenomena, and perhaps the purely motor spasm – are, as we saw above, not caused by ideas, but are a direct consequence of the fundamental abnormality of the nervous system.

Closest to these are the ideogenic phenomena that are simply conversions of affective excitation (pp. 204–5). They arise as the consequences of affects in people of a hysterical disposition and are at first simply an 'abnormal expression of emotions' (Oppenheim).[19] Through repetition, this becomes a real, apparently purely somatic hysterical symptom, while the precipitating idea becomes imperceptible (p. 208) or is fended off and so repressed from consciousness.

Most of the fended-off and converted ideas – and the most important of them – have a sexual content. They are the basis of a large deal of pubertal hysteria. Girls who are maturing – and it is they who are primarily concerned – respond in very different ways to the sexual ideas and feelings that crowd in on them. Some respond without any inhibition, and this includes those who ignore and overlook the whole area. Others accept it like boys: this tends to be the rule with peasant or working-class girls. Another group snatches with a more or less perverse curiosity at anything that conversation and reading can tell them about sexuality. And finally, those fine-tuned natures whose great sexual excitability is equalled by their great moral purity perceive everything sexual as irreconcilable with their moral substance, as soiling and sullying.[20] This last group represses sexuality from their consciousness, and affective ideas that have this content and have caused somatic phenomena are 'fended off' and become unconscious.

The tendency to fend off the sexual is further intensified by the fact that sensual excitation in female virgins has an element of anxiety, the fear of what is unknown but suspected, of what will come, whereas in natural, healthy young men it is an unmixed aggressive drive. Girls sense in Eros the terrible power that controls and determines their fate and are frightened by it. The inclination to look away and repress what is frightening from consciousness is, then, all the greater.

Marriage brings new sexual traumas. It is surprising that the wedding night does not have a pathogenic effect more frequently, since very often it is regrettably not a matter of erotic seduction but of rape. It is, however, true that hysteria in young married women can not infrequently be traced back to this and that it disappears when in the course of time sexual pleasure has been established and the trauma has faded. Sexual traumas also occur later on in many marriages. The case histories that we are obliged to refrain from publishing contain a large number of these, perverse demands on the part of the husband, unnatural practices, and so on. I do not believe that I am exaggerating when I claim that *the great majority of severe neuroses in women originate in the marital bed*.[21]

Some aspects of sexuality that are noxious and consist principally in insufficient satisfaction (*coitus interruptus, ejaculatio praecox*, etc.) lead, according to Freud's discovery, not to hysteria but to anxiety neurosis.[22] In my opinion, however, the excitation of the sexual affect in cases such as this is converted into hysterical somatic phenomena with reasonable frequency.

It is self-evident and also follows amply from our observations that the non-sexual affects of fright, anxiety or anger lead to the development of hysterical phenomena. But it does perhaps bear repeating that the sexual factor is by far the most important and, in terms of pathology, the most fruitful. The naïve observations of our predecessors, the traces of which are preserved in the word 'hysteria', came nearer to the truth than the more recent view that puts sexuality almost last in order to protect patients from moral reproach. The sexual needs of hysterics vary just as much from person to person and are no more powerful than in healthy people. Hysterics, however, fall ill from them and, for the most part, precisely by fighting them, that is, by fending off sexuality.

Alongside sexual hysteria we should at this point recall hysteria due to fright – genuinely traumatic hysteria. It is one of the best-known and recognized forms of hysteria.

Occupying what may be called the same stratum as phenomena that have arisen through the conversion of affective excitation are those that owe their origin to suggestion (mostly auto-suggestion) in individuals who are innately suggestible. High-level suggestibility, i.e. an uninhibited predominance of newly excited ideas, is not an essential feature of hysteria, but it does occur as a complication in those disposed to hysteria, in whom precisely this idiosyncrasy of the nervous system enables the physical realization of ideas that have too great a value. In any case, it is mostly only affective ideas that can be realized by suggestion as somatic phenomena, and so the process can also frequently be understood as a conversion of the accompanying affect of fright or anxiety.

These processes – *affect conversion* and *suggestion* – remain identical even in the more complicated forms of hysteria that are to be considered now. They simply find more favourable conditions in such cases, but psychically determined hysterical phenomena always develop by one of these two processes.

The third constituent of the hysterical disposition is the *hypnoid state*, the tendency to auto-hypnosis (p. 216), which in a number of cases occurs together with those discussed above; it favours and facilitates both conversion and suggestion to the highest degree and in so doing builds, as it were, on top of the small hysterias, which display only individual hysterical phenomena, the next level of major hysteria. The tendency to auto-hypnosis constitutes what is at first only a transitory state alternating with the normal one. We can attribute to it the same heightening of psychical influence on the body as is observed under artificial hypnosis. This influence is all the more intense and far-reaching here when it affects a nervous system that is already abnormally excitable outside hypnosis.[23] We do not know to what extent and in which cases the tendency to auto-hypnosis is an innate idiosyncrasy of the organism. I voiced the opinion above (p. 219) that it develops from affect-laden reverie. But it is certain that innate disposition also plays a part. If this opinion is correct, then here too it becomes clear how great an influence is to be attributed to sexuality in the development of hysteria. For, apart from nursing, there is no psychical factor quite so well suited to engendering reverie filled with affect as the lover's longing. Moreover, the wealth of affect and restriction of consciousness in sexual orgasm itself are closely related to hypnoid states.

The hypnoid factor becomes most clearly visible as a hysterical attack and in that state which can be described as acute hysteria and which, it seems, plays such a significant role in the development of major hysteria (p. 236). These are long, clearly psychotic states, often of several months' duration, which must frequently be described as nothing other than hallucinatory confusion. Even when the disturbance is not so far-reaching, a variety of hysterical phenomena emerge in this state, some of which persist subsequently. The psychical content of these states consists in part precisely of those ideas which in waking life have been fended off and repressed from consciousness ('hysterical deliria in saints and nuns, abstinent women, and well brought-up children').

Since these states are so often virtually psychoses and yet stem directly and exclusively from hysteria, I cannot join Möbius in his view that 'with the exception of the deliria attached to attacks, it is impossible to speak of an actual hysterical insanity'.[24] These states are in many cases precisely this, and in the further course of the hysteria, too, psychoses of this kind are repeated that are in essence, it is true, nothing other than the psychotic stage of an attack, but they can hardly be described as attacks because they last for months.

How do these acute hysterias arise? In the best-known case (Case 1), it developed from the accumulation of hypnoid attacks, in another case (of pre-existing, complex hysteria), in connection with withdrawal from morphine. The process is for the most part quite opaque and awaits clarification from further observations.

Möbius's proposition that 'The essential change that occurs in hysteria is that the mental state of the hysteric resembles that of the hypnotized subject either temporarily or permanently' therefore applies to the cases of hysteria discussed here.

The fact that hysterical symptoms that have arisen in the hypnoid state persist during the normal one corresponds fully to our experiences of post-hypnotic suggestion. This already implies, however, that complexes of ideas that are inadmissible to consciousness co-exist with series of ideas whose course is conscious, that the *splitting of the psyche* is complete (p. 226). It seems certain that this can also develop without a hypnoid state, from the wealth of ideas that have been fended off and repressed from consciousness, but not suppressed. In one way or the other an area of psychical life develops that is sometimes rudimentary and lacking ideas, sometimes more or less similar to waking thought, and it is thanks above all to Binet and Janet that we are able to identify it. The splitting of the psyche marks the completion of hysteria: how it explains the principal character traits of the illness was explained above (section 5). One part of the patient's psyche is constantly in the hypnoid state, albeit with varying ideational intensity, ever ready, when waking thought wanes, to gain control over the entire person (attack, delirium). This happens as soon as a powerful affect disrupts the normal course of ideas, as in twilight states or states of exhaustion. From this persistent hypnoid state unmotivated ideas, alien to normal association, press up into consciousness, hallucinations are cast into perception, motor acts are innervated independently of conscious volition. This hypnoid psyche is capable of affect conversion and suggestion to the highest degree, and thus new hysterical phenomena develop easily, which, in the absence of psychical splitting, would have arisen only with great difficulty under the pressure of repeated affect. The split-off psyche is the *demon* by which the naïve observation of early, superstitious times believed the sick to be possessed. It is true that a spirit alien to the patient's waking consciousness prevails within him; save that it is not really alien, but a part of himself.

The attempt made here to construct hysteria from a synthesis of our present-day knowledge is open to the reproach of eclecticism, if such a reproach can be justified at all. So many formulations of hysteria from the old 'reflex theory' to the 'dissociation of the personality' have had to find a place in it. But it can scarcely be otherwise. So very many excellent observers and acute minds have engaged with hysteria, that it is unlikely that there was not some truth in all their formulations. In the future when the true state of affairs is represented it will undoubtedly contain them all, merely combining all the one-sided views of the object to create a physical reality. Eclecticism, therefore, does not seem to me a blemish.

But how far we still are today from the possibility of any such complete understanding of hysteria! With what uncertain strokes the contours have been outlined, with what crude hypotheses the yawning gaps have been covered up rather than filled in. Only one consideration is of some comfort – that all physiological representations of complicated psychical processes are flawed in this way, and necessarily so. What Theseus says of tragedy in *A Midsummer Night's Dream* is true of these representations: 'The best of this kind are but shadows'. And even the weakest is not without value if it attempts, in truth and modesty, to capture the outlines of shadows cast upon the wall by objects that are real but unknown. For then we are still justified in hoping that there will be some measure of agreement and resemblance between the real processes and our idea of them.

(1895)

Notes

1. Möbius, 'Über den Begriff der Hysterie' ['On the Concept of Hysteria'], reprinted in *Neurologische Beiträge*, vol. I, 1894.

2. This perceptual apparatus, including the sensory areas of the cortex, must differ from the organ that stores and reproduces sense impressions as memory-images. For the basic precondition for the function of the perceptual apparatus is the swiftest possible restitution of its *status quo ante*; without this it would no longer be possible for proper perception to occur. The precondition for memory, on the other hand, is that a restitution of this kind does not take place, but that every perception creates lasting changes. It is impossible for one and the same organ to satisfy these two contradictory conditions; the mirror of a reflecting telescope cannot simultaneously be a photographic plate. I am in agreement with Meynert in the sense that the excitation of the perceptual apparatus gives hallucinations their objective character, though not as regards the more specific claim that the excitation of the subcortical centres is involved. If, however, the perceptual organ is excited by the memory-image, then we have to assume that its excitability has been abnormally altered and that this does in fact make hallucination possible.

3. Oppenheim's 'lability of molecules'. In time it may be possible to replace what is expressed very vaguely above with a more precise and meaningful formula.

4. Permit me to give a brief indication of the underlying idea of the exposition given above. We usually think of the sensitive and sensory nerve cells as passive organs of reception – wrongly so. For the very existence of the system of associative fibres is proof that there is also a flow of excitation from these cells into the nerve fibres. If excitation flows from two sensory cells into a nerve fibre that connects them, whether *per continuitatem* or *per contiguitatem*, then a state of tension must be present in it. This state bears the same relation to the outward flow of excitation from, for example, a peripheral motor fibre as does hydrostatic pressure to the living force of flowing water or electric tension to an electric current. If all the nerve cells

are in a state of mean excitation and are exciting their nerve processes, this immense network will in its entirety create a unified reservoir of 'nervous tension'. So, in addition to the potential energy latent in the cell's chemical reserves and to that unknown form of kinetic energy that drains away when the fibres are in a state of excitation, we have to assume that there is a dormant state of nervous excitation, *tonic excitation* or *nervous tension*.

5. There is a long-standing conception of the energy of the central nervous system as a quantity whose distribution throughout the brain fluctuates and changes. 'La sensibilité', wrote Cabanis, 'semble se comporter à la manière d'un fluide dont la quantité totale est déterminée et qui, toutes les fois qu'il se jette en plus grande abondance dans un de ses canaux, diminue proportionellement dans les autres.' ['Sensibility', wrote Cabanis, 'appears to behave like a fluid whose total quantity is predetermined and which, whenever it flows more plentifully into one of its channels, causes a proportional decrease in the others.'] (Janet, *Etat mental* [*The Mental State of Hysterics*], 1894, II, p. 277.)

6. Lange, *Über Gemütsbewegungen* [*On the Emotions*], 1887.

7. The drive for revenge, which is so powerful in natural man and is more disguised than suppressed by civilization, is really nothing more than the excitation of a reflex that has not been released. Defending oneself against injury in a fight and thereby injuring the opponent is the appropriate, preformed psychical reflex. Should it be insufficiently performed, or not performed at all, it will repeatedly be released by recollection and the 'revenge drive' arises, which, as with all 'drives', is an irrational impulse of the will. The proof of this is precisely its irrationality, its lack of regard for usefulness or efficacy, indeed its victory over any consideration for one's own safety. As soon as the reflex has been released, this irrationality can enter consciousness.

> 'Ein anderes Antlitz, bevor sie geschehen,
>   ein anderes trägt die vollbrachte Tat.'
> ['An act bears one face before it happens,
>   Another once it has been completed.']

8. I have no wish to flog the comparison with an electrical system to death; indeed, in view of the fundamentally different conditions it is barely able to illustrate the processes of the nervous system and certainly cannot explain them. But we would still do well to call to mind how the insulation of a lighting system is damaged by high tension, producing a 'short circuit' at one point; should electrical phenomena (such as heating, sparking and so on) now appear at this point, the lamp at the end of the wire will not light.

In the same way the affect will not arise if the excitation flows off as an abnormal reflex and is converted into a somatic phenomenon.

9. See, on this point, some interesting communications and remarks by Benedikt (1889), reprinted in the text *Hypnotismus und Suggestion* [*Hypnotism and Suggestion*], 1894, p. 51 and ff.

10. There is an observation in Mach's 'Bewegungsempfindungen' ['Sensations of Movement'] that it is well worth recalling here:

'It has repeatedly been shown in the experiments (on dizziness) described here that a feeling of nausea tended to come on when it was difficult to bring the sensations of movement into harmony with the optical impressions. It appeared that one part of the stimulus being emitted by the labyrinth had been forced to abandon the optical paths that had been closed off to it by another stimulus and to take up quite different paths ... I have also repeatedly observed a feeling of nausea when the attempt is made to combine stereoscopic images which differ greatly from one another.'

This is precisely the physiological schema for the genesis of pathological, hysterical phenomena as a result of the co-existence of vivid, irreconcilable ideas.

11. I am grateful to Herr Assistent Dr Paul Karplus for this case.

12. These and later references to ideas that are effective in the present, albeit unconscious, rarely involve single ideas (as, for example, Anna O.'s hallucination of a large snake that set off her contracture), but almost always complexes of ideas, connections, memories of external processes and the subject's own trains of thought. Occasionally, all of the single ideas contained within such complexes are consciously thought. Only the specific combination is excluded from consciousness.

13. Möbius, 'Über Astasie-Abasie' ['On Astasia-Abasia'], *Neurologische Beiträge*, vol. I, p. 17.

14. By this description Möbius may mean nothing other than that the flow of ideas is inhibited, as indeed occurs when there is an affect, even if the reasons for it are quite different from those under hypnosis.

15. Cases 1 and 2.

16. This expression ['*bewußtseinsunfähig*'] is not unambiguous and therefore leaves much to be desired; it is formed by analogy with '*hoffähig*' ['admissible at court'] and we hope that, for want of a better term, it will serve.

17. I must add, however, that in precisely the best known and most transparent case of major hysteria with manifest *double conscience*, that is, the case of Anna O. (Case 1), no residue was transferred from the acute stage into the chronic one, and all the phenomena in the latter had already been

engendered during the 'incubation period' in hypnoid and affective states.

18. Oppenheim's 'lability of molecules'.

19. This disposition is precisely what Strümpell describes as 'the disruption in the psycho-physical domain' which is at the basis of hysteria.

20. Some observations lead us to believe that this is very frequently the origin of the fear of touching, which is in fact a fear of being soiled and which compels women constantly to wash their hands. The washing stems from the same internal process as in Lady Macbeth.

21. It is undoubtedly unfortunate that medical practice ignores or only delicately hints at this, one of the most important pathological factors. This is certainly a matter in which the experience of the experienced should be communicated to the young doctor, who usually blindly overlooks sexuality – at least as far as his patients are concerned.

22. Freud, 'Über die Berechtigung, von der Neurasthenie einen bestimmten Symptomenkomplex als "Angstneurose" abzutrennen' ['On the Grounds for Detaching a Particular Syndrome from Neurasthenia under the Description "Anxiety Neurosis"'], *Neurol. Zentralblatt*, 1895, 14(2) [*Standard Edition*, vol. III].

23. It is tempting to identify the disposition to hypnosis with innate abnormal excitability, since artificial hypnosis also displays ideogenic changes in secretion and local blood-supply, the formation of blisters and so on. This seems to be the opinion of Möbius. In my opinion, however, this is a circular argument. As far as I can see, the miracle-work of hypnosis can in fact be observed only in hysterics. We would then be attributing the effects of hysteria to hypnosis, only to derive them from hypnosis again.

24. Möbius, 'Gegenwärtige Auffassung der Hysterie' ['On the Contemporary Conception of Hysteria'], *Monatsschrift für Geburtshilfe und Gynäkologie*, 1895, vol. I, p. 18.

IV

On the Psychotherapy of Hysteria

(Freud)

In the 'Preliminary Statement' we reported that during our research into the aetiology of hysterical symptoms we had come upon a therapeutic method which we held to be of practical importance. *'We found, at first to our great surprise, that the individual hysterical symptoms disappeared immediately and did not recur if we succeeded in wakening the memory of the precipitating event with complete clarity, arousing with it the accompanying affect, and if the patient then depicted the event in the greatest possible detail and put words to the affect.'* (p. 10).

We further sought to gain an understanding of how our therapeutic method works: ['It] *removes the effectiveness of the idea that had not originally been abreacted by allowing its trapped affect to drain away through speech; it then submits the idea to associative correction by drawing it into normal consciousness (under light hypnosis) or by using the doctor's suggestion to remove it, as occurs in somnambulism with amnesia.'* (p. 19).

I will now try to set forth coherently the range of the method, the nature of its advantages over others, how it operates in terms of technique, and the kinds of difficulties it encounters. I will do so even though much of the substance is already given in the preceding case histories and I will not, therefore, be able to avoid repeating myself in this account.

1

For my own part, I too may say that I can still stand by the contents of the 'Preliminary Statement'. I must admit, though, that in the years that have passed since then – during which I have ceaselessly been occupied with the problems touched on in it – new perspectives have occurred to me that have resulted in what is at least in part a different grouping and conception of the factual material I knew of at the time. It would be unjust to burden my honourable friend J. Breuer with too much of the responsibility for this development. The following remarks are, therefore, advanced predominantly in my own name.

When I attempted to apply Breuer's method of curing hysterical symptoms by investigation and abreaction under hypnosis to a greater number of patients, I encountered two difficulties and in following them through arrived at a modification of both technique and conception. 1. Not all of those who displayed unambiguously hysterical symptoms, and who were in all probability governed by the same psychical mechanism, could be hypnotized. 2. I had then to take a view on the question of what the principal characteristics of hysteria were and how it was demarcated from other neuroses.

I will defer my account of how I mastered the former difficulty and what I learnt from it until later. First, I want to go into the attitude that I adopted towards the second problem in daily practice. It is very difficult really to penetrate a case of neurosis until one has subjected it to a thorough analysis, that is, to an analysis that results only from the application of Breuer's method. But the decision about the diagnosis and type of therapy has to be made before one has a thorough knowledge of this kind. I had no choice, then, but to select the cathartic method for the kind of case that could provisionally be diagnosed as hysteria and in which one or several of the stigmata or characteristic symptoms of hysteria were recognizable. Sometimes it then happened that, despite the diagnosis of hysteria, the therapeutic results proved very poor indeed and even the analysis itself failed to bring anything significant to light. On other occasions

I used Breuer's method in an attempt to treat neuroses that certainly would not have struck anyone as hysterical, and found that they could be influenced and even solved in this way. This was my experience of obsessive ideas, genuine obsessions according to Westphal's model, in cases where no single trait was reminiscent of hysteria. This meant that the psychical mechanism exposed in the 'Preliminary Statement' could not be pathognomonic for hysteria. I was also unable to bring myself to throw in so many other neuroses with hysteria simply because of this mechanism. In the end I was released from all the doubts that had been aroused by the plan of treating all the neuroses in question as I would a hysteria, of searching everywhere for the aetiology and nature of the psychical mechanism, and of letting the decision as to the justifiability of diagnosing hysteria depend on the outcome of the investigation.

So, proceeding from Breuer's method, I came to be occupied principally with the aetiology and mechanism of neuroses. I then had the good fortune of achieving some useful results in a relatively short period of time. What struck me initially was the recognition that in as much as one could speak of how the *acquisition* of neuroses is caused, the aetiology was to be sought in *sexual* factors. In addition to this it was found that a variety of sexual factors, in the most general sense, also engenders a variety of pictures of neurotic disorders. And so, in the degree to which this relation was confirmed, one could also venture to use aetiology to characterize the neuroses and to establish sharp distinctions between the clinical pictures of the different neuroses. If the aetiological characteristics constantly coincided with the clinical ones, this was indeed justified.

In this way I realized that *neurasthenia* really corresponds to a monotonous clinical picture in which, as the analyses demonstrated, 'psychical mechanisms' play no part. There is a clear demarcation between neurasthenia and obsessive neurosis, the neurosis of genuinely obsessive ideas, which can be identified by its complicated psychical mechanism, its aetiology (similar to that of hysteria), and the far-reaching possibility of reducing it by psychotherapy. On the other hand it seemed to me unreservedly necessary to isolate from neurasthenia a complex of neurotic symptoms that depends on a quite different aetiology, one which is basically antithetical; the individual symptoms making up this complex are unified by the characteristic distinguished by E. Hecker.[1] They are in fact either the symptoms or equivalents and rudiments of *expressions of anxiety* and for this reason I have called this complex that is to be separated from neurasthenia, *anxiety neurosis*. I have asserted that it comes about through the accumulation of physical tension, which is itself again sexual in origin. This neurosis is also lacking a psychical mechanism, but it has a quite regular influence on psychical life, so that it is regularly expressed as, among other things, 'anxious expectation', phobias, hyperaesthesia to pains, and so on. This anxiety neurosis, as I understand it, coincides in part with the neurosis that in so many accounts is acknowledged alongside hysteria and neurasthenia under the name 'hypochondria', save that I cannot take the demarcation of this neurosis in any of the works in question to be correct and find that the usefulness of the term hypochondria is impaired by its fixed connection with the symptom of 'fear of illness'.

Once I had fixed in this way the simple pictures of neurasthenia, anxiety neurosis and obsessive ideas, I tackled the interpretation of the commonly occurring cases of neurosis that are involved in the diagnosis of hysteria. I had to say to myself at this point that it is not appropriate to stamp a neurosis as hysterical in its entirety just because a few hysterical signs stand out from its complex of symptoms. It was easy enough for me to account for this practice, since hysteria is after all the most ancient, best-known and most striking of the neuroses in question; but it still constituted a misuse, the same misuse that allowed hysteria to be held accountable for so many traits of perversion and degeneration. Whenever a sign of hysteria, such as an anaesthesia, or characteristic attack, was uncovered in a complicated case of psychical degeneracy, the whole condition was called 'hysteria', and so the worst and most contradictory things could readily be brought together under this label. But if it was certain that *this* diagnosis was incorrect, it was equally certain that one might also separate out the neuroses, and since neurasthenia, anxiety neurosis and so on were known in their pure state, there was no longer any need to overlook them when combined with each other.

The following interpretation seemed, therefore, to be more legitimate: commonly occurring neuroses are, for the most part, to be described as 'mixed'; neurasthenia and anxiety neurosis are easily found in their pure forms as well, most often in young people. Pure cases of hysteria and obsessive neurosis are rare, as both are usually combined with an anxiety neurosis. Mixed neuroses occur with such frequency because their aetiological factors are so frequently intermixed, sometimes simply by chance, sometimes as a result of causal relations between the processes from which the aetiological factors of the neuroses issue. This can be demonstrated and proven without difficulty; but for hysteria it follows that it is hardly possible to wrench it from the interconnected sexual neuroses for inspection, that as a rule it represents only one side, one aspect of the complicated case of neurosis, and that only in, as it were, borderline cases can it be uncovered and treated as an isolated neurosis. In a number of cases one might say, *a potiori fit denominatio* [it has been named according to its most important feature].

I want to test the case histories reported here to see if they speak in favour of my view that hysteria is not an independent clinical entity. Anna O., Breuer's patient, seems to be an illustration of a purely hysterical illness and so to present a contradiction. But this case, which has proved so fruitful in the recognition of hysteria, was never considered by its observer from the perspective of sexual neurosis and has now simply become unusable in this respect. When I began to analyse the second patient, Frau Emmy von N., I was quite far from expecting to find a sexual neurosis as the basis of hysteria; I had come straight from the school of Charcot and considered it a form of insult to connect hysteria with the theme of sexuality – rather as the female patients themselves tend to. When I glance through my notes on this case now, there is no doubt but that I have to recognize a case of severe anxiety neurosis, with anxious expectation and phobias, which stemmed from sexual abstinence and had been combined with hysteria.

Case 3, the case of Miss Lucy R., is perhaps most likely to be

Studies in Hysteria

termed a borderline case of pure hysteria. It was a short hysteria
that ran an episodic course and its aetiology was unmistakably sexual,
as would correspond to an anxiety neurosis. The patient was an
over-mature girl, in need of love, whose affection was too quickly
awakened by a misunderstanding. Yet the anxiety neurosis could not
be proved or escaped me. Case 4, Katharina, is practically a model
of what I have termed virginal anxiety: it is a combination of anxiety
neurosis and hysteria in which the former creates the symptoms and
the latter repeats and works with them. This is, incidentally, a typical
case for so many neuroses suffered by the young that are termed
'hysteria'. Case 5, that of Elisabeth von R., was once again not
investigated as a sexual neurosis and I could only voice but not
confirm my suspicion that its foundation was a spinal neurasthenia.
But I must add that pure hysterias have, in my experience, become
far rarer since then. That I was able to put together these four cases
as hysteria, and in discussing them to disregard aspects that were
decisive as regards sexual neuroses, is due to the fact that these are
relatively old cases and that at the time I had not yet undertaken
deliberate and penetrating research into their neurotic, sexual foundation. And I have refrained from replacing my account of these
four cases with an analysis of twelve which would produce a confir-
mation of the psychical mechanism of hysterical phenomena proposed by us, simply because the analysis revealed that these cases
were, simultaneously, sexual neuroses, although it is certain that no
one making the diagnosis would have refused to call them 'hysteria'.
But the elucidation of sexual neuroses such as these oversteps the
bounds of our joint publication.

I would not want to be misunderstood as not wanting to let
hysteria count as an independent neurotic affection, as if I grasped
it only as the psychical expression of anxiety neurosis, as if I ascribed
only 'ideogenic' symptoms to it and were transferring the somatic
symptoms (hysterogenic points, anaesthesias) to the anxiety neurosis. Nothing of the sort; in my opinion, hysteria that has been
purified of all additional factors can be dealt with as independent in
every respect save that of therapy. For in therapy it is a matter of
practical goals, of removing the state of suffering in its entirety, and

if hysteria occurs mostly as the component of a mixed neurosis, then the case is probably similar to a mixed infection in which the task is to preserve life, a task which does not coincide with that of fighting the effect of any one pathogen.

It is of great importance to me to distinguish hysteria's share in the clinical pictures of mixed neuroses from that of neurasthenia, anxiety neurosis and so on, because, once this separation has been made, I can give a concise formulation of the therapeutic value of the cathartic method. I would, then, venture to say that it is – in principle – highly capable of removing any kind of hysterical symptom, but, as can easily be seen, utterly powerless against the phenomena of neurasthenia and that it only rarely and circuitously influences the psychical consequences of anxiety neurosis. Thus in individual cases its therapeutic effectiveness will depend on whether the hysterical components of the clinical picture can claim a position of practical significance by comparison with the other neurotic components.

As has already been indicated in the 'Preliminary Statement', there is a further limitation to the efficacy of the cathartic method. It does not influence the basic causes of hysteria and is therefore unable to prevent new symptoms developing in the place of those that have been removed. All in all, then, I have to claim a prominent place for our therapeutic method within the framework of a therapy of neuroses, but would like to advise against valuing or applying it outside this context. Since in this context I cannot give a 'neurosis therapy' of the kind needed by practising doctors, the above statements amount to a postponement of my account until some later publication. I believe that I can, however, append the following remarks in the way of an exposition and elucidation.

1. I do not claim actually to have removed all the hysterical symptoms that I undertook to influence with the cathartic method. But in my opinion the obstacles concerned the individual circumstances of the cases and were not of a theoretical nature. In passing judgement, I can disregard these failed cases in the same way that the surgeon puts aside cases of death during anaesthesia as a result of post-operative haemorrhage, or of chance sepsis and so on, when

making a decision about a new technique. When later I come to deal with the difficulties and ills of the procedure, failures originating in this way will again be given due consideration.

2. The cathartic method does not lose its value because it is *symptomatic* and not *causal*. For causal therapy is on the whole really only a prophylactic: it hinders the continuing effect of the harmful agent, but does not necessarily remove what it has already produced. As a rule, a second operation is usually required to solve this latter problem, and for this purpose in cases of hysteria the cathartic method really cannot be bettered.

3. When a period of hysterical production, that is, an acute hysterical paroxysm, has been overcome and only the hysterical symptoms remain in the form of residual manifestations, the cathartic method is sufficient for all indications and its results are completely and permanently successful. It is not unusual for a favourable therapeutic constellation like this to occur precisely in the area of sexual life, as a consequence of the great variations in the intensity of sexual needs and of the complicated conditions needed to bring about sexual trauma. In this area the cathartic method accomplishes everything that one might ask of it, for the doctor cannot make it his business to change a constitution like that of the hysteric. He must content himself with removing the illness to which a constitution such as this inclines and which can arise from it when assisted by external conditions. He will be satisfied if the patient has recovered her stamina. Nor does he lack consolation for the future when he considers the possibility of a relapse. He knows the main characteristic in the aetiology of neuroses, that their genesis is on the whole *overdetermined* and that several factors must coincide for this to take effect, and he may hope that even if individual aetiological factors are still operative they do not coincide again too soon.

The objection could be made that in cases where hysteria has run its course, the remaining symptoms in any case disappear spontaneously. In response, however, one might say that the course of a spontaneous cure of this kind is very often neither swift enough nor sufficiently complete, and that it can be assisted immeasurably by the intervention of therapy. For now we can be content to leave unanswered the question of whether cathartic therapy cures only what can be cured spontaneously, or if it sometimes cures other things that would not have been resolved spontaneously.

4. When one encounters an acute hysteria, a case that is in the period of the most active production of hysterical symptoms and in which the self is consistently overpowered by the products of the illness (hysterical psychosis), even the cathartic method will change little in the appearance and course of the illness. This means that one is probably in the same position *vis-à-vis* the neurosis as that taken by a doctor towards an acute infectious disease. The aetiological factors have taken effect sufficiently during a time that has passed and is now beyond influence; once the incubation period has been overcome, these same factors become manifest; the affection cannot be broken off, one has to let it run its course and in the meantime create the most beneficial conditions for the patient. If during an acute period such as this one removes the products of the illness, the newly developed hysterical symptoms, one must be prepared for those that have been removed to be replaced immediately by new ones. The doctor will not be spared the depressing sense that this is a Sisyphean task, an endless whitewashing. The immense expenditure of effort and the dissatisfaction of the patient's family, who will hardly be as familiar with the necessary duration of an acute neurosis as in the analogous case of an acute infectious disease, these and other factors are on the whole likely to make it almost impossible to apply the cathartic method consistently in the case posited here. Yet it remains a matter for serious consideration whether the regular removal of the products of the illness, even in an acute hysteria, might not exercise a curative influence by supporting the patient's normal self, which is occupied with fending them off, and by preserving it from being overpowered, from falling into a psychosis and perhaps even a permanent state of confusion.

What the cathartic method is able to achieve, even in cases of acute hysteria, and how it even limits the production of new pathological symptoms in a way that is of practical importance, is undoubtedly illuminated by the history of Anna O. in which Breuer first learnt how to practise this psychotherapeutic procedure.

5. Those cases in which the course of the hysteria is chronic and the production of hysterical symptoms moderate but incessant may cause us most keenly to regret that there is no causally effective therapy, but also to value most highly the importance of the cathartic procedure as a symptomatic therapy. In this instance one is concerned with the damage done by an aetiology that continues to have a chronic effect; the primary concern is then to strengthen the capacity for resistance of the patient's nervous system, and one has to remind oneself that the existence of a hysterical symptom indicates a weakening of the resistance of the nervous system and represents a factor predisposing to hysteria. As can be seen from the mechanism of monosymptomatic hysteria, a new hysterical symptom is most readily formed in connection and analogy with a pre-existing one; the place where it has already 'broken through' once before (see pp. 205–6) represents a weak point at which it will break through again on the next occasion. Once the psychical group has been split off, it plays the part of a growth-provoking crystal: a crystallization that would otherwise have failed to occur develops from it. Disposing of the symptoms that are already present and removing the psychical changes that underlie them means restoring the patients' capacity for resistance to its full extent, so that they can successfully withstand the effects of the harmful agent. A great deal can be done for patients such as this by means of prolonged periods of supervision and periodic 'chimney-sweeping' (p. 34).

6. It remains for me to revisit the apparent contradiction between the admission that not all hysterical symptoms are psychogenic and the claim that they can all be disposed of by a psychotherapeutic procedure. The solution lies in the fact that although some of these non-psychogenic symptoms are signs of the illness (such as stigmata), it is impossible to describe them as ailments. Whether or not they persist beyond the therapeutic resolution of the illness is then of no practical importance. It seems to be true of other symptoms of this kind that in some roundabout way they are swept away with the psychogenic symptoms, for after all it is probable that they too, in some roundabout way, depend on psychical causation.

*

I have now to mention the difficulties and negative aspects of our therapeutic procedure in so far as these may not become clear to everyone from the preceding case histories or the subsequent observations on the technique of this method. – I will list and give an indication of these difficulties rather than supplying a detailed description. The procedure is laborious and time-consuming for the doctor; it demands a great interest in psychological incidents as well as empathy for the patient. I could not imagine myself able to become absorbed in the psychical mechanism of a hysteria in someone who seemed to me base or repellent, and who would not on closer acquaintance be able to arouse human sympathy, whereas I can of course carry out the treatment of someone suffering from tabes or rheumatism independently of whether or not they appeal to me personally. The demands on the patient are no less great. The procedure is not at all applicable below a certain level of intelligence; any element of feeble-mindedness makes it extraordinarily difficult. One needs the patients' full consent and full attention, but above all one needs their trust, since the analysis leads regularly to the most intimate and secret psychical processes. A good number of patients who would be suited to this treatment withdraw from the doctor as soon as the suspicion dawns on them of the direction that will be taken by his investigation. For these patients the doctor has remained a stranger. Others have taken the decision to put themselves in the hands of their doctor and to place their confidence in him – an action that is normally only ever made of one's own free will, but is never demanded – and in the case of these patients it can scarcely be avoided that the personal relationship with the doctor should, at least for a time, be pushed unduly to the fore. Indeed, it seems that for the doctor to exercise an influence of this kind might even be the sole condition under which the problem can be solved. I do not think that there is a significant difference here between being able to use hypnosis or having to avoid and replace it. Yet it is only right to stress that although our procedure is inseparable from these negative aspects it cannot be blamed for them. Rather, it is perfectly comprehensible that they have their basis in the preconditions of the neuroses that are to be cured and that they will necessarily be involved in any medical activity that is accompanied by an intense concern with the patient and introduces a psychical change in him. I was never able to trace any damage or danger back to the application of hypnosis, however extensive my use of this method in some cases. Where I did cause damage the reasons lay elsewhere and went deeper. If I take an overview of the therapeutic efforts made during the years since the reports made by my distinguished teacher and friend J. Breuer placed the cathartic method in my hands, I believe that I have, in fact, done far more good and more frequently done good than harm, and that I have achieved some things that no other therapeutic means would have managed. To quote the 'Preliminary Statement', its 'therapeutic advantages' were, on the whole, considerable.

There is another advantage of applying this procedure that I must emphasize. I know no better means of working out a severe case of complicated neurosis in which there is a greater or lesser element of hysteria than subjecting it to Breuer's method. The first thing that happens is that whatever is exhibiting the hysterical mechanism disappears. But this analysis also taught me how to interpret the remaining manifestations and how to trace their aetiology, thereby securing the grounds for deciding which of the therapeutic instruments for combating neuroses is appropriate to the case in question. If I think of how much my judgement of a case of neurosis differs *before* and *after* having made such an analysis, I am almost tempted to believe that this analysis is indispensable to our understanding of a neurotic illness. I have, in addition, taken to combining the application of cathartic psychotherapy with a rest-cure, which, if required, can be built up to the complete Weir-Mitchell feeding treatment. This has the advantage for me of on the one hand avoiding the influence of new psychical impressions, which is highly disruptive during psychotherapy, and on the other hand ruling out the boredom of the feeding treatment in which it is not uncommon for the patient to lapse into harmful dreaming. It might be expected that the often quite considerable burden of psychical work that is placed on the patient in the course of a cathartic cure, and the excitations resulting from the reproduction of traumatic experiences, would be contrary to the spirit of the Weir-Mitchell *rest-cure* and would prevent the success that one usually sees it achieve. Yet the opposite is true; by combining Breuer's therapy with that of Weir-Mitchell one achieves all the physical improvement that one would expect of the latter, and a far-reaching psychical influence of the kind never achieved by the rest-cure without psychotherapy.

2

I want now to take up the observations that I made earlier, namely that when I tried to apply Breuer's method more extensively I came across the problem that a number of patients could not be placed under hypnosis although their diagnosis was one of hysteria, and in all likelihood the psychical mechanism that we have described applied. I needed hypnosis, of course, to expand the patient's memory so that I could find pathogenic recollections that were not present in normal consciousness: I had, therefore, either to give up treating these patients or try to bring about this expansion by some other means.

I was just as little able as anyone else to explain why some people can be hypnotized and others not, and so could not pursue a causal path to resolve this difficulty. All that I noticed was that in a number of patients the obstacle lay still further back; they refused even the attempt to hypnotize them. I then came upon the idea that the two cases might be identical and that both might signify an unwillingness. The person who cannot be hypnotized has a psychical objection to hypnosis, regardless of whether this is expressed as unwillingness or not. I am still not clear whether I can maintain this interpretation.

But the issue was to bypass hypnosis and still obtain the pathogenic recollections. This I achieved in the following way.

When on the first meeting with my patients I asked if they remembered what first gave rise to the symptom in question, some would say that they did not know at all, others would produce something that they described as a dim recollection and were unable to pursue any further. If, according to Bernheim's example of waking

impressions that had supposedly been forgotten from a somnambulistic state, I then became pressing, assured both groups that they
did know, that they would think of it, and so on (see pp. 112 ff.),
then something would occur to the first group, and in the case of
the others, the recollection would reach a little further back. Now I
would become still more pressing, tell the patients to lie down and
make themselves close their eyes so as to 'concentrate', which at
least produced a degree of resemblance to hypnosis, and at this
point I discovered that without any hypnosis new and more remote
recollections were emerging that probably were of relevance to us.
Experiences such as this gave me the impression that simply by
pushing the patients it would in fact be possible to bring to light a
series of pathogenic ideas that were undoubtedly present. And since
pushing in this way demanded exertion on my part and suggested
that there was a resistance to be overcome, I simply converted this
fact into the theory that *through my psychical work I had to overcome a psychical force in the patients that was opposed to the
pathogenic ideas becoming conscious (being recollected)*. A new
understanding now seemed to be opening up to me, as it occurred
to me that this might well be the same psychical force that had
contributed to the genesis of the hysterical symptom and prevented
the pathogenic idea from becoming conscious at the time. What sort
of force was likely to have been effective here and what could the
motive be that had brought it into effect? It was easy for me to form
an opinion on this matter, since I already had a few completed
analyses at my disposal in which I had become familiar with examples
of ideas that were pathogenic and had been forgotten and removed
from consciousness. These allowed me to see the general character
of ideas like this: they were all of a distressing nature, fit to arouse
the affects of shame, self-reproach, psychical pain and the feeling of
impairment; all represented the kind of affect that one would like
not to have experienced and would prefer to forget. What resulted
from all of this, as if of its own accord, was the thought of *defence*.
It is, after all, generally admitted by psychologists that the acceptance
of a new idea (acceptance in the sense of believing or recognizing
as real) depends on the nature and direction of the ideas that are

already united in the self, and they have created particular technical terms for the process of censorship to which the new arrival is subject. The patient's self had been approached by an idea that proved to be intolerable, and aroused on the part of the self a force of repulsion, which had aimed to *defend* itself against this intolerable idea. This defence was in fact successful, the idea in question was forced out of consciousness and memory, and its psychical trace was, it seems, not to be found. Yet the trace had to be present. When I endeavoured to draw the patient's attention to it, I became aware of this same force that had manifested itself as *repulsion* in the genesis of the symptom in the form of *resistance*. If I could now make a plausible case for the idea having become pathogenic precisely as a result of its having been expelled and repressed, then the chain would seem to be complete. In several of the discussions of our case histories and in a short study of 'Die Abwehr-Neuropsychosen' ['The Neuro-Psychoses of Defence'] (1894) [*Standard Edition*, vol. III] I have tried to give an indication of the psychological hypotheses that can also help to illustrate this connection – the fact of *conversion*.

A psychical force, then, aversion on the part of the self, had originally pushed the pathogenic idea out of association and was now opposing its return to memory. The hysteric's not-knowing was, therefore, a more or less conscious not-wanting-to-know, and the therapist's task consists in overcoming this *resistance to association* through psychical work. This can be accomplished first by means of 'pushing', through the application of psychical compulsion in order to direct the patient's attention to the traces of ideas that are being sought. But this is not the end of his work, since in the course of an analysis, as I will show, it will take on other forms and call further psychical forces to its aid.

But first I want to dwell a little longer on the 'pushing'. One still doesn't get very far with simple assurances such as 'You do know really', 'Just tell me', 'It will come to you in a minute'. Even a patient who is in a state of 'concentration' will find that their thread is broken after just a few sentences. It must be borne in mind, however, that a quantitative comparison – the conflict between motives of varying strength and intensity – is always involved. For an unfamiliar doctor who is unacquainted with the matter, 'pushing' will be no match for the 'resistance to association' of a serious hysteria. More powerful means must be devised.

At this point I turn first to a small technical trick. I tell the patient that in a moment I am going to apply pressure to his forehead, assure him that throughout the application of this pressure a memory will appear to him either in the form of an image or as an idea coming to mind, and I make him promise to tell me about this image or idea, whatever it may be. He is not allowed to keep it to himself because he thinks, say, that it is not what is being sought after, not the right thing, or because it is too unpleasant for him to say it. No criticism, no reserve, whether for emotional reasons or because the patient has a poor opinion of the idea. This was the only way that we could find what we were looking for, but in this way we would unfailingly find it. So for a few seconds I press on the forehead of the patient lying in front of me, then release it, and ask in a calm tone of voice, as if disappointment were out of the question, 'What did you see?' or 'What occurred to you?'

This procedure taught me a great deal and always achieved its aim. Nowadays I cannot do without it. Of course I know that I could replace this pressure on the forehead with some other signal or by exercising some other physical influence on the patient, but when the patient is lying in front of me, applying pressure to the forehead or taking his head in my hands proves to be the most comfortable action for my purpose, and the action most conducive to suggestion. To explain the effectiveness of this trick, I could say something to the effect that it corresponds to a 'hypnosis that is momentarily intensified', save that I find the mechanism of hypnosis so puzzling that I would not like to draw on it as a means of explanation. I believe rather that the advantage of the procedure lies in its enabling me to dissociate the patient's attention from his conscious searching and reflecting, in short, from everything which is an expression of his will, rather as must happen when one stares into a crystal ball or such like. But the lesson that I draw from the fact that what I am looking for always appears under the pressure of my hand is as follows: the pathogenic idea that has supposedly been forgotten is always lying ready 'close by' and can be reached through associations that are easily accessible – it is simply a matter of clearing away some kind of obstacle. This obstacle, once again, seems to be the person's will and different people have a greater or lesser facility for learning how to relinquish their intentionality and become the perfectly objective observers of the psychical processes within them.

What emerges under the pressure of my hand is not always a 'forgotten' recollection; indeed, truly pathogenic recollections are very rarely to be found so close to the surface. It is far more frequent for an idea to emerge that is an intermediary link in the chain of association between the initial idea and the pathogenic idea that we are looking for, or an idea that forms the starting point in a new series of thoughts and memories, of which the endpoint is the pathogenic idea. The pressure has not, then, uncovered the pathogenic idea – which would in any case be incomprehensible were it torn precipitately from its context – but pointed the way to it and indicated the direction in which the investigation has to proceed. The idea that has initially been wakened by the pressure can, in this instance, take the form of a well-known recollection that has never been repressed. If, when moving towards the pathogenic idea, the context is again broken off, all that is required is a repetition of the procedure, of the pressure, to establish new bearings and a new point from which to begin.

In other instances, the pressure of one's hand wakens a recollection that is in itself well known to the patient but whose appearance nevertheless amazes him because he had forgotten its connection to the idea from which we started. This connection is then proven in the later course of the analysis. Everything that results from the application of pressure gives the deceptive impression that there is a superior intelligence exterior to the consciousness of the patient, which has specific reasons for keeping a large amount of psychical material in order and has made a meaningful arrangement by which this material may return to consciousness. I suspect, however, that this second intelligence exists in appearance only.

In every complicated analysis one's work is repeatedly, in fact continuously, aided by this procedure (pressure on the forehead). Sometimes, if the patient becomes incapable of tracing thoughts back when awake, the procedure will show the way ahead by means of recollections that have not been forgotten; sometimes it will draw attention to connections that have been forgotten; sometimes call up and append recollections which, although withdrawn from association for many years, are still recognizable as recollections; and finally, its greatest achievement in terms of reproduction, the procedure allows ideas to emerge which the patient will never acknowledge as his own, which he does not *remember*, although he admits that the context calls for them inexorably, and yet at the same time he becomes convinced that precisely these ideas will bring about the conclusion of the analysis and the cessation of his symptoms.

I want to try to list a few examples of the excellent results of this technical procedure.

I was treating a young girl with an unbearable *tussis nervosa* [nervous cough] that had dragged on for six years, was clearly being fed by common catarrh, yet had to have strong psychical motives. Every other therapy had long since proved impotent, so I attempted to remove the symptom by means of psychical analysis. All that the patient knows is that her nervous coughing began when at the age of fourteen she was boarding with an aunt; she denies that she was ever psychically excited during this period and does not believe that there was any motive for her ailment. Under the pressure of my hand her first memory is of a large dog. She then recognizes the visual memory: it was a dog belonging to her aunt which became attached to her, went everywhere with her, and so on, and now, without any further assistance, it occurs to her that this dog died, that the children gave him a solemn burial, and that on the way back from this funeral her cough started. I ask her why, but have to use the pressure to help her. Then the thought comes to mind, 'Now I am quite alone in the world. Nobody here loves me, this animal was my only friend, and now I have lost him.' – Now she continues her story, 'The coughing disappeared when I left my aunt's, but reappeared eighteen months later.' 'What was the reason then?' 'I don't know.' I press again. She remembers hearing the news that her uncle had died, at which there was another outbreak of coughing, and remembers too having a similar train of thoughts. Her uncle was, it seems, the only member of her family who was fond of her, who loved her. This, then, was the pathogenic idea: she was not loved, others were liked better, nor did she deserve to be loved, and so on. Yet something was attached to the idea of 'love' which when spoken of aroused a keen resistance. The analysis broke off before this was clarified.

Some time ago I was asked to relieve an elderly lady of her attacks of anxiety; her character traits meant that she was hardly suited to being influenced in this way. Since the menopause she had become excessively devout and greeted me each time armed with a small ivory crucifix that she buried in the palm of her hand as if I were the devil incarnate. Her attacks of anxiety, which were of a hysterical character, dated back to her early girlhood, and stemmed, allegedly, from the use of an iodine preparation that was supposed to reduce a moderate swelling of the thyroid gland. Naturally I rejected this derivation and sought to replace it with another that would be more in keeping with my views on the aetiology of neurotic symptoms. In response to my first question about whether there was an impression from her youth that had a causal connection to her anxiety attacks, there emerged, under the pressure of my hand, the memory of reading a so-called 'edifying' book in which a pious enough reference to sexual processes was made. The passage in question made an impression on the girl that ran quite counter to the author's intentions: she burst into tears and flung the book away. This was before the first anxiety attack. A second pressure on the forehead conjured up another reminiscence, the recollection of a tutor of her brother's who showed a very high regard for her and for whom she herself had had feelings of some warmth. This recollection culminated in the reproduction of an evening at the family home, during which they were all sitting around the table with the young man, having a delightful time engaged in stimulating conversation. In the night following this evening she was woken by her first anxiety attack, which probably had more to do with her rebelling against a sensual impulse than with the iodine that was being used at about the same time. – What other method would have given me the prospect of uncovering a connection such as this that went against the opinion and assertions of this stubborn patient who was prejudiced against me and every form of secular therapy?

Another instance involved a happily married young woman who, as far back as her earliest youth, was for a time found every morning in a dazed state, her limbs stiff, mouth open and tongue sticking out, and who was now experiencing similar attacks, if not with quite the same degree of acuity, on waking up. It proved impossible to reach a deep hypnosis, so I began by investigating when she was in a state of concentration and, on the first application of pressure, assured her that she would now see something that had a direct connection with what caused the state in her childhood. She behaved calmly and willingly, saw once more the apartment in which she had spent her earliest youth, her room, the position of her bed, her grandmother who was living with them at that time, and one of her governesses of whom she had been very fond. There followed several small scenes that had occurred in these rooms and between these people, all, in truth, of little consequence; the last of these involved the departure of the governess who was leaving the house to get married. I could make nothing at all of these reminiscences and was unable to establish a relation between them and the aetiology of the attacks. And yet it was clear from various circumstances that this was the same time at which the attacks had first appeared.

However, before I was able to continue the analysis I had the opportunity of speaking to a colleague who had been my patient's family doctor some years ago. He gave me the following explanation: at the time when he was treating the girl – who was approaching maturity and physically very well developed – for her first attacks, he was struck by the excessively affectionate relationship between her and the governess living in the house. This made him suspicious and he arranged for the grandmother to take on the supervision of this relationship. Not long afterwards the old lady was able to report that the governess was in the habit of paying the child nightly visits in bed and that in the morning after these nights the child was regularly found suffering an attack. Now they had no hesitation at all in silently removing this corrupter of youth. The children and even the mother were kept under the impression that the governess was leaving the house to get married. The therapy, which was immediately successful, then consisted in my passing on to the young woman the explanation that had been given to me.

Occasionally the information given by the pressure technique appears in a very strange form and in circumstances that make it all the more tempting to assume the existence of an unconscious intelligence. I remember, for example, a lady who had been suffering from obsessive ideas and phobias for many years and who referred me to her childhood to explain the genesis of her affliction, yet was unable to indicate anything at all that could be held to blame for it. She was sincere and intelligent and put up only a remarkably slight conscious resistance. (I may add in parenthesis here that there is a strong internal relationship between the psychical mechanism of obsessive ideas and that of hysterical symptoms and that the analytic technique for both is the same.)

When I asked this lady if she had seen or remembered something under the pressure of my hand, she answered, 'Neither of the two, but a word did suddenly come to me.' – 'A single word?' – 'Yes, but it sounds too silly.' – 'Tell me anyway.' – 'Concierge.' – 'Nothing else?' – 'No.' – I pressed for the second time and again a single word appeared that shot through her mind, 'night-gown'. – I now realized that this was a new way of responding and by means of repeated pressure brought out a seemingly meaningless series of words, 'Concierge – night-gown – bed – town – farm-cart'. 'What does that mean?' I asked. She pondered for a moment and then it occurred to her. 'It can only be this one story that is coming to mind now. One night when I was ten years old and my next elder sister twelve, she had a raving fit and had to be tied up and taken into town on a farm-cart. I know for sure that it was the concierge who overpowered her and he too who took her to the institution.' – We now continued with this style of investigation and came to hear other series of words from our oracle, not all of which, it is true, we were able to interpret, but which did allow the continuation of this story and could be used to initiate a second. The significance of this reminiscence also came quickly to light. Her sister's falling ill had made such a deep impression on her because the two of them shared a secret: they slept in the same room and had one night both submitted to sexual assaults by a certain man. The mention of this sexual trauma from her early youth revealed not only the origin of the first obsessive ideas but also the trauma that had later had a pathogenic effect. – The peculiarity of this case consisted only in that single key words emerged which we then had to work into sentences, for the appearance of there being no connection or context is characteristic of all the ideas and scenes that generally arise on the application of pressure, just as it was characteristic of these words which were emitted as if from an oracle. When pursued further, it is generally found that the apparently unconnected reminiscences are in fact closely linked by bands of thought and that they lead quite directly to the pathogenic factor that we are looking for.

That is why I take pleasure in remembering a case of analysis in which my confidence in the results of the pressure was at first put to a hard test, but then brilliantly justified. A very intelligent and apparently very happy young woman had consulted me because of a persistent pain in her abdomen that was resistant to therapy. Recognizing that the pain was located in the abdominal walls and had to be related to a palpable thickening and hardening of the muscles, I prescribed local treatment.

When, months later, I saw the patient again, she said to me, 'After the recommended treatment, the pain I had went away and remained absent for a long time, but now it has returned as a nervous pain. I know this because I am no longer in pain when I move, as I was before, but only at specific times, in the morning when I wake up, for example, or when I get agitated in a certain way.' The lady's diagnosis was quite accurate. The issue now was to find the cause of this pain and while in an uninfluenced state she was unable to help me in this. When she was in a state of concentration and I asked her under the pressure of my hand if something occurred to her, or if she could see something, she opted for seeing and began to describe her visions to me. She saw something like a sun with rays, which I, naturally, took to be a phosphene, induced by pressure on the eyes.

I expected something useful to follow, but she continued, 'Stars of a peculiarly pale blue light, like moonlight', and so on, nothing but shimmering, gleaming and luminous spots before her eyes, or so I thought. I was already prepared to count this attempt among the failures and was thinking about how I might inconspicuously extract myself from the affair, when one of the apparitions that she was describing attracted my attention. A large black cross, as she saw it, leaning over; at its edges was the same shimmer as of moonlight which had illuminated all of the previous images and on its crossbeam a small flame flickered. Clearly there was no longer any question of this being a phosphene. Now I sat up: a huge number of images came bathed in the same light, strange signs that looked somewhat similar to Sanskrit, also figures like triangles, a large triangle among them; the cross once more . . . This time I suspect an allegorical significance and ask, 'What does this cross mean?' – 'It probably means pain,' she replies. – I object that by 'cross' one usually means a moral burden and ask her what is hidden behind the pain. – She doesn't know and carries on with her visions: a sun with golden rays, which she also knows how to interpret – 'That is God, the elemental force'; then a giant lizard, which observes her in an inquiring manner, but without fear; then a pile of snakes, then a sun again, but with mild silver rays, and in front of her, between her person and this source of light, a grille concealing the central point of the sun from her.

I have known for some time now that I am dealing with allegories and immediately ask about the significance of the last image. Without a second thought she answers, 'The sun is perfection, the ideal, and the grille, my weaknesses and failures, which stand between myself and the ideal.' 'So do you reproach yourself, are you dissatisfied with yourself?' 'Of course I am.' 'Since when?' 'Since I have been a member of the Theosophical Society and have been reading its publications. I always did have a low opinion of myself.' 'What last made a deep impression on you?' 'A translation from Sanskrit which is currently appearing in instalments.' A minute later my initiation into her spiritual struggles and self-reproaches is complete. I am told of a minor experience that gave her cause for self-reproach and during which what had previously been an organic pain made its first appearance as the result of a conversion of excitation. – The images that I had at first taken for phosphenes were symbols of occult trains of thought, perhaps even emblems from the title-pages of occult books.

Having now praised the achievements of the auxiliary pressure technique with such warmth and having throughout largely neglected the perspective of defence or resistance, I am bound to have given the impression that this small trick puts one in the position of mastering the psychical impediment to a cathartic cure. But to believe this would be a grave mistake. As far as I can see, there are no such profits in therapy. For there to be a great change, here as elsewhere, demands a great deal of work. The pressure technique is nothing more than a trick for catching the defensive self unawares for a while. In all fairly serious cases the self remembers its intentions and resumes its resistance.

I must recall the various forms in which this resistance occurs. First, as a rule, the application of pressure fails on either the first or second occasion. The patient then says with great disappointment, 'I believed that something would come to mind, but all that I thought was how much I wondered what it would be – nothing actually came to me.' The patient's putting himself on guard like this cannot yet be counted as an obstacle; one says in response, 'It is precisely because you were too curious, but it will work the next time.' And it really does work then. It is remarkable how often even the most obedient and intelligent patients are able completely to forget the arrangement that they did in fact agree to beforehand. They have promised to say everything that occurs to them under the pressure of my hand, regardless of whether it seems to have a connection or not and regardless of whether it is pleasant for them to say it or not, that is, without making a selection, or being influenced by criticism or affect. But they do not keep to this promise, it is clearly not in their powers to do so. The work keeps on being brought to a stop, and they keep on claiming that nothing has occurred to them this time. This is not to be believed, one has always to assume and also to say that they are holding something back because they think it is unimportant or find it embarrassing. One is insistent, repeats the pressure, pretends to be infallible, until one really is told something. Then the patient will add, 'I could have told you that the first time.' – 'Why didn't you say it then?' – 'I couldn't believe that it would be *that*. I only decided to say it when it kept coming back.' Or, 'I hoped that it wouldn't be that of all things. I could do without having to say that. But when it couldn't be repressed, I realized that I wasn't going to be let off.' Thus, in retrospect, the patient gives away the motives for a resistance that initially he did not want to admit at all. He is evidently unable to do anything but put up a resistance.

This resistance often hides behind some curious excuses. 'I am distracted today; the clock or the piano-playing in the next room is disturbing me.' I have learnt to respond, 'Not at all; now you have come across something that you don't want to say. That won't do you any good. Think about it for a while.' – The longer the pause between the pressure of my hand and the statement made by the patient turns out to be, the more distrustful I become and the more it is to be feared that the patient is sorting out what has occurred to him and mutilating it when he reproduces it. The most important elucidations are frequently announced as being superfluous additions, like princes disguised as beggars in opera. 'Now something has occurred to me, but it has nothing to do with the matter. I'm only telling you because you insist on knowing everything.' This then tends to usher in the long-awaited solution. I always sit up and pay attention when I hear a patient speak so disparagingly of an idea that has occurred to him. It is, in fact, a sign of successful defence that pathogenic ideas which re-emerge seem of such little significance. What was involved in the process of defence can be inferred from this, namely that a strong idea has been turned into a weak one, stripped of its affect.

Pathogenic memories can then be recognized, among other characteristics, by the fact that the patient describes them as unimportant, yet always utters them under resistance. There are also cases in which the patient tries to deny them even when they have returned. 'Now something has occurred to me, but it's clear that you have talked me into it,' or 'I know what you are expecting with this question. You obviously mean that I have thought such and such.' A particularly clever way of denying something lies in saying, 'Now something *has* occurred to me: but I have the impression that it is a deliberate addition on my part. It doesn't seem to me to be a thought that has been reproduced.' – In all of these instances I remain absolutely firm, I don't go into any of these distinctions but rather explain to the patient that they are simply the forms and pretexts for resisting the reproduction of a memory which we must, nevertheless, acknowledge.

It is on the whole easier to deal with images that return than thoughts. Hysterics, who are for the most part visual types, are less trouble for the analyst than people with obsessive ideas. Once an image has emerged from memory, the patient can be heard to say that it is crumbling and becoming unclear in proportion to the development of his depiction of it. *The patient is, as it were, clearing it away by converting it into words*. We then take our bearings from the visual memory itself, in order to find the direction in which the work is to proceed. 'Have another look at the image. Has it disappeared?' – 'On the whole, yes, but I can still see this detail.' – 'Then it must still mean something. Either you will see something new in addition to this residue, or something will occur to you in connection with it.' – When the work is finished and the visual field appears free again, we can lure out another image. But on other occasions an image such as this remains stubbornly lodged before the patient's inner eye, in spite of his having described it, and for me that is a sign that he still has something important to say on the subject of the image. As soon as he has completed this, the image vanishes, like a rescued spirit being laid to rest.

It is, of course, extremely important for the progress of the analysis that one should always be in the right as regards the patient, otherwise one is dependent on what he sees fit to impart. It is, therefore, comforting to hear that the pressure technique never really fails, save for one single case to which I will have to give proper attention later, but which I can characterize straight away by noting that it corresponds to a particular motive for resistance. It is true that the technique can be applied under circumstances in which it is impossible to unearth anything; if, for example, one inquires about the further aetiology of a symptom when it has already been brought to a close, or if one investigates the psychical genealogy of a symptom, a pain of some kind, which was in truth a somatic pain. In cases such as these the patient will similarly claim that nothing has occurred to him and he will be right. We can avoid doing him an injustice, if we make it a general rule not to let the countenance of the quietly recumbent patient out of our sight during the analysis. We then have no difficulty in learning how to distinguish the psychical peace that results from the genuine absence of reminiscence from the tension and signs of affect with which a patient in the service of defence tries to deny the emerging reminiscence. Incidentally, experiences of this kind also mean that the pressure technique can be used for differential diagnosis.

Even with the help of the pressure technique, then, this is no easy task. We simply have the advantage of having learnt from the results of this procedure which direction to take in our investigation and which things have to be forced on the patients. For a fair number of cases this is sufficient. The main thing after all is for me to guess the secret and say it to the patient's face; on the whole he then has to give up his rejection of it. In other cases more is needed. What survives of the patient's resistance is manifest in the tearing apart of connections, the non-appearance of solutions, and the unclear and incomplete remembering of images. On looking back from a later period of analysis to an earlier one, one is often astonished by how mutilated all the ideas and scenes were that were extracted from the patient by means of the pressure technique. What was lacking was precisely the most important thing, the relation to the person or the theme, and thus the image remained incomprehensible. I want to give one or two examples of how a process of censorship such as this operates when pathogenic memories first emerge. For example, the patient sees the upper part of a female body and it has been left partly uncovered, as if out of carelessness. Not until much later does he add a head to this torso so as to reveal a person and his relation to her. Or he recounts a childhood reminiscence involving two lads;

he cannot make out their appearance, but knows that they were accused of some misdeed. Many months and a great deal of progress in the course of the analysis are required before he sees this reminiscence again and recognizes himself in one of the children and his brother in the other. What are the means at our disposal for overcoming this constant resistance?

Few, but almost all are those by which one person usually exercises a psychical influence on another. The first thing we have to remind ourselves of is that psychical resistance, particularly resistance that has been constituted over a long period of time, can only be resolved slowly, step by step; we have to wait patiently. Thereafter we can count on the intellectual interest that will begin to stir in the patient after a short period of work. In enlightening him and informing him of the wondrous world of psychical processes, into which we have ourselves gained an insight only by analyses such as this, we win him over as a co-worker, bring him to observe himself with the objective interest of the researcher, thereby repelling any resistance which has an affective base. But ultimately – and this still affords the strongest leverage – we must try, having guessed the motives for his defence, to lessen the value of these motives or even to replace them with stronger ones. This is probably the point at which it ceases to be possible to express psychotherapeutic activity in formulas. One operates, as best one can, as an enlightener (where shyness is born of ignorance), as a teacher, as the representative of a freer or superior philosophy of life, as a confessor, who by his continuing compassion and respect for the confessions that are made, as it were grants absolution. One tries to do something for the patient in human terms, as far as is allowed by the capacity of one's own personality and the degree of sympathy that one can find for the case in question. For psychical activity of this kind it is an essential precondition that we have more or less guessed the nature of the case and the motives for the defence that are operative here, and luckily the technique of pushing the patient and applying pressure can bring us just this far. The more riddles of this kind we have already solved, the easier it is likely to be to guess others and the sooner we will be able to take the truly curative psychical work in hand. For it is worth making sure that one is quite clear about the following things: even if the patient is not freed of the hysterical symptom until he has reproduced the pathogenic impressions that caused it and talked them through with an expression of affect, the therapeutic task still consists *only in inducing him to do so*; once the task is complete there remains nothing for the doctor to correct or remove. Whatever is needed to do this in the way of counter-suggestions has already been expended during the struggle against the patient's resistance. The case might be compared to unlocking a locked door – once this has been done, opening it by turning the handle ceases to be a problem.

Alongside the intellectual motives enlisted to overcome resistance, there is an affective factor that can rarely be dispensed with, the personal influence of the doctor. And in a number of cases only this second factor will be capable of removing the resistance. This is no different from general medical practice and one should not expect any therapeutic method wholly to do without the involvement of this personal factor.

3

The explanations of the previous section give an unreserved exposition of the difficulties of my technique, which, incidentally, I have assembled from among the most difficult cases – things are often far easier. In view of these facts, then, people will undoubtedly ask whether it would not be more effective to avoid all this bother and instead put more effort into hypnosis or limit the application of the cathartic method to those patients who can be put under a deep hypnosis. In answer to this second suggestion, I would have to say that the number of suitable patients, as far as *my* skill is concerned, would be too much diminished; I would counter the first piece of advice with the conjecture that we would be spared little resistance by forcing hypnosis. I have curiously little experience of this, which is why I cannot advance anything more than a conjecture, but when I have conducted a cathartic cure under hypnosis instead of in a state of concentration, I found that the work that fell to me was not reduced. I have only recently completed a treatment of this kind, in the course of which I caused a hysterical paralysis of the legs to clear up. The patient got into a state that was psychically very different from when she was awake and whose somatic characteristics were that it was impossible for her to open her eyes or get up until I had called out to her, 'Now wake up'. And yet it was in this, of all cases, that I encountered the greatest resistance. I did not attribute any significance to these physical signs and towards the end of the treatment, which lasted ten months, they had ceased to be noticeable. Yet in spite of this the patient's state while we were working lost none of its characteristics, namely the capacity to remember things that were unconscious and the quite special relation to the person of the doctor. In the history of Frau Emmy v. N., on the other hand, I have given an example of a cathartic cure that was carried out in very deep somnambulism and in which resistance played almost no part whatsoever. But nor did I learn anything from this woman that needed particularly to be overcome before she could impart it, nothing that she would not have been able to tell me – given a longer acquaintance and a degree of regard – when awake. I never discovered the real causes of her illness, which were undoubtedly identical to the causes of its recurrence following my treatment – this was just my first attempt at this therapy – and the only time that I happened to ask her for a reminiscence involving an erotic element, I found her to be just as reluctant and unreliable in her statements as any of my non-somnambulistic female patients were later. I have already discussed this woman's resistance to other requests and demands, even in a somnambulistic state, in her case history. In general, I have become doubtful of the value of hypnosis in facilitating cathartic cures since I have experienced absolute therapeutic recalcitrance from patients in a state of deep somnambulism who have otherwise been perfectly obedient. I gave a brief account of such a case on pp. 106–7 (note 28); I could cite others in addition. I admit, too, that this experience corresponded pretty well to my requirement that there be a quantitative relation between cause and effect in the psychical domain.

In this exposition thus far the idea of *resistance* has come forcefully to the fore. I have shown how in therapeutic work one comes to conceive of hysteria as developing through the repression – motivated by defence – of an intolerable idea; the repressed idea then persists as a weak (low intensity) memory trace and the affect which is torn from it is used for a somatic innervation: the conversion of excitation. Precisely because it is repressed, the idea then becomes the cause of pathological symptoms, that is, it becomes pathogenic. A hysteria that demonstrates this psychical mechanism may be termed '*defence hysteria*'. Now, both Breuer and I have repeatedly spoken of two other types of hysteria for which we introduced the terms '*hypnoid*' and '*retention hysteria*'. Hypnoid hysteria was the very first form of which we became aware. I can cite no better example of this kind of hysteria than Breuer's first case, which takes first place among our case histories. Breuer attributes a psychical mechanism to this kind of hypnoid hysteria which is significantly different from that of defence by conversion. In this instance an idea is thought to become pathogenic in that, having been conceived in a particular psychical state, it has from the outset remained outside the self. No psychical force has then been needed to keep it apart from the self and it can awaken no resistance when, with the aid of somnambulistic mental activity, it is introduced into the self. Nor, in fact, does the case history of Anna O. show any sign of this kind of resistance.

I believe this difference to be of such significance that on the basis of it I willingly adhere to the proposition that there is a hypnoid hysteria. Curiously, in my own experience, I have not encountered any genuine cases of hypnoid hysteria. What I took on turned into defence hysteria. Which is not to say that I have never had to deal with symptoms that had demonstrably arisen in separated states of consciousness and had therefore to remain barred from being taken up into the self. I did come across this in my cases too, but was then able to prove that the so-called hypnoid state owed its separation to the fact that a psychical group that had previously been split off by defence had come into effect within it. In short, I cannot suppress the suspicion that the roots of hypnoid and defence hysterias meet at some point and that defence is the primary factor here. But I have no knowledge of this.

My judgement is at the moment equally uncertain as regards 'retention hysteria', in which therapeutic work is also supposed to ensue immediately and without resistance. I had a case that I took to be a typical retention hysteria. I was looking forward to an easy and sure success, but this success was not forthcoming despite the fact that the work really was very easy. I suspect, then, again with all the reserve fitting to ignorance, that even at the basis of retention hysteria there is a bit of defence that has driven the whole process to become hysterical. Future experience will, I hope, determine whether or not my inclination to extend the concept of defence to hysteria in its entirety runs the risk of lapsing into one-sidedness and error.

I have thus far dealt with the difficulties and technique of the cathartic method, and would like to give a few additional indications as to how an analysis takes shape using this technique. This theme is of great interest to me, but can hardly be expected to excite a similar interest in those who have not yet carried out an analysis of this kind. We will, in fact, be talking about technique again, but this time about inherent difficulties for which the patient cannot be held responsible and which would in part have to be the same for a hypnoid or retention hysteria as for the defence hysterias which are the model that I have in mind. I am approaching this last part of the exposition in the expectation that the psychical characteristics that will be disclosed could at some point assume a certain value as raw material for a dynamics of ideation.

The first and most powerful impression that one has in an analysis of this kind is undoubtedly that the pathogenic psychical material, which has ostensibly been forgotten and is not at the disposal of the self, plays no part in association or recollection, yet in some way is not just ready, but ready in correct and proper order. It is simply a question of setting aside the resistances that bar the way to this material. In other respects the material is known,[2] in the same way that we are able to know anything: the correct connections between the individual ideas and those with non-pathogenic, frequently remembered ideas are present, having been completed at some time and preserved in memory. The pathogenic psychical material appears to be the property of an intelligence that is not necessarily inferior to that of the normal self. The semblance of a second personality is often produced in the most deceptive way.

I do not yet – and not at this point in the discussion – want to consider whether or not this impression is justified and whether it might not mean taking the arrangement of the psychical material which results after recovery as having happened at the time of the illness. There is no more convenient or vivid way of describing the experiences that this kind of analysis brings than from the standpoint that one can adopt *after* recovery, which offers an overview of the matter in its entirety.

The situation is rarely as simple as has been depicted in particular cases, as, for example, in the case of a single symptom resulting from a major trauma. One does not, on the whole, have a single hysterical symptom but rather a number of them, which are in part independent of each other, in part connected. One cannot expect a single traumatic recollection with a single pathogenic idea at its nucleus, but rather must be prepared for series of partial traumas and pathogenic trains of thought that are interlinked. Monosymptomatic traumatic hysteria is, as it were, an elementary organism, a single-celled creature in comparison with the complicated structure of severe hysterical neurosis as it is commonly encountered.

The psychical material of a hysteria such as this presents itself as a multidimensional construct with at least *three strata*. I hope shortly to be able to justify this figurative expression. Present at first is a *nucleus* consisting of those recollections (of experiences or trains of thought) in which the traumatic moment peaked or the pathogenic idea found its purest form. Surrounding this nucleus there is often an incredibly copious amount of other memory material which has to be worked through in analysis and which, as mentioned earlier, is arranged in three parts. First, there is unmistakably a *linear*, *chronological* arrangement that occurs within every single theme. As an example of this I need only cite the arrangements in Breuer's analysis of Anna O. The theme is that of becoming deaf, of not-hearing (p. 40). This was then differentiated according to seven conditions, and under every heading ten to over a hundred individual memories were grouped chronologically. It was as if one were examining an archive that had been kept in good order. Similar, if less fully described, memory dossiers were contained in the analysis of my patient Emmy v. N. These dossiers are, in fact, a quite common occurrence in every analysis, always appear in a chronological order that is as infallibly reliable as is the sequence of days of the week or months of the year in those who are psychically normal, and make the work of analysis difficult in that when reproduced they characteristically reverse the order in which they arose – the freshest, most recent experience in the dossier comes first as a 'cover sheet', and the conclusion is formed by the impression with which the sequence in fact began.

I have described the way in which similar kinds of memory form large groups made up of linear strata – like a bundle of documents, a package, etc. – as constituting *themes*. These themes then display a second kind of arrangement. They form, and I can find no other way of expressing it, *concentric strata around the pathogenic nucleus*. It is not difficult to say what determines this stratification and according to what decreasing or increasing magnitude the arrangement occurs. There are *strata* of equal *resistance* and this resistance increases towards the nucleus; hence the presence of *zones in which there is an equal change in consciousness* through which the individual themes extend. The most peripheral strata contain the recollections (or dossiers) of various themes that are easily remembered and were always clearly conscious; the deeper one goes the more difficult it is to recognize the recollections that are surfacing, until, near to the nucleus itself, we encounter those that the patient will deny even when they are reproduced.

It is this particular characteristic of the concentric stratification of the pathogenic psychical material which, as we shall see, lends the course of the analysis its characteristic traits. Now a third kind of order remains to be mentioned, which is the most significant and the most difficult to make a general statement about. This is the arrangement according to thought-content, the connection along the logical thread which extends to the nucleus and may take a highly irregular and frequently branching path, different in every case. This arrangement has a dynamic character, in contrast to the morphological character of the two previously mentioned types of stratification. Whereas the latter could be depicted by fixed, arched and straight lines in a schema laid out spatially, the course of the logical chain would have to be followed with a pointer that would move along the most winding paths, from superficial to deep strata and back, but in general penetrating from the periphery to the central nucleus and in doing so having to touch every stopping-place, similar to the zig-zag that results when one solves a chess problem by moving a Knight across the squares of the board.

I want to hold onto this last comparison for a moment longer in order to emphasize one point in which it does not do justice to the properties of what is being compared. The logical connection does not merely correspond to a broken zig-zag line, but rather to a line that branches and in particular to a system of converging lines. It has nodal points at which two or more threads converge, then continue as a single group, and as a rule several threads – either running independently or in places connected by side-paths – flow into the nucleus. In other words, it is quite remarkable how often a symptom is *multiply determined*, or *overdetermined*.

My attempt to picture the organization of the pathogenic psychical material will be complete once I have introduced one last complication. Namely that it is possible for the pathogenic material to have more than one nucleus, as, for example, when one has to analyse a second outbreak of hysteria which, despite having its own aetiology, is connected with an initial outbreak of acute hysteria that was overcome years ago. In this instance, it is easy to imagine what additions there must be to the strata and thought-paths in order to establish a connection between the two pathogenic nuclei.

I want to bring one or two further remarks to the picture established thus far of the organization of the pathogenic material. We have said of this material that it behaves like a foreign body and that the therapy operates as if it were removing a foreign body from the living tissue. We are now in a position to see how this comparison is lacking. A foreign body does not enter into any connection with the layers of tissue surrounding it, although it does alter them and triggers a reactive inflammation. Our pathogenic psychical group, on the other hand, cannot be cleanly extracted from the self, its outer strata pass over into parts of the normal self on all sides and ultimately belong just as much to it as to the pathogenic organization. In analysis the border between the two is placed in a purely conventional fashion at one point or another and in certain places cannot be indicated at all. The inner strata are increasingly estranged from the self, yet the point at which the border of the pathogenic material begins does not become visible. The pathogenic organization does not really behave like a foreign body, but far more like an infiltration. In this comparison, the resistance must be taken as that which is doing the infiltrating. Nor does the therapy consist in extirpating something – psychotherapy is not at present capable of this – but rather of bringing the resistance to melting point and so breaching a path for the circulation to enter an area that was previously blocked.

(I am using a series of similes here that all have a very limited resemblance to my theme and that in addition are not compatible with each other. I am aware of this and am not in danger of overestimating their value, but my guiding purpose is to illustrate from various angles a highly complicated thought-object, such as has never before been depicted, and so, although this method is not without its faults, I hope I may take the liberty of continuing to introduce comparisons over the following pages.)

If, having completely resolved the pathogenic material into what is now recognized as its complicated, multidimensional organization, one could show it to a third party, they would quite justifiably raise the question, 'How did a camel like this get through the eye of the needle?' For one is not wrong to speak of a 'narrowing of consciousness'. The term becomes meaningful and vivid for a doctor who carries out an analysis of this kind. Recollections can only ever enter the self's consciousness one at a time; the patient who is occupied with working through this one recollection sees nothing of the throng behind it and forgets what has already made its way through. If there are difficulties in managing this one pathogenic recollection, if, for example, the patient does not relax his resistance to it, if he wants to repress or mutilate it, then the narrow pass is, so to speak, blocked, the work is held up, nothing else can come, and the one memory that is in the process of breaking through remains in front of the patient until he has taken it up into the expanse of the self. The entire spatially extended mass of pathogenic material is thus drawn through a narrow fissure and so reaches consciousness as if broken down into pieces or strips. It is the psychotherapist's task to reassemble this material according to its suspected organization. For readers who still crave comparisons, this may be taken as reminiscent of a puzzle.

If we are about to begin such an analysis in which it might be expected that the pathogenic material will be organized in this way, then what experience has taught us can be put to good use: namely, that *there is no point at all in advancing directly to the nucleus of the pathogenic organization*. Even if it were possible for us to guess this, the patient would not know what to do with the elucidation given to him and would not be altered by it psychically.

The only possibility is to begin by keeping to the periphery of the pathogenic psychical construct. We begin by letting the patient recount what he knows and remembers, at which point we are already directing his attention and overcoming slight resistances by applying the pressure technique. Whenever we have opened up a new path by pressure, we can expect the patient to continue it a stretch further without any new resistance.

Once we have worked in this way for a while a co-operative activity begins to stir in the patient. A wealth of reminiscences now occurs to him, without our having to ask him questions and set him tasks, for we have, precisely, breached the path into an inner stratum within which the patient can spontaneously access material of equal resistance. It is wise to let him reproduce for a while without being subjected to any influence. While he is not in a position to uncover important connections himself, he can be left to clear away material within the same stratum. The things that he supplies in so doing often seem disconnected but they provide the material that will be activated by a connection that is recognized at a later stage.

We have, in general, to beware of two things here. If we inhibit the patient when he is reproducing the ideas that are flooding into him, we can 'bury' much that it would later take great effort to free up. On the other hand we should not overestimate his unconscious 'intelligence' and allow all the work to be guided by it. If I were to schematize the mode of work, then I could say that we take on the opening up of the inner strata ourselves, and advance radially, while the patient takes care of the peripheral extension.

Advances are made by overcoming resistance in the way indicated previously. But as a rule another problem has to be solved first. We have to get hold of a piece of the logical thread, for only when guided by this can we hope to penetrate to the interior. We should not expect that what is freely imparted by the patient, the material at the most superficial strata, will make it easy for the analyst to recognize those places at which it runs deep, the starting-points of the thought-connections which he is seeking. On the contrary, it is this of all things that is carefully veiled; what the patient has presented sounds complete and self-contained. At first we stand before it as if before a wall blocking every view and preventing us from sensing whether something is behind it and what that something might be.

But once we have taken a critical eye to inspect the presentation that the patient has given without much effort or resistance, we will not fail to discover gaps and faults in it. At one point the connection is visibly broken and supplemented by the patient in a makeshift way with a turn of phrase or inadequate information; at another we come across a motive that in a normal person would be described as weak. The patient refuses to acknowledge these gaps when his attention is drawn to them. But the doctor is right to look behind these weak spots for access to material at the deeper strata, or to hope to discover, at precisely these points, the threads of the connection that he is tracking through the pressure technique. Then we say to the patient, 'You are mistaken. What you're telling me can't have anything to do with the subject. We have to come upon something else now and it will occur to you under the pressure of my hand.'

The same demand for logical connection and sufficient motivation can be made of hysterics' trains of thought, even if they do extend into the unconscious, as of those in normal individuals. It is not within the power of the neurosis to loosen these connections. If the links between ideas in neurotics, and in particular in hysterics, make a different impression, and if the relative intensities of different ideas seem inexplicable in purely psychological terms, we have already become aware of precisely what the reason for this is and can describe it as *the existence of hidden, unconscious motives*. We may suspect such secret motives wherever we can detect that there is a fault in the connection or an exceeding of the degree of motivation that is normally justifiable.

This kind of work of course demands that we remain free of the theoretical prejudice that we are dealing with the abnormal brains of *dégénérés* or *déséquilibrés* in whom the liberty of overturning the common psychological laws of ideational connection is a peculiar stigma, and in whom a random idea can undergo intense and excessive growth, while another can be indestructible, for no psychological reason. Experience proves that the opposite is true of hysteria; if we have found out and brought to account motives – often those that have remained unconscious – then there is no longer anything puzzling or irregular in hysterical thought-connections.

In this way, then, by tracking down gaps in the patient's first presentation that are often covered by 'false links', we take hold of a piece of the logical thread at the periphery and use the pressure technique to breach a way ahead from that point.

It is extremely rare to succeed in working along the same thread right to the interior; it tends to break off along the way as the pressure fails and delivers either no result at all or one which cannot be clarified or continued no matter how hard we try. We soon learn how to protect ourselves from the errors that are likely to occur in this instance. The patient's facial expression has to be decisive in whether or not we really have reached an end point, or whether we have come across a case that does not require psychical elucidation, or if there is an excessive resistance that is putting a stop to the work. If this resistance cannot be defeated straightaway, then we have to assume that we have pursued the thread through to a stratum which for the time being is still impermeable. We let it go in order to pick up another thread, which may perhaps be pursued for the same distance. If we have arrived at this stratum along all the threads and discovered the knots there which prevented us from pursuing any of the single threads in isolation, then we may think again about tackling the resistance with which we are faced.

It is easy to imagine how complicated this kind of work can become. By constantly overcoming resistance we force our way through to the inner strata, getting to know the themes that are accumulated in one such stratum and the threads that run through it; we test how far the means currently at our disposal and the knowledge gained will allow us to advance; we reconnoitre, using the pressure technique, to discover the contents of the next strata; we let the threads go and take them up again, pursue them to their point of intersection, are all the time catching up and, by going into dossiers of recollections, constantly ending up on side-paths that ultimately join up with the others again. In this way we finally reach a point at which we can abandon the method of working stratum by stratum and advance directly along a main path straight to the nucleus of the pathogenic organization. At this point the battle has been won but is not yet over. The other threads have to be followed up, the material exhausted; but now the patient has become an energetic helper his resistance is for the most part already broken.

In these later stages of the work it is useful to have guessed the connection and told the patient about it before having actually uncovered it. If we have guessed correctly, we will speed up the course of the analysis, but even an incorrect hypothesis will help us to progress in that it forces the patient to take sides and entices vigorous denials from him which betray that he certainly knows more than it seems.

It is astonishing to realize that *we are not in a position to force anything on the patient that involves things of which he is seemingly unaware or to influence the results of the analysis by exciting his expectation.* Not once has a prediction of mine managed to alter or falsify the reproduction of memories or the connection of events – had it done so it would undoubtedly eventually have been given away by a contradiction in the structure of the thing. If something occurred as I had predicted, multiple reminiscences that were quite above suspicion testified to my having guessed correctly. There is, then, no need to be frightened of voicing an opinion in front of the patient about what connection will follow next; no harm is done by this.

Another observation that is constantly repeated relates to the reproductions made independently by the patient. It can be claimed that not one reminiscence surfaces during an analysis like this that is devoid of significance. There is never really any intrusion of unrelated memory images that are in some way associated with the important ones. An exception that does not contradict this rule might be postulated for those recollections that are in themselves unimportant yet are indispensable as switch-points because the association between two recollections that are rich in connections can only occur through them. – How long a recollection will linger in the narrow pass in front of the patient's consciousness is, as indicated previously, directly proportionate to its significance. An image that will not fade still calls for acknowledgement; a thought that will not allow itself to be dismissed still needs to be pursued further. Nor will a reminiscence return for a second time if it has been dealt with and an image that was talked away will never be seen again. But should this happen, we can confidently expect that the second time a new thought-content will be attached to the image, or the idea will have different implications, i.e. that they have not in fact been fully dealt with. It is, however, common for there to be recurrences at varying degrees of intensity, just a hint at first, then with complete clarity, but this does not contradict the assertion that has just been made.

The analytic tasks may include removing a symptom that is capable of increasing in intensity or of recurring (pains, symptoms such as vomiting which are due to stimuli, sensations and contractures). During this work the interesting and not undesirable phenomenon of the symptom *'joining in the conversation'* may be observed. The symptom in question reappears or appears with increased intensity as soon as we have entered the region of the pathogenic organization containing the symptom's aetiology, and will then continue to accompany the work with characteristic and, for the doctor, instructive fluctuations. The intensity of this symptom (the desire to vomit, say) increases the deeper we penetrate into one of the recollections that are pathogenic in this respect, reaches its highest point shortly before the talking through of the recollection, and suddenly subsides once it has been fully talked through and may even disappear completely for a while. If resistance causes a patient to delay talking through for a long time, the tension of the sensation – the desire to vomit – becomes unbearable and if we cannot force him to talk things through then vomiting really will occur. This gives a vivid sense of how the 'vomiting' stands in for a psychical action (in this instance, talking things through), as is maintained by the conversion theory of hysteria.

The fluctuation of intensity on the part of the hysterical symptom is then repeated whenever we are dealing with a new memory that is pathogenic in this respect: the symptom is, as it were, *on the agenda* all the time. If one is forced to drop the thread to which this symptom is attached for a while, the symptom too will retreat into obscurity, only to resurface at a later period of the analysis. This game will persist until, by working over the pathogenic material, the symptom is disposed of definitively.

The behaviour of the hysterical symptom here is, strictly speaking, not in the least different from that of a memory-image or reproduced thought, which we conjure up under the pressure of our hand. In both cases there is the same obsessively stubborn recurrence in the patient's memory that demands to be disposed of. The difference lies only in the apparently spontaneous appearance of the hysterical symptoms, whereas, as we very well remember, we ourselves provoked the scenes and thoughts. In reality, however, there is an uninterrupted progression from the unaltered *memory-residues* of affect-laden experiences and acts of thought through to the hysterical symptoms that are their *memory-symbols*.

The phenomenon of the hysterical symptom joining in the conversation during the analysis brings with it a practical difficulty to which we should be able to reconcile the patient. It is quite impossible to undertake the analysis of a symptom in one go or to distribute the breaks in the work in such a way that they coincide precisely with the calm points in the process of dealing with the symptoms. Rather, the interruption that is dictated by incidental circumstances of the treatment, such as the hour being late and so on, often occurs at the most awkward points, precisely when we might be able to approach a decision or when a new theme emerges. These are the same difficulties that spoil anyone's reading of a novel serialized in a daily newspaper, when the heroine's decisive speech or, say, the ringing out of a shot is immediately followed by the words: 'To be continued'. In our case the theme that has been roused but not resolved, the symptom that is for the moment intensified and not yet explained, persists in the patient's inner life and is perhaps a greater burden to him than was otherwise the case. But he will simply have to be capable of coming to terms with this; there is no alternative arrangement. There are patients who, during an analysis like this, cannot let go of the theme once it has been touched on, who remain obsessed by it in the interval between two sessions of treatment, and, since they can come no closer to dealing with it on their own, at first suffer more than they did before the treatment. Yet even patients such as these eventually learn to wait for the doctor and postpone their entire interest in dealing with the pathogenic material to the time of their treatment; they then begin to feel freer in the intervening periods.

The patient's general condition during an analysis of this kind also seems worthy of note. For a while, uninfluenced by the treatment, it continues to be an expression of the factors that had been operative at an earlier stage, but a moment then arrives when the patient is 'gripped', his interest is caught, and from then on his general health will become increasingly dependent on the state of the work. With every new elucidation and whenever an important section in the structure of the analysis has been accomplished, the patient also feels relieved and takes pleasure in the anticipation of his impending release. Whenever the work is held up, whenever confusion threatens, the psychical burden which is oppressing him grows, his feeling of unhappiness increases, his stamina grows less. Both, though, last for only a short time: for the analysis goes on, disdaining to boast about those moments of well-being, and proceeding regardless of the periods of bleakness. On the whole we feel glad to have replaced the spontaneous fluctuations in the patient's condition with those that we have ourselves provoked and understood, just as we are glad to see the spontaneous succession of symptoms replaced by an agenda that corresponds to the state of analysis.

At first the work tends to become more obscure and difficult the deeper we penetrate into the stratified psychical construct described above. But once we have worked our way through to the nucleus, light dawns, and the patient's general condition is no longer at risk of periods of severe gloom. The rewards of the work, however, the cessation of the symptoms of illness, cannot be expected until the full analysis of each individual symptom has been achieved. Indeed, where individual symptoms are attached to each other at several nodal points we cannot even be encouraged in our work by partial success. By dint of the abundant causal connections which are present each unresolved pathogenic idea operates as the motive for all the products of the neurosis and not until the last words of the analysis does the clinical picture disappear in its entirety, just as happens with recollections reproduced individually.

If a pathogenic recollection or a pathogenic connection that was previously withdrawn from the self's consciousness is uncovered by the work of analysis and inserted into the self, it can be seen that the psychical personality that has been so enriched has various modes for expressing its acquisition. A particularly frequent occurrence is that we go to great lengths to force a piece of knowledge on a patient, only for him to declare, 'But I've always known that, I could have told you that earlier.' The more insightful among them then recognize this to be a form of self-deception and accuse themselves of ingratitude. Otherwise the position adopted by the self in response to the new acquisition tends to depend on which stratum of the

analysis it originates from. Everything belonging to the outermost
strata is acknowledged without difficulty, for it had remained in the
self's possession and only its connection with the deeper strata of
the pathogenic material was a novelty to the self. What is unearthed
from these deeper strata will also be recognized and acknowledged,
but often only after prolonged hesitation and reflection. Visual
memory-images are of course more difficult to deny here than the
memory-traces of mere trains of thought. It is far from rare for the
patient to begin by saying, 'It is possible that I thought this, but I
can't remember', and only when he has over time become familiar
with this supposition does he come to recognize it too. The patient
remembers and also confirms by means of secondary links that he
once really had this thought. During the analysis, however, I make
it a rule that the evaluation of an emerging reminiscence be kept
independent of the patient's acknowledgement of it. I never tire of
repeating that we are bound to accept everything that we bring to
light by our own means. Should this contain something inauthentic
or incorrect, the context would later show us how to remove it. I
should say, in passing, that I have hardly ever had cause subsequently
to repudiate a reminiscence that had provisionally been accepted.
Whatever surfaced, even if it gave the most deceptive appearance
of being a glaring contradiction, turned out to be correct in the end.

The ideas that originate from the greatest depth and form the
nucleus of the pathogenic organization are also the most difficult for
patients to acknowledge as recollections. Even when everything is
over, when the patients have been overwhelmed by the force of
logic and convinced of the curative effect that accompanied the
emergence of precisely these ideas – even, I must say, when the
patients themselves have accepted that they thought such and such,
they will often add, 'But *remember* that I thought that? That I can't
do.' An understanding can then easily be reached, by telling them
that they were *unconscious* thoughts. But how might this state of
affairs be incorporated into our own psychological views? Should
we dismiss the denial of recognition on the part of the patient, which,
now that the work is done, lacks any motive? Should we suppose
that we are really dealing with thoughts that did not materialize,

whose existence was only ever potential, and that the therapy consisted in accomplishing a psychical act that did not occur at the time? It is clearly impossible to say something about this, that is, about the state of the pathogenic material prior to the analysis, before we have thoroughly clarified our fundamental psychological views, concerning in particular the nature of consciousness. It is still well worth considering that in analyses like these we can pursue a train of thought from the conscious into the unconscious (that is, into something that is in no way recognized as a memory), from there draw it a stretch further through consciousness, and see it ending back in the unconscious without this alternation of 'psychical illumination' changing anything about the train of thought itself, its logical consistency, or the connection of its individual parts. Once I have this train of thought before me in its entirety I would not be able to guess which section would have been recognized by the patient as a memory and which would not. All that I can see to a certain extent are the tips of the train of thought dipping into the unconscious, the reverse of what has been claimed of our normal psychical processes.

One last theme remains to be treated, which plays an undesirably large part in carrying out cathartic analyses of this kind. I have already admitted that it is possible for the pressure technique to fail, to elicit no reminiscence despite every reassurance and insistence. Then I said that there were two possibilities: either there really is nothing to be found in the place where we are investigating, as can be recognized from the patient's completely calm expression; or we have encountered a resistance that it will not be possible to overcome until later on, we are faced with a new stratum which cannot yet be penetrated, and this is once again legible from the patient's tense expression, indicative of psychical strain. But there remains a third possibility, which likewise denotes an obstacle but one that is external rather than relating to the material itself. This occurs when the relationship of patient to doctor is disturbed and represents the worst obstacle that can be encountered. We can, however, count on it occurring in every serious analysis.

I have already indicated the important part played by the person of the doctor in creating motives to defeat the psychical force of resistance. In no small number of cases, particularly those with women and where the clarification of erotic thought processes is involved, the patient's collaboration becomes a personal sacrifice that has to be repaid by some kind of surrogate for love. The trouble taken by the doctor and his steady friendliness have to suffice as a surrogate of this kind. Should this relationship of patient to doctor be disturbed, the patient's willingness will also fail. When the doctor tries to find out about the next pathogenic idea, the patient's consciousness of the complaints that have built up in her against him intervenes. In my experience so far, this obstacle occurs in three major cases.

1. Personal estrangement. If the patient believes herself to be neglected, undervalued or insulted, or if she has heard anything undesirable about the doctor and his method of treatment. This is the least serious case. The obstacle is easily overcome by explanation and talking things through, although the sensitivity and suspiciousness of hysterics can sometimes assume undreamt-of proportions.

2. If the patient is seized by a fear of becoming too accustomed to the doctor personally, of losing her independence in relation to him, or even of becoming sexually dependent on him. This case is more significant because it is less conditioned by the individual. The reason for this obstacle lies in the very nature of the therapeutic care. The patient now has a new motive for resistance, that is expressed not only when there is a particular reminiscence but whenever treatment is attempted. It is quite common for the patient to complain of a headache when the pressure technique is used. On the whole she remains unconscious of her new motive for resistance and expresses it by creating a new hysterical symptom. The headache signifies her aversion to allowing herself to be influenced.

3. If the patient is fearful of transferring the distressing ideas emerging from the content of the analysis onto the person of the doctor. This happens frequently and in a number of analyses is even a common occurrence. The transference onto the doctor occurs by

means of a *false connection* (see p. 99 (note 19)). I should probably give an example here: the origin of a particular hysterical symptom in one of my patients was a wish that she had felt many years previously and immediately relegated to her unconscious, namely that the man she was talking to at the time would just take swift and firm action and give her a kiss. Once, after the end of a session, a wish like this arose in my patient with regard to myself. She is horrified about it, spends a sleepless night, and the next time, although she does not refuse treatment, is quite unfit for the work. After I have discovered and removed the obstacle, the work proceeds and lo and behold! the wish that so frightened the patient appears as the next of the pathogenic memories logically demanded by the context. What happened is as follows. The content of the wish first appeared in the patient's consciousness without there being any memory of the surrounding circumstances that could have transposed this wish to the past. The wish that was now present was linked, by the compulsion to associate prevalent in the patient's consciousness, with my person, which was a quite legitimate concern, and through this *mésalliance* – what I call a false connection – the same affect is wakened that had at the time forced the patient to repudiate this forbidden wish. Now that I have experienced this once, I can assume that, whenever I am involved personally in this way, a transference and false connection have again occurred. Curiously, the patient herself will fall victim to every new occurrence of this deception.

No analysis can be brought to an end if we do not know how to counter the resistance that results from these three incidents. But we can find a means of doing so if we decide to treat the new symptom that has been produced according to the old pattern in the same way that we treated the old symptom. The first task is to make the patient conscious of the 'obstacle'. In the case of one of my patients, for example, with whom the pressure technique suddenly failed and I had reason to suspect the presence of an unconscious idea like those mentioned in point 2, I first managed this by taking her by surprise. I told her that an obstacle to the continuation of the treatment must have occurred, but that it was at least within the power of the pressure technique to show her this obstacle, and I applied pressure to her head. She said, astonished, 'But that's a nonsense, I can see you here, sitting in the armchair. What is that supposed to mean?' At this I was able to enlighten her.

In another patient the 'obstacle' did not tend to appear in direct response to pressure, but I could detect it every time by taking the patient back to the moment at which it had arisen. The pressure technique never failed to bring back this moment. In discovering and establishing the obstacle the first difficulty was disposed of, but a greater one remained. It consisted in persuading the patient to communicate when seemingly personal relations were involved in which the third person coincided with that of the doctor. I was, at first, quite indignant about this increase in my psychical work, but then I learnt to see that the whole process followed a law, at which point I noticed too that no great increase in effort was demanded by this kind of transference. The patient's work remained the same, that is, overcoming the painful affect that she could harbour a wish of this kind even momentarily, and whether she made this psychical repulsion the theme of her work in the historic instance or in the recent one connected with me seemed to make no difference to its success. The patients, too, gradually learnt to see that these kinds of transference to the person of the doctor were a matter of a compulsion and an illusion that would melt away when the analysis was brought to a close. I do, however, believe that had I neglected to make the nature of the 'obstacle' clear to them, I would simply have provided them with a new, if milder, hysterical symptom as a substitute for another that had developed spontaneously.

I have now, I think, given sufficient indications of how the analyses were carried out and what was learnt from them. It may be that they make some things appear more complicated than they are; much is self-explanatory when one is involved in work of this kind. I have not listed the difficulties of the work so as to give the impression that these kinds of demands on doctor and patient make it worthwhile undertaking a cathartic analysis in only very rare cases. I let my practice as a doctor be influenced by the opposite assumption. – Admittedly, I cannot draw up the surest indications for the application of the therapeutic method depicted here without going into the weightier and more extensive theme of the therapy of neuroses. In my own work, I have frequently compared cathartic psychotherapy with surgical interventions, describing my treatments as *psychotherapeutic operations*, which in turn leads to analogies with opening up a cavity filled with pus, scraping out a carious area and so on. Analogies of this kind are not so much justified in terms of removing what is diseased as they are in terms of establishing conditions that in the course of the process are more favourable to the cure.

When I have promised my patients help or relief by means of a cathartic treatment, I have repeatedly had to listen to the following objection: 'You yourself tell me that what I am suffering from is probably connected with my circumstances and fate. You can't change anything about that. So how are you going to help me?' And I have been able to answer: 'I do not doubt that it would be easier for fate to take away your suffering than it would for me. But you will see for yourself that much has been gained if we succeed in turning your hysterical misery into common unhappiness. Having restored your inner life, you will be better able to arm yourself against that unhappiness.'[3]

(1895)

Notes

1. E. Hecker, *Zentralblatt für Nervenheilkunde*, December 1893.
2. ['Conscious', or *'bewußt'*, is given in all later editions. It is possibly a typographic error for *'gewußt'*, 'known', which is given in the first edition and makes better sense.]
3. [In the editions prior to 1925, 'Nervensystem' (nervous system) is given in place of 'Seelenleben' (inner life).]

Hysterical Phantasies and their Relation to Bisexuality

(Freud)

We are all familiar with the delusional writings of paranoiacs whose subject is the greatness and suffering of their own self and which assume quite typical, almost monotonous forms. In addition, numerous accounts have acquainted us with the peculiar performances through which certain perverts stage their sexual satisfaction, whether in their thoughts or in practice. Nevertheless, some readers may be surprised to learn that quite analogous psychical formations occur regularly in all psychoneuroses, in particular hysteria, and that these so-called hysterical phantasies can be seen to have important connections with the development of neurotic symptoms.

What are termed the daydreams of youth are a common source and normal model for all these phantastical creations and they have already received a certain, if as yet insufficient, degree of attention in the literature.[1] It is possible that they occur with equal frequency in both sexes: in girls and women they appear without exception to be erotic and in men to be either erotic or ambitious. But even in men, the significance of the erotic factor should not be relegated to second place. Closer inspection of a man's daydreams usually reveals that all his heroic acts are performed and all his achievements won with the sole purpose of pleasing a woman and of her preferring him to other men.[2] These phantasies are wish-fulfilments that stem from privation and longing. They are rightly called 'daydreams', for they are the key to understanding the dreams we have at night in which the nucleus of dream-formation is established by nothing other than these complicated, distorted day phantasies that are misunderstood by the conscious psychical agency.

These daydreams are invested and charged with great interest, carefully tended and on the whole shyly protected as if they were among the most intimate treasures of one's personality. But it is easy enough to recognize someone in the street who is involved in a daydream from the way they give a sudden smile, as if absent, talk to themselves or quicken their pace as if to a run, all of which mark the peak of the situation that is being dreamt. – Every hysterical attack that I have been able to investigate turned out to be the involuntary onset of a daydream of this kind. Having observed this, one is left in no doubt that phantasies of this kind can just as well be unconscious as conscious, and as soon as the latter have become unconscious they can also become pathogenic, i.e. be expressed in symptoms and attacks. Under favourable conditions an unconscious phantasy like this can still be caught hold of by the conscious. One of my patients, whose attention I had drawn to her phantasies, told me that once in the street she had suddenly found that she was crying, and on rapid reflection as to why she was really crying she got hold of the phantasy that she had begun an affair with a virtuoso pianist who was well known in the town (but with whom she was not personally acquainted), had had a child with him (she had no children), and she and the child had then been abandoned by him and left in poverty. At this point in the romance she burst into tears.

Unconscious phantasies are either those that have always been unconscious and were formed in the unconscious or, as is more frequently the case, those that were once conscious phantasies, daydreams which have then deliberately been forgotten and got into the unconscious through 'repression'. Their content has then either remained the same or undergone distortions such that the phantasy that is now unconscious represents a descendant of the phantasy that was once conscious. The unconscious phantasy now occupies a very important relationship with the person's sexual life, namely that it is identical with the phantasy which gave this person sexual satisfaction during a period of masturbation. The masturbatory act (onanistic in the broadest sense) was at the time composed of two items, the calling up of the phantasy and the active behaviour leading to self-gratification at the height of the phantasy. This compound is itself known to be soldered together.[3] Originally, the action was a purely auto-erotic undertaking to gain pleasure from a specific area of the body which may be called erogenous. Later the action merged with a wishful idea from the sphere of object love and served partially to realize the situation in which this phantasy culminated. If the subject then gives up this kind of satisfaction, which is derived from both phantasy and masturbation, the action is omitted but the phantasy turns from being conscious to unconscious. If no other means of sexual satisfaction appears, if the subject remains abstinent and does not succeed in sublimating the libido, that is, in diverting his or her sexual excitation to higher aims, then the condition is established for the unconscious phantasy to be refreshed and to proliferate and, as regards at least a part of its content, to put itself into effect with the whole force of the need for love, in the form of a pathological symptom.

These kinds of unconscious phantasies are the earliest psychical stages of a large number of hysterical symptoms. Hysterical symptoms are nothing other than unconscious phantasies whose representation has been brought about by 'conversion', and, in as much as they are somatic symptoms, are drawn with reasonable frequency from the sphere of the same sexual sensations and motor innervations that had originally accompanied the phantasies when they were still conscious. In this way the attempt to break the habit of masturbation really is cancelled out, and the ultimate aim of the entire pathological process, the restoration of the original primary sexual satisfaction, is always reached by a kind of approximation – if never completely achieved.

Anyone studying hysteria will quickly turn their interest from its symptoms to the phantasies from which they arise. The technique of psychoanalysis first enables these unconscious phantasies to be guessed from the symptoms and then for them to become conscious in the patient. In this way it has now been found that the unconscious phantasies of hysterics correspond completely in terms of content to the situations in which perverts consciously obtain gratification. And should one be at a loss for examples of this kind one need only recall the world-famous performances of the Roman emperors, the madness of which was of course determined only by the enormous and unrestrained power of the creators of these phantasies. The delusional creations of paranoiacs are similar kinds of phantasy, although they have become directly conscious; they are borne by the sado-masochistic component of the sexual drive and likewise may find their exact counterpart in certain of the unconscious phantasies of hysterics. Moreover, cases are also known – and this is of practical significance – in which hysterics do not express their phantasies as symptoms but as conscious realizations, and in so doing fabricate and stage assassination attempts, and acts of cruelty and of sexual aggression.

This method of psychoanalytic investigation, which leads from symptoms which are conspicuous through to phantasies which are hidden and unconscious, conveys everything that can be discovered about the sexuality of psychoneurotics, including the fact that is the focus of this short preliminary publication.

Probably as a consequence of the difficulties that stand in the way of the unconscious phantasies in their endeavour to find expression, the relationship between phantasies and symptoms is not a simple one, but rather one which is complicated in numerous ways.[4] As a rule, that is, once the neurosis has developed fully and existed for some time, a symptom no longer corresponds to one single unconscious phantasy but to a number of them, and not in an arbitrary way but according to a regular pattern of composition. It is unlikely that all of these complications will be developed at the beginning of the illness.

For the sake of general interest I want at this stage to go beyond the immediate context of this paper and add a series of formulations that attempt to give an increasingly exhaustive description of the nature of hysterical symptoms. They do not contradict each other; rather, they constitute either conceptions that are sharper and more complete, or that are taken from different points of view.

1) Hysterical symptoms are memory-symbols of certain (traumatic) impressions and experiences that are active.
2) Hysterical symptoms are substitutes, engendered by 'con-

version', for the associative return of these traumatic experiences.

3) Hysterical symptoms express – as do other psychical formations – the fulfilment of a wish.

4) Hysterical symptoms are the realization of an unconscious phantasy that serves the fulfilment of a wish.

5) Hysterical symptoms serve sexual satisfaction and represent a part of the subject's sexual life (corresponding to one of the components of his or her sexual drive).

6) Hysterical symptoms correspond to the return of a means of sexual satisfaction that was real in infant life and has since been repressed.

7) Hysterical symptoms arise as a compromise between two opposing stirrings of the affects or of the drives, one of which endeavours to express a partial drive or a component of the sexual constitution and the other to suppress it.

8) Hysterical symptoms can stand in for various unconscious non-sexual stirrings, but they cannot be devoid of sexual significance.

Of these various definitions it is the seventh that most exhaustively expresses the nature of hysterical symptoms as the realizations of unconscious phantasies, and with the eighth a proper acknowledgement of the sexual factor is given. Some of the previous formulations are preliminary stages of this formulation and are contained within it.

This relationship between symptoms and phantasies means that it is not difficult to move from the psychoanalysis of these symptoms to a knowledge of the components of the sexual drive which controls the individual, as I have set out in the *Three Essays on Sexual Theory* [*Standard Edition*, vol. VII]. In a number of cases, however, this investigation produces an unexpected result. It shows that many symptoms cannot be resolved by an unconscious sexual phantasy or a series of phantasies of which the most significant and earliest is sexual in nature. To remove the symptom two sexual phantasies are needed, one of which has a masculine and the other a feminine character, so that one of these phantasies arises from a homosexual impulse. This development does not affect the proposition given in formulation 7; in other words, hysterical symptoms necessarily represent a compromise between a libidinous and a repressive impulse, but they may additionally represent a union of two libidinous phantasies of opposite sexual character.

I will refrain from giving examples of this proposition. Experience has taught me that short analyses condensed into extracts can never give the impression of decisive proof which was one's intention in citing them. The report of fully analysed cases will, however, have to be reserved for another occasion.

I will content myself then with putting forward the proposition and elucidating its significance:

9) A hysterical symptom is the expression, on the one hand, of an unconscious sexual phantasy that is masculine and, on the other, of one that is feminine.

I want to draw particular attention to the fact that I cannot attribute the same general validity to this proposition as I have claimed for the other formulations. It applies, as far as I can see, neither to all the symptoms of one case, nor to all cases. On the contrary, it is not difficult to point to cases in which the impulses of the opposite sexes have been expressed as separate symptoms so that the symptoms of hetero- and homosexuality can be as sharply distinguished from one another as the phantasies concealed behind them. Yet the relationship put forward in the ninth formula is common enough and, where it occurs, significant enough to deserve particular emphasis. It seems to me to signify the highest level of complexity that can be attained by the determination of a hysterical symptom, and is therefore only to be expected of a neurosis that has existed for some length of time and within which a great deal of organizational work has gone on.[5]

The bisexual meaning of hysterical symptoms that is, in any event, demonstrable in numerous cases is undoubtedly interesting as evidence for the claim I have advanced,[6] that man's postulated bisexual disposition can be observed with particular clarity in the psychoanalysis of psychoneurotics. A completely analogous process occurs in the same field when someone masturbating tries in their conscious phantasies to empathize with both the man and the woman in the imagined situation. Further counterparts indicate certain hysterical attacks in which the patient plays both parts in the underlying sexual phantasy at once, as, for example, in a case I observed, where the patient holds her gown against her body with one hand (as the woman), and tries to tear it off with the other (as the man). This contradictory simultaneity is to a fair degree responsible for the incomprehensibility of the situation which is otherwise so vividly represented in the attack and is therefore extremely well suited to veiling the unconscious phantasy that is at work.

In psychoanalytic treatment it is very important to be prepared for a symptom to have a bisexual meaning. We need not then be surprised or disconcerted if a symptom seems to persist undiminished even though one of its sexual meanings has been solved; it may be maintained by a meaning that belongs to the opposite sex and that we may not have suspected. During the treatment of cases like this we can also observe that while one sexual meaning is being analysed, the patient finds it convenient constantly to switch the thoughts that come to him into the field of contrary meaning, as if onto a neighbouring track.

(1908)

Notes

1. See Breuer and Freud, *Studies in Hysteria*, P. Janet, *Névroses et idées fixes* [*Neuroses and idées fixes*], 1898, vol. 1, Havelock Ellis, *Studies in the Psychology of Sex*, 1899, Freud, *Die Traumdeutung* [*The Interpretation of Dreams*], 1900 [*Standard Edition*, vols IV, V], A. Pick, 'Über pathologische Träumerei und ihre Beziehung zur Hysterie', ['On pathological daydreaming and its relation to hysteria'], *Jb. Psychiat. Neurol.*, vol. 14, 1896.
2. H. Ellis draws a similar conclusion [*Studies in the Psychology of Sex*, 3rd edn., 1910, pp. 185 ff.].
3. See Freud, *Drei Abhandlungen zur Sexualtheorie* [*Three Essays on Sexual Theory*] (1905) [Chapter I, section 1A].

4. The same thing applies to the relationship between the 'latent' dream-thoughts and the elements of the 'manifest' dream-content. See the section on 'dream-work' in Chapter VI of *The Interpretation of Dreams*.

5. I. Sadger recently discovered the proposition under discussion in his own independent psychoanalytic work. However, he does claim that it has general validity. 'Die Bedeutung der psychoanalytischen Methode nach Freud' ['The significance of the psychoanalytic method according to Freud'], *Zentbl. Nervenheilk. Psychiat.*, 1907, N. F. 18, 41.

6. *Three Essays on Sexual Theory* [*Standard Edition*, vol. VII].

The Psychopathology of Everday Life
Translated by Anthea Bell
Introduction by Paul Keegan
Starting with the story of how he once forgot the name of an Italian painter—and how a young acquaintance mangled a quotation from Virgil through fears that his girlfriend might be pregnant—this volume brings together a treasure trove of muddled memories, inadvertent action, and verbal tangles. Freud's dazzling interpretations provide the perfect introduction to psychoanalytic thinking in action.

ISBN 0-14-243743-3

The Uncanny
Translated by David McClintock
Introduction by Hugh Haughton
Freud was fascinated by the mysteries of creativity and the imagination. His insights into the roots of artistic expression in the triangular "family romances" (of father, mother, and infant) that so dominate our early lives reveal the artistry of Freud's own writing. Freud's first exercise in psycho-biography, his celebrated study of Leonardo, brilliantly uses a single memory to reveal the childhood conflicts behind Leonardo's remarkable achievements and his striking eccentricity.

Coming in November 2004

The Psychology of Love
Translated by Shaun Whiteside
Introduction by Jeri Johnson
This volume brings together Freud's illuminating discussions of the ways in which sexuality is always psychosexuality—that there is no sexuality without fantasy, conscious or unconscious. In these papers Freud develops his now famous theories about childhood and the transgressive nature of human desire.

CLICK ON A CLASSIC
www.penguinclassics.com

The world's greatest literature at your fingertips

Constantly updated information on more than a thousand titles, from Icelandic sagas to ancient Indian epics, Russian drama to Italian romance, American greats to African masterpieces

•

The latest news on recent additions to the list, updated editions, and specially commissioned translations

•

Original essays by leading writers

•

A wealth of background material, including biographies of every classic author from Aristotle to Zamyatin, plot synopses, readers' and teachers' guides, useful web links

•

Online desk and examination copy assistance for academics

•

Trivia quizzes, competitions, giveaways, news on forthcoming screen adaptations

FOR THE BEST IN PAPERBACKS, LOOK FOR THE

In every corner of the world, on every subject under the sun, Penguin represents quality and variety—the very best in publishing today.

For complete information about books available from Penguin—including Penguin Classics, Penguin Compass, and Puffins—and how to order them, write to us at the appropriate address below. Please note that for copyright reasons the selection of books varies from country to country.

In the United States: Please write to *Penguin Group (USA), P.O. Box 12289 Dept. B, Newark, New Jersey 07101-5289* or call *1-800-788-6262*.

In the United Kingdom: Please write to *Dept. EP, Penguin Books Ltd, Bath Road, Harmondsworth, West Drayton, Middlesex UB7 0DA*.

In Canada: Please write to *Penguin Books Canada Ltd, 10 Alcorn Avenue, Suite 300, Toronto, Ontario M4V 3B2*.

In Australia: Please write to *Penguin Books Australia Ltd, P.O. Box 257, Ringwood, Victoria 3134*.

In New Zealand: Please write to *Penguin Books (NZ) Ltd, Private Bag 102902, North Shore Mail Centre, Auckland 10*.

In India: Please write to *Penguin Books India Pvt Ltd, 11 Panchsheel Shopping Centre, Panchsheel Park, New Delhi 110 017*.

In the Netherlands: Please write to *Penguin Books Netherlands bv, Postbus 3507, NL-1001 AH Amsterdam*.

In Germany: Please write to *Penguin Books Deutschland GmbH, Metzlerstrasse 26, 60594 Frankfurt am Main*.

In Spain: Please write to *Penguin Books S. A., Bravo Murillo 19, 1° B, 28015 Madrid*.

In Italy: Please write to *Penguin Italia s.r.l., Via Benedetto Croce 2, 20094 Corsico, Milano*.

In France: Please write to *Penguin France, Le Carré Wilson, 62 rue Benjamin Baillaud, 31500 Toulouse*.

In Japan: Please write to *Penguin Books Japan Ltd, Kaneko Building, 2-3-25 Koraku, Bunkyo-Ku, Tokyo 112*.

In South Africa: Please write to *Penguin Books South Africa (Pty) Ltd, Private Bag X14, Parkview, 2122 Johannesburg*.